M

The British Left Wing
and
Foreign Policy

THE BRITISH LEFT WING
AND FOREIGN POLICY

A Study of the Influence of Ideology

by

Eugene J. Meehan

Rutgers University Press

New Brunswick, New Jersey

Manufactured in the United States of America
by Edwards Brothers, Inc., Ann Arbor, Michigan

This book has been published with
the assistance of a grant
from the Ford Foundation

FOREWORD

Throughout the history of mankind, there have been those who felt that their own generation marked a milestone of some sort in the development of man. Such beliefs are difficult to support, and even more difficult to evaluate should they be true. Twentieth century man, for example, can claim one truly unique though somewhat dubious distinction: he has finally obtained an instrument that renders him capable of encompassing his total self-destruction. The instrument may be refined, made more efficient, cheaper, speedier, but it can do no more than raise the level of probability that extermination will be complete. Dead is already a superlative.

It has often been said—too often, perhaps—that this new development has an abiding importance for the student of international affairs. This study does not pretend to evaluate the significance of the development of atomic weapons. But the existence of atomic weapons has greatly increased the importance of the subject matter with which the study deals. The present structure of social organization ensures that the decision for or against self-immolation will be taken by those who direct the policies of the great political societies of our time. That is to say that any future war, should it occur, will almost certainly result from some aberration in the relations between states and not from some internal stress that cannot be solved within the existing political system. Widespread recognition of this principle has produced a lively and almost universal interest in international affairs, centered particularly on those nations capable of beginning a nuclear war. Interestingly enough, the number of states whose behavior might conceivably lead to war on such a scale has increased substantially in recent years as a consequence of the numerous military alliances concluded between those states possessing atomic weapons and those less fortunately endowed. The failure of the general public to take cognizance of this aspect of international politics is perhaps due to the unfailing regularity with which the creators of such alliances have argued that they constitute additional bulwarks against hostilities.

No one would argue that there would be no interest in international affairs if there were no atomic weapons, and if man's destructive potential was still limited to the relatively insignificant ability to erase from the earth a few thousands of its inhabitants in a single effort. The people of the United States and of the Soviet Union, together with those unfortunate enough to occupy the intervening territories, would undoubtedly have developed an active and personal interest in their mutual relations after 1945. What is new in the situation, and perhaps the most significant contribution of atomic energy to international politics, is the extension of this interest to third parties far removed from the seat of conflict. In all history, few nations were able to arouse universal concern over international relations. It is true enough that fear of war has always been present in every society, so far as we know, but people feared war in their own geographical area, not in some land far off across the seas. This much has changed. Great power conflict can no longer be confined within geographic limits so long as the principle of self preservation is accepted as valid for political society. Talk of "limited war" is futile if the nations involved believe that their own continued existence depends upon victory and act upon that belief. This is the catalyst which brought about world-wide concern with "western" politics. The famous dictum of Louis XIV loses its fatuity on the lips of the modern rulers of the great political societies. This state of affairs, as is often pointed out, underlines the interdependence of all men; it likewise underscores just as heavily the exasperating inability of the weak to control the strong, and the many to control the few. Little real satisfaction can be derived from either observation.

The advent of atomic energy has resulted in an enormous increase in the prestige of "science," though what is meant by the term is not always clear. In a special and limited sense, some responsibility for the present impasse in international affairs rests with modern science, although the generalizations sometimes made about the nature and scope of that responsibility are not always valid. The marriage of immense natural resources to rapidly advancing technology, with government playing the marriage broker, has produced the new tools, new weapons, and new sources of energy which are the title deeds to national power in the modern world. Nevertheless, it seems grossly unfair to charge science with responsibility for the use made of these developments as is so often done, sometimes by the scientists themselves. Not only is it unfair, it also tends to divert attention from the real culprit, government. For it is the men who govern, not the men who occupy the laboratories, that bear the responsibility for the present state of international affairs. The scientist, for his part, has the same responsibilities as any other citizen, perhaps slightly accentuated by his understanding of the forces moulded by his work. It is a travesty to ask him to refuse to explore certain areas because of the potential his explorations might release. All energy sources can be used for either good or evil. The real technological "problem" lies in the need to control the use of the new instruments which technology develops, not to limit such development.

One corollary of the immense prestige which science enjoys at the present time has been a growing belief that its working principles, the "scientific method," should be applied to every sort of problem which man must solve. This is not the proper place to deal adequately with a question of these dimensions, but certain general observations are perhaps in order. Physical science has produced magnificent results in the areas to which it applies its energies. The results have induced a sense of optimism, a faith in the efficacy of human intelligence, and a belief in the inevitability of human progress, usually undefined, that would be ludicrous if the results were less pernicious. It is often assumed that scientific progress stems from the application of human intelligence, methodical observation, and some system of measurement, to specified data. By analogy, the application of similar methods to human data should produce similar results. The study of inanimate objects and the lower life forms has yielded substantial results when these methods were applied. The application of human intelligence to human problems has only infrequently led to agreement; more often the result has been confusion, discord, and conflict. Indeed, science may be construed as a definite handicap in the process of studying man if dogmatic insistence upon the use of "scientific" tools, usually meaning observation and measurement, leads to the use of these tools on materials to which they are not suited. The careful, objective, empirical approach to a field of study is infinitely to be preferred to any other approach available to us at present, but its limitations must be observed. What science produces, man must dispose, and disposal requires a value system that will make the actions meaningful. The fundamental problems of politics, as I hope to demonstrate in a future work, are moral or ethical, and not scientific.

This rather dreary background is the milieu in which the student of international affairs must function, willing or not. It is also the measure of the political scientist's accomplishments. The objectives of this book, viewed in this broad context, are quite limited. It does not contain a panacea for the ills of international society, nor even much solace for those who are genuinely concerned with the future of man. If anything, the theses advanced here, if true, render a peaceful solution to international disagreements even less likely than they presently appear unless radical changes in human behavior occur.

The aim is to provide additional insight into one small area of international affairs which has not yet been fully explored. Specifically, the book attempts to illustrate the manner in which ideology influences human thought about the factual data of international relations, taking ideology to mean simply a pattern of beliefs which an individual or group accepts. This is a specific example of the general problem of examining the manner in which human beliefs condition human thought. The study deals with beliefs and thought about political matters only, on the assumption that the relationship is less likely to be obscured by this approach. It is realized, of course, that beliefs which are not related to politics nevertheless affect political judgments, and conversely, that not all political beliefs affect every political decision. But this appeared to be the most satisfactory method of arriving at a useful result. The specific content of the ideology must, of course, be used in the study; but the effect of content is ignored in the conclusions, which seek to determine the influence of ideology *qua* ideology, and not the influence of a particular body of beliefs. If the method is valid, the conclusions so drawn should have relevance to all ideologies, whatever their content. One may either approve or disapprove of the effect which the ideology of the British Left Wing—the group used to illustrate the theses—has upon its thinking about international affairs. But this does not really matter very much as compared with the approval or disapproval elicited by recognition of the principles which appear to govern that relationship.

One of the secondary purposes of this study is to serve as an antidote to the current tendency to generalize about the nature of ideology and its influence by making reference only to the specific ideology of the Soviet Union. The need for students of international affairs to concentrate upon Soviet ideology is understandable, but regrettable as well. It has had the effect of astricting the meaning of ideology into a synonym for communism, which is grossly inadequate as a description of the Soviet ideology at the present time. Further, since the American ideology presently contains an attitude, real or presumed, toward Soviet ideology that is extremely hostile, this limited meaning of ideology renders it more difficult to obtain an objective appreciation of the real content of the Soviet ideology. A careful catalog of the occasions on which the leaders of the Soviet Union have come into conflict with "their own" ideology presumes that the definition of the ideology made by the cataloging agent is correct. The possibility of an error in judgment by the person making such assertions, which seems in fact quite likely to occur, is all too frequently ignored. The generalizations which have been drawn about the effect of ideologies using communism as the sole example have in many cases involved even more serious errors. The assumption that all ideologies are expansive and warlike can be drawn, and has been drawn, on this basis. Yet many ideologies are in fact pacific and strongly opposed to war. One need only mention the Quakers, and certain elements of European socialism as suitable examples. Finally, modern mass ideologies are enormously complex systems of thought, relative in meaning to time and circumstances, constantly changing in meaning. Nationalism, perhaps the most important ideology in the world today, is not a single ideology at all but a characteristic of the political societies which we call states, and one which varies in content from one society to the next, and from one generation to the next. To assume that the meaning of ideology can be fixed and studied seems a serious error. In very large measure, its meaning is really determined by its consequences.

The method selected for this study of ideology is a combination of theoretical generalization and historical verification. In the first chapter, ideology is subjected to an analysis which provides the working theory which the remainder of the study can be used to verify. The verification consists of a survey of the manner in which a particular group of persons, who maintain an ideology that can be reasonably well delineated, view the course of international affairs over a specific period of time. This approach limits the validity of the conclusions, and these limits must be clearly understood. First, the theory of ideology stated in Chapter I is tested against the actual behavior of only one group, and the results are therefore much less conclusive than might have been the case if a number of ideologies had been used. On the other hand, the use of a single ideology permits both depth and detail without excessive length, thus allowing ample opportunity for error in detail to make its appearance. The validity of the theory can, in any case, be subjected to further test as additional studies appear. A second problem, which appears in every study of opinion, is that the material on which the study is based is limited to what is produced by the vocal elements of a particular group. It is not possible to state the degree to which these vocal elements are representative of the whole group. It can be argued, for example, that group leaders appear and gain support simply because they do state, in some way, the general attitudes of the group. For the moment, however, little real evidence can be adduced in favor of this argument, though I feel the argument to be substantially true. Finally, it must be realized that changes in opinion cannot really be ascribed to ideology with complete certainty, therefore only the assumption of probability is made throughout the book. The manuscript has been examined by a number of authorities on British politics, and there is general agreement with the assumptions that have been made. But this is only an indication of probability, not certainty, and the reader is left to evaluate the relative influence of ideology and the numerous other factors which enter into opinion formation.

The ideology chosen to test the theory on which the study is based is the form of socialism held by the Left Wing of the British Labour movement, excluding known members of the British Communist party. The time period covered by the study extends from the General Election of 1945 through the summer of 1951. The general trends of socialist opinion in the years between the two world wars, and the early part of World War II, are set forth in Chapter II. The material is meant to illustrate the actual content of the ideology of the Left Wing at the beginning of the study. This combination of ideology and time period has definite advantages for a study of this sort. The British Left Wing is a reasonably well-defined group, and spokesmen for particular viewpoints within the group are well known. The Left Wing is an extremely self-conscious group, that is, it tends to think of itself as the Left Wing and to take pride in its own convictions. This has the advantage of heightening the effect of the ideology, and thus producing trends which are easy to follow. The Left Wing took a great interest in international affairs after 1945, perhaps more than any other similar group in Great Britain. The signs of their interest took the form of frequent writings or speeches about international affairs, hence a wealth of material is available for the study. Finally, the fact that the British Labour party was forming a government during the 1945-1951 period is a distinct advantage, in that it reduces the element of partisan opposition to government policy that might otherwise be expected. There is, after all, some measure of truth in the view that one function of an Opposition is to oppose. Elimination of this facet of political discussion removes a very important variable from the study, and makes it much more likely that ideological conviction led to the results which are observed in Left Wing behavior. This situation has a corollary advantage, in that direct opposition to government policy by the Left Wing can be taken to indicate very strong feelings about a particular issue, otherwise, the disadvantage, politically speaking, of opposition to one's own government would more than outweigh the strength of personal conviction. Formal opposition to party policy is not a matter to be undertaken lightly by active British politicians, and the data obtained during such conflicts are particularly valuable.

Readers will notice that the survey of international affairs from 1945 to 1951 is far from complete. Many events were omitted because they added little to the data already available, or because they required an inordinate amount of detailed explanation. Colonial questions, including the highly controversial problems raised by British policy in India and in Palestine, have been omitted completely. Certain problems arising out of World War II were reluctantly laid aside, as for example the Polish settlement, which was included in detail in the original draft but finally omitted because it added little that could not be seen in the Left Wing reaction to the Greek crisis, which is considered fully. In one sense, all of these matters are part of the text, since they were carefully weighed before the final selection was made. The material that remains is representative and typical of a vast body of material that could not be included. The selection was made on the basis of generality, that is, those materials were included which demonstrate most clearly the type of reaction met most often in the study of Left Wing opinion.

So far as is possible the material has been organized into chapters which accord with the major phases of Left Wing opinion rather than with the various phases of international affairs. Thus Chapter IV, which deals with the liberation of Greece from Germany, is typical of the attitude of the Left Wing toward the whole liberation process, whether of Italy, of western Europe, or of eastern Europe. Chapters V and VI deal with the gradual deterioration of great power cordiality during the last half of 1945 and most of 1946, and the response of the Left Wing to the publication of the details of this breakdown of political relations. Chapter VII covers the crucial months in 1947 when the western nations openly and publicly renounced the need for Soviet agreement prior to a postwar settlement and began to make decisions applicable to their own sphere of influence. Chapter VIII deals with the Left Wing view of the Soviet response to this western decision to go forward alone, centering, of course, on the blockade of Berlin. The final chapter deals with the principal problem facing both sides after 1948, i.e., to determine how seriously the security of the western world was threatened, what the appropriate actions were under these circumstances, and what each side was likely to do. In this period, the Korean War plays the dominant part.

We must make a clear distinction, throughout the study, between the timing of events as they appeared in public, and the actual decisions made by the governments concerned. This study deals with opinion, and opinion responds to known data, and not to decisions which are not communicated to the public. Thus we can assume a time lag between the western decision that agreement with the Soviet Union could not be obtained, and the actual operation of that policy. Yet public opinion cannot function until the second stage in the process is reached, and one sometimes wonders whether it is in fact possible for public opinion to have the slightest influence on policy under these circumstances. One is struck again and again by the extent to which the general public remains in complete ignorance of the actual course of events in international affairs. One of the results of this condition is a decided increase in the influence of ideology in the opinion-forming process.

Perhaps the most important consequence of ideology to appear in the study is the rigidity which it produces in the opinions of its adherents. One exception to this generalization appears in the study when the behavior of one group within the Left Wing undergoes a substantial change toward the end of the period covered. Because a change of this magnitude might seriously impair the hypothesis that ideology gives continuity and stability to patterns of thought, the sequence of events leading to the change have been examined with great care in the body of the text. It is the considered opinion of this writer that the motive in this particular case was relevant to internal Labour politics and not to ideology. That is, those who forced the new trend in Left Wing thought did so quite deliberately in an effort to obtain the support of the Labour movement as a whole against the leadership of the Labour party. The final judgment must rest with the reader, and the data have been included in sufficient detail to make this judgment possible.

Eugene J. Meehan

New Brunswick, New Jersey
August, 1960

ACKNOWLEDGMENTS

The author acknowledges permission to quote passages from the following:

Into a Dangerous World, by Woodrow Wyatt, published by George Weidenfeld & Nicolson, Ltd., London.

The Labour Party in Perspective, by C. R. Attlee, and *The Intelligent Man's Guide to the Postwar World*, by G. D. H. Cole, published by Victor Gollancz, Ltd., London.

I cannot hope to acknowledge the whole of my scholarly debts in one brief paragraph. To all those who took time from their own work to explain the subtleties of British politics to an American, I offer my heartfelt thanks. I also am indebted to Mr. R. Bassett of the London School of Economics, whose unrivaled knowledge of British politics in this century was always at my disposal. Finally, I must thank Miss Ellen McCullough of the Transport and General Workers Union, who taught me the things about Labour politics that cannot be learned from books. She and her colleagues, particularly Miss Violet Cleveland, helped me to avoid countless errors of judgment. My colleague, Professor E. M. Burns, kindly read the introduction and offered a number of helpful suggestions. None of these persons is in any way responsible for either the data or the conclusions in the book. This responsibility lies with me.

I dedicate the book to my wife, Alice. It is a totally inadequate recompense for endless hours of silence, typewriter noise, and fits of extremely bad temper. But it is all that I have to offer, and I can only hope it will suffice.

CONTENTS

CONTENTS

I

IDEOLOGY: AN ANALYSIS

An ideology, in the most general sense possible, is simply a pattern of beliefs relating to some particular aspect of social, political, or economic life. The term also implies a system or theorem—a program of action—flowing from the basic pattern of beliefs. Further, it implies an element of the irrational which is absolute and must be accepted as a matter of faith. This is a commonplace in most religions, and seems equally true of social, political, or economic ideologies. As the word is used here, ideology is taken to include all of these shades of meaning.

Political ideologies have a direct and immediate relation to international affairs which is comparatively easy to isolate. Hence the data presented here are derived from a political ideology, but it is assumed that any ideology will have the same consequences, though the specific effect will vary with the content of the ideology. In the sense in which ideology is used here, every individual accepts a number of ideologies each of which is relevant to some part of the total behavior of the person. In many, and perhaps in most cases, the individual does not recognize his own adherence to an ideology, and its influence may be so much a part of normal behavior in the society in which the individual functions that it completely escapes notice, even by others. Nevertheless, ideology plays a vital part in human behavior, and the exact nature of its influence is well worth exploration. The study assumes that a detailed examination of the relationship between an ideological group, e.g., those who accept a particular ideology, and international affairs, as demonstrated in the opinions of the group, will produce data that will bring out some of the basic principles governing that relationship. Since it is assumed that the principles so obtained will be valid for any ideology, political or otherwise, the analysis of ideology made in this chapter is not necessarily limited to political ideologies, although they are a prime source of the data on which the analysis is based. Similarly, the hypotheses posed throughout the chapter are relevant to any ideology, and to the manner in which its influence will be exerted.

Ideologies are so numerous, and their external characteristics

1

are so diverse, that extensive generalization about these externals would involve a long and detailed examination of past history, premises, goals, scope, and similar data that is not really suitable to our purpose. To mention only three of the principal external characteristics of ideology—the scope of the area of human behavior which they affect, the demands which they make upon their supporters, and the complexity of their fundamental doctrines—the possible variation in particulars involved in these three aspects of ideology alone is enormous.

A more promising approach to the analysis of ideology is offered by a detailed study of two major characteristics which all ideologies possess: first, it is impossible to construct an ideology which does not contain absolutes, unless the definition of ideology be expanded to include every system of thought, and this would render the word meaningless; second, ideologies acquire significance as they acquire mass support, and mass support is a consequence of some form of social organization. The implications of these two characteristics of ideology are sufficient for the formulation of the hypotheses suggested here regarding the influence of ideology.

The characteristic feature of an ideology which distinguishes it from all other approaches to social or political questions is its dependence upon absolutes not its irrationality. By definition, a system of thought cannot be irrational unless by irrationality we mean thought which is not empirically based. This latter case is impossible unless thought is made synonymous with *logical* thought. Since it is not possible to move from "Is" to "Ought" in any logical system, any system of thought which involved values would be irrational on this basis. This attitude is sometimes adopted, and political beliefs which are not confined strictly to empirical data are thereby condemned as irrational. Yet empirical evidence by itself cannot provide an adequate basis for political action. This paragraph may appear unnecessary, yet it is desirable to be certain at the outset that a clear distinction has been made between an ideology and a pattern of political beliefs which involves irrational beliefs, but does not pose them as absolute truths. Both approaches to politics, or any other subject matter, may involve certain beliefs and a program of action. But the approach to politics which is based upon the best information available, which embodies beliefs tentatively held and subject to constant criticism and revision as new data appear, cannot be called an ideology. In fact, this pragmatic or empirical approach to politics seems the least ideological attitude which is possible given the present state of human knowledge of social behavior. It denies the existence of absolutes by denying that the outcome of any worthwhile process of verification can be predicted with certainty, while at the same time it insists that all beliefs must be subjected to such verification as often as circumstances demand.

The strength of political ideologies, and of religious ideologies as well, derives from the nature of the subject with which they deal. Both politics and religion appear to exclude the possibility of a completely empirical approach, though this is more easily seen in the latter case. In the case of politics, the absence of an agreed end, and indeed the serious doubt that such an end exists, undermines the validity of any basis for action which may be suggested. The universals of politics, and of religion, are questions of value, of good and bad, right and wrong. Such problems are an exercise in judgment, or the application of general principles to specific situations, not an exercise in mathematics. Moral judgments do not yield to empirical investigation, even with the use of some hedonistic calculus such as that associated with Jeremy Bentham and the English Utilitarians. The necessary quantification seems inevitably to require the use of subjective judgment. This is only another way of saying that basic political beliefs are value judgments and assumptions predicated upon value judgments, while value judgments are themselves always relative and subject to argument. Careful empirical analysis can and should be used to insure that the premises from which the value judgments are derived are the best and most accurate available. Such analysis cannot be used to determine the values.

What might be called the dilemma of politics, then, is the genuine need for beliefs and principles of action, and man's present inability to provide them on an empirical basis. Any approach to politics which pretends to be significant must produce a set of behavioral standards. The tentative standards produced by the pragmatic approach to politics have the great disadvantage that they leave the individual who accepts them with uncertainty as a constant companion. Psychologically, this is profoundly unsatisfactory, particularly for those charged with the responsibility for making social decisions. The great strength of ideology derives from its ability to fill this gap by postulating absolute values. It is one of the peculiarities of human nature that individuals presume that their own absolute requirements are in some manner binding upon the universe. If the continued existence of mankind depended upon the acquisition of a particular piece of knowledge, it is quite reasonable to assume that mankind might very well perish. Yet this possibility is habitually excluded from human thought. The hard-pressed governmental agent, faced with a problem that demands action, will seldom if ever agree that no action is possible, although logic and reason may so dictate. He is far more likely in these circumstances to grasp at the "answer" which ideology provides. There have never been any pessimistic ideologies; they are, more usually, solutions to the insoluble, or at least what is presently insoluble.

The assertion of absolute first principles, once made, forces an ideology to concentrate its attention upon means and restricts discussion of these first principles. The extreme political ideologies, which display this characteristic most clearly, claim absolute and exclusive knowledge of the ends of politics and forbid on pain of expulsion from the ideological group any discussion whatever of these ends. Such ideological beliefs are commonly based on the assumption that life is teleological, and that progress toward the ultimate goal is in some manner inevitable. Political ideologies of this type, like their religious counterparts, accept the dictum that their own sphere of activity is the highest form of human endeavor, as did Aristotle in his *Politics*. Their prophets and priests lay claim to have touched the hem of eternity, and even lifted it long enough to catch a clear view of what lies on the other side. These political ends may be eminently practical, as in the doctrine of "the world under a single roof" that was so popular in Japan before 1945, or as mystical and other-worldly as pure communism and the world of non-coercive co-operation envisioned by some anarchists. Whatever the ends postulated by the ideology, the absolute nature of the end seriously increases the danger that any means may be considered satisfactory so long as the end is one prescribed by the ideology. This danger is greatly reinforced by the absolute character of the value system which ideology produces. Historically, much of the world's misery has been due to the work of those who believed that their own values were correct and their own ends were absolute. Modern ideologies, if the sample studied here is typical, retain this characteristic to an alarming degree.

We have already noted that the existence of absolute fundamental postulates in a system of thought tends to discourage or interdict completely any effort on the part of the supporters of the ideology to examine or attempt to verify these assumptions. These absolutes have the further and perhaps even more significant effect of multiplying the doctrines of the ideology, rendering them more complex, and increasing the danger of internal inconsistencies as the absolutes are applied to the changing pattern of day to day affairs. A closed system of thought, whether simple or elaborate in the beginning, that must adapt to a society that is dynamic, and all societies are such, cannot permit an open contradiction to exist within itself. Flat contradiction, permitted to remain, undermines belief since the most basic method of disproving a proposition is simple contradiction. Given the proposition that a thing is both "A" and "not-A," the mind boggles and disbelief in one or the other of the propositions will usually follow.

This is clearly recognized by those who direct the activities of ideological groups. Two methods are relied upon very heavily as means of avoiding internal contradictions: the first technique, which might be termed a system of distributed contradictions, is most common in politics; the second, reliance upon deductive methods from given principles, is most frequently met in religious ideologies. The use of "distributed contradiction" avoids the entire problem by a technique that can scarcely be considered intellectually honest. It is based upon the logical truth that a subject without a predicate has no meaning whatever, hence contradiction is a function of predicates. The possibility of conflict among predicates is avoided by ignoring completely whatever relation may exist among them. It may be asserted for example, that "X," "Y," and "Z," are predicates of the subject "A." None of these predicates can contradict "A," and if each predicate is discussed separately in relation to "A" and to "A" only, contradiction is wholly avoided. This is most familiar, perhaps, in the election speech, wherein the speaker (subject "A") asserts predicates about his own future behavior which may involve a total contradiction, that is, the predicates may be as mutually exclusive as hot and cold. Converts to socialism or communism very often follow this same practice of making assertions about their respective ideologies which are not really compatible.

When a group of first principles are taken as absolutely true, and deduction from these principles is the only permitted form of intellectual activity, much the same result ensues. A given number of predicates are postulated as true for a particular subject, usually the ideology itself. All further predicates employed by the ideology are deduced from these original premises. Extremely elaborate and coherent systems can be produced by this method, witness the work of Thomas Acquinas. The usual corollary to this technique is an absolute injunction against examination of the agreed premises, for if all of the non-verifiable absolutes in such systems are rejected, the edifice collapses. The number of serious drawbacks of too extensive a reliance upon deduction make it somewhat less suitable for politics than for religion. No body of dogma relating to social matters has yet proved so fertile that all the needs of daily existence can be derived from the initial premises without the introduction of new data. As a consequence, we find that the Popes of the Catholic Church, the Supreme Court of the United States, Lenin and Stalin, and other high priests of ideological movements have frequently introduced into their respective ideologies, under the guise of interpretation, conceptions that are entirely new, and even in contradiction to previous dogma. The results of this practice are fairly obvious to anyone who has compared the Sermon on the Mount with modern Catholic dogma, the opinions of John Marshall with those of the present-day Supreme Court, or Marx with Lenin and Stalin. Casuistry has not been confined to religion; all ideologies have their interpreters. The role which the interpreter has played depends upon a number of factors affecting the historical development of the ideology. In any event, interpretation has usually had the effect of still further restricting the area open to the free play of the intellect, since each deduction made by an "authorized" source was usually meant to fill some lacuna in the original theory of the ideology. Anyone familiar with the development of the Christian religion, Confucianism, Marxism, or American constitutional law will be aware of the manner in which these restrictions develop.

The development of ideologies appears to move through three historical stages: first, the initial statement of principles is made by the prophet or founder of the ideology; second, these principles are elaborated by a group of disciples; third, a "priesthood" develops, claiming authority to apply the principles of the ideology to current problems. This is, of course, most reminiscent of the origins and development of Christianity, but the circumstances appear to have a parallel in every major political ideology of our time. The classical political prophet is naturally Karl Marx. But Sun Yat-sen performed much the same task for the Nationalist party of China with his "Three People's Principles," Mahatma Gandhi served as prophet to the Indian Congress party, Jefferson and Lincoln are the classical prophets of "Americanism," Hitler and Mussolini were the prophets of German National Socialism and Italian Fascism respectively, and so on. The writings of the prophet may be very brief, or even nonexistent so long as a verbal tradition remains, as with Christ and Confucius. Such writings acquire enormous authority within the ideology, and in most instances are used as an authoritative means of "proving" various contentions. The massive reliance upon the writings of Lincoln and Jefferson, often lifted completely out of context, in American patriotic speeches is an illustration of the use of the principle that the word of the prophet is, or ought to be, sufficient evidence of the validity of an argument. For this reason, the ideal prophet is one whose works are rather vague, highly generalized, and perhaps even contradictory since this allows those who rework the ideology more latitude in their behavior. One of the great merits of the Bible is that its length, complexity, obscurity, and the fact that few have read it, has made it a working text for centuries despite the social change that has taken place since it was written.

Although the prophets are eulogized, and their works made holy, the role of the disciples and the priesthood seems to have been rather more important in the development of ideologies. St. Paul's services to Christiantity are paralleled by the contribution which Lenin and Stalin made to Marxism, and Chiang Kai-shek to the modernized version of Sunyatsenism. It is a characteristic of ideology, however, that all of these interpreters would firmly deny that they had made any addition whatever to the original principles of the prophet. All changes in doctrine are usually repudiated, and each new principle is attributed to the original data of the prophet. This acts to create an ever-deepening body of myth about the person of the prophet as his omniscience is more clearly revealed with each new discovery. Obviously it is desirable that the person so treated be removed as far as circumstances permit from the possibility of exhibiting merely human foibles, and the best means of accomplishing this is death. One of the reasons why a prophet is without honor in his own era is simply that a living prophet can hardly be considered omniscient. The deliberate rejuvenation of emperor worship in Japan after the Meiji restoration of 1868 is atypical, and an example to the contrary, since the emperor was actually put forward as a living deity. But the example is peculiar, in that the quiescence of the Japanese emperors, and their willingness to be seldom seen and never heard, had a long and involved history which made it possible to develop and maintain this fiction for a remarkably long time. In most instances, eulogizing a deceased prophet is both simpler and safer. In the absence of a true prophet, and this is a prominent feature of nationalism, national heroes can help fill the gap. No political society is without its Washingtons and Wellingtons, Nevskys or Nelsons. The action of the leaders of the Soviet Union in recent years, when they deliberately ripped down the myth surrounding Stalin, is unusual, and must represent the outcome of a very complex internal political situation. It can hardly be viewed as anything but a serious error of judgment from the standpoint of the Soviet ideology.

The constant process of interpretation, given sufficient time and energy, produces an increasingly bulky and unwieldy store of accretions to the fundamental dogma of the ideology. In the Catholic Church, which has one of the oldest ideologies that remains alive at the present time, this process led to increasing demand for a return to the primitive or original doctrines of the church, and eventuated in the Reformation. By analogy, one would suppose that any ideology which endured long enough would tend toward a similar position and the growth of similar pressures. The state of the world being what it is, this is an engaging possibility, and there is even some evidence that supports it, but the pressures that have emerged within political ideologies are as yet insignificant. Perhaps centuries are needed for dissatisfaction to emerge. Perhaps it is not in the nature of politics to produce this sort of effect, for one vital function of any political system is to produce necessary internal changes without resorting to violence or bloodshed. Indeed, this is one of the best criteria available to us for judging the worth of political systems. By and large, political societies have performed this function quite well in the past. While it must be said that the ideologies of the rulers of Russia, France, and Britain hardened at one stage in history into a static system and thus led to revolution, the significance of this statement is rather dubious.

Nevertheless, there are some warning signs of what may be called a hardening process within political ideologies. The communist ideology has produced rebels like Djilas, though it may be only wishful thinking to assume that this is symptomatic of greater things. Nationalism too shows signs of this hardening process. Complete freedom of criticism of national behavior is being discarded; the imperatives of the national ideology are growing more difficult to attack with impunity, particularly in periods of stress. But aside from nationalism, most of the political ideologies in the world today are new, and many are weak and in opposition to the existing regime. Oppositions cannot afford to become static if they wish to achieve power; only after power is achieved can they afford this luxury, and succumb to the allures of certainty, allowing arteriosclerosis to set in. It is nonetheless a point that bears watching, and even now a careful study of nationalism might show that in fact there has been extensive hardening of dogma in recent decades and perhaps the beginning of a reaction against the process that might issue in a political "reformation."

These few aspects of ideology as a pattern of absolute beliefs may, perhaps, help to explain the rather peculiar "flavor" of ideological controversy and lead us to expect a somewhat rigid and dogmatic approach to international affairs among those who are committed too firmly to an ideology. If the ideology is held by only a single person, or even a small group, the consequences at the international level can hardly be serious. Ideologies become a major social force when and if they acquire sufficient organization to obtain mass support or at least mass acceptance; for the Christian religion without the Christian church, or communism without the communist party, or nationalism without the state, are unthinkable. The great ideologies in the history of man all owe their success to a strong organization. Even Confucianism, perhaps the least organized of the great political ideologies, was only one among several competitors until it was adopted by the Han as an official or semi-official doctrine. Those which have failed to achieve great influence are legion, and their failure can usually be traced to the lack of organization, often, of course, because organization was not desired. Sun Yat-sen's doctrines had little real influence in post-Manchu China until he allied himself with the Chinese Communist party and organized his followers along communist party lines.

The mass organization of ideologies both supports and controls those who accept the ideology, and in effect it acts to concentrate the diffuse social power of individuals into a single functional social unit which can apply its power effectively. Ideological conviction breeds aspirations to power as a means of satisfying conviction, and the means to power is always organization. The most successful of all ideologies owes much of its remarkable vitality to its organization, which was "modern" at a time when the political regimes of the West were still the personal property of the ruler and scarcely institutionalized at all. The organization of the Soviet Communist party owes much to the structure of the Catholic Church, which embraced the principle of "democractic centralism" centuries before Marx was born.

Ideologies, then, tend to produce organization. Conversely, organizations tend to produce ideologies, and one of the greatest of modern ideologies, nationalism, is a clear example of the strength of purpose that organization can produce even where it has not been clearly directed toward a specified end. Since modern man lives at the center of an extremely complex and interlocking structure of social organizations, even in the so-called backward areas, the influence of ideology is considerably enhanced. Even the most trivial of societies produces basic rules of behavior; in fact, this is perhaps the best definition of social organization—a group of persons bound by a set of common rules. While the importance of information organizations is small in the field of international affairs, such organizations play a vital part in the private life of the individual, and must be calculated into the immensely complicated structure of nationalistic thought.

In the remainder of this chapter, we shall examine three fundamental characteristics of social organization on a mass scale. In the first place, it is clear that mass support involves the adherence of very large numbers of people with diverse backgrounds and possibly quite different cultural patterns to the fundamental principles and purposes of the ideology. Secondly, individuals who accept the same basic principles of thought and program of action form what sociologists call a secondary group, and secondary groups tend to behave in a particular manner toward other groups and individuals. Finally, purposeful social organization tends to concentrate authority in the hands of a relatively small number of persons, or more briefly, purposeful social organization clearly demonstrates authoritarian tendencies. Each of these characteristics, taken in conjunction with the general aspects of ideology already considered, has substantial consequences in the field of international affairs, and of course in other social situations as well.

It is certainly true that not every ideology obtains mass support, but it is equally true that ideologies which do not obtain mass support have little practical importance, particularly in the field of politics. In modern times, the need to appeal to the masses is a corollary to the peculiar virtues now attributed to number, and commonly expressed in terms of majority and minority. Number has become the key to power in our age; it is also the hallmark of legitimacy, as Maurice Duverger pointed out in his work on political parties. Modern political ideologies, well aware of these circumstances, have tended to frame their basic principles *ad captandum vulgus* since the road to power lies in this direction. The appeal is to the mass and not to the elite, a truly amazing transformation in a relatively short period of time. From the time of Plato until the eighteenth century at least, political thought and political propaganda ignored the masses and concentrated on the elite; the trend was completely reversed in the nineteenth century, and the emphasis on this new type of appeal has been sharply accentuated in the first few decades of the twentieth century. There are occasional signs of a return to the appeal to elites—academic writers commonly aim their products at their peers—but even elitism would now require mass support to be workable since the legitimacy of mass support has been institutionalized in most countries.

One possible explanation of this phenomenon may lie in the proposition that ideologies, in the sense in which they are used here, only appear when men begin to seek power by appealing to the many and not to the few; but the proposition is not provable, and the converse can be argued. Certainly there was a time in the history of man when the equal importance of each individual was rejected, rightly or wrongly. At some point, the emphasis began to change. In one sense, individualism, which is the father of mass politics, was a product of Christianity, though the sophisticated precision of Thomas Aquinas is not designed for mass consumption, and the practices of the church are hardly amenable to this interpretation.

Most of the classics of political thought, ancient and modern, were in fact meant for limited audiences. The *Vindicia Contra*

Tyrannos appealed to the nobles and gentlemen of the reformed church of France and not to the French people. The *Federalist Papers* can hardly be construed as an appeal to the masses of colonial America. Even Rousseau, one of the guiding spirits of the new era, did not really write for mass consumption. Marx, whose *Das Kapital* defies intelligible study even by the elite, prepared one of the most famous appeals to the masses ever written, but the thundering declamation of the *Communist Manifesto* had little influence at first though it did presage the new approach to the dissemination of political beliefs. Perhaps the chief cause of the prestige and "legitimacy" of mass appeals has been the growing acceptance of democracy as the sole legitimate political method. The articles of faith of the ideology we call democracy assume as a matter of course that this change in the locus of power in society has had admirable results. The opposite view is denounced as reactionary, and in fact this negative aspect of democracy has been even more important than its positive contributions, that is, the value of democracy has been asserted to lie in preventing elitism, rather than in any positive function it may have. Whether or not this attitude can be sustained in the face of available data is quite another matter, and the actual consequences of numerical politics need very serious and uninhibited criticism. The role of democratic dogma in the "ideologizing" of modern politics, for example, is a subject well worth further research.

The appeal to the masses plays a vital part in the development of ideology, and the fact that such an appeal is made has important consequences for the ideology which we will now examine. As a general rule, the larger the number of persons who must agree to a proposition, the simpler the proposition must become, precision must be sacrificed, and meaning must become ambiguous. A few persons with similar backgrounds and tastes may agree to a very carefully constructed, relatively complicated doctrine. But when millions must adhere to a proposal, this is no longer possible. The level of complexity must be lowered to a common denominator within the reach of all those whose approval is needed. The complexity of the proposition will be limited by the sophistication of the potential adherents to the doctrine. Otherwise, it must be assumed that agreement and understanding are totally unrelated. Now, realistic and reasonable propositions about involved social questions cannot, a priori, be simple and uncomplicated, hence it seems out of the question to assume mass agreement to either the cause or the solution to such questions.

It is doubtful, to say the least, that an appeal to the masses can be reasonable and realistic—if this line of reasoning is accepted. Most of the early proponents of democracy, for example, recognized this very clearly, and offered as a solution to the dilemma the concept of the enlightened public which they hoped to achieve by education. This rather optimistic attitude ignored the question whether it was genuinely possible to achieve the educational level required for meaningful political discussion by mass education, though it did recognize the need for some leavening of the mass mind. Others, less reasonable perhaps, turned to the meaningless concept of "mass wisdom," that is, they assumed that large groups of people could demonstrate intuitively a collective wisdom which was adequate to the needs of mass political action.

The ideologists took still a third alternative and posed their own social absolutes, thus rendering the whole problem academic. The difficulty lies in the need to give very simple answers to extremely complicated questions, and it must be confessed that only ideologies have solved the problem, though we may dislike the manner in which it was solved. The validity of simple answers to complicated questions is, a priori, very questionable. The simpler the statement, the greater the likelihood of error, and the greater the margin left free for individual interpretation. The wider the margin free for interpretation, the more agreement is made possible. The technique employed to further this mass agreement is the widespread use of symbols, which play a key role in every ideology.

Ideological symbols, which may be short phrases or single words, or even proper names, play a crucial role in every mass ideology. They make possible widespread agreement to very complex and elaborate doctrines among a diversified population. Symbols are usually accepted without understanding, that is, the individual responds to the symbol without fully realizing what he is doing. The symbol is thus a mechanism for evoking a particular conditioned reflex. But symbols also play a part in more thoughtful adherence to ideologies in that they make it possible for those who actually inquire into the meaning of their own behavior to agree on a program of action by making their own interpretation of the nature of that program. To illustrate the first of these cases, assume an individual who simply responds favorably to the word "democracy" without any real understanding of what it means beyond, perhaps, the mores of his own society; in the second case, democracy might have a genuine meaning, highly particularized, which the individual accepts, thus giving the illusion of agreement with others who support democracy.

Most important political symbols have dozens of possible meanings, and often no agreed upon meaning whatever. Consider the possible interpretations and uses of words like "liberty," "freedom," "democracy," "equality," "socialism," "communism." Each term has a powerful appeal in one or more of our major political societies and arouses great enthusiasm among its supporters. Yet not one of these symbols has a meaning that would be agreed to by every person who claims to support the concept involved. Such terms are the political equivalent of the "call name" attached to canines with unpronounceable kennel names. In terms of strict meaning, one might just as well discuss yesterday's menu.

How did these meaningless terms come to occupy such an honorable and influential position in political belief? The best answers to date seem to have been provided by the Russian physiologist, Ivan Pavlov, who demonstrated by his experiments with dogs that suitable "conditioning" can lead to a desired response even though stimuli are used which have little or no relevance to the response pattern itself. By suitable conditioning, a dog can be made to salivate at the sight of a brick, just as men can be made to voluntarily sacrifice their lives in the name of a political symbol. Political symbols, in this context, are stimuli which evoke a value response among those who have been suitably conditioned. Undoubtedly, a more elaborate conditioning period is needed but the complexity of the human mind seems to permit the use of totally abstract symbols, which makes the task much easier. Consider the response of the average American citizen to the series of vibrations in the air which we identify as our National Anthem. As a musical composition, it has no merit whatever. The words, which are seldom intelligible and little known, relate to a sequence of events in the past which are little remembered, perhaps because they are somewhat embarrasing. The tune did not become "official" until 1931, and even then was adopted over strong opposition. It is frequently heard in a pitch only faintly related to the original, sung by screeching and raucous sopranos. Yet, as the writer can testify, it produces a definite emotional response in the individual, and cannot be criticized within the society with complete impunity. The process by which this result is obtained seems to fall within the terms of the definition of preconditioning. One major task of an ideology seeking mass support is certainly to condition a group of persons to respond in a particular manner to a given stimulus.

Unthinking response to symbol-stimuli as a substitute for thought seems one of the common features of ideological groups, and indeed similar behavior seems to characterize the whole political process in these days of mass politics. It is a truism that religious worship consists, for the most part, of this same type of behavior. One is tempted to assert that the conditioned response accounts for the vast majority of social behavior for the whole of humanity, and in a certain sense of the phrase, this is quite possibly true. Consciously or not, ideologies have always made considerable use of this technique, and this accounts for the peculiar flavor of ideological discussion (to the uninitiated). For the behavior of Pavlov's dogs is absurd to anyone who does not know the conditioning process. This may account in part for the great difficulty experienced in cross-cultural understanding or international understanding. Whether or not it is truly possible to appreciate the nature of social behavior which is largely a consequence of symbol conditioning without having seen subjected to the conditioning oneself is a matter for conjecture. On the face of it, it seems rather unlikely.

Even if this much is accepted, however, it remains to account for the unquestioned fact that many highly intelligent and well-trained individuals can and do accept ideologies of various sorts, and that the leadership of ideological movements usually derives from precisely these sources. The application of Pavlovian methods to such persons seems unlikely, and the invidious explanation, that ideologies are used by such persons as a ladder to power, cannot really account for many of the known instances. Perhaps the first point that needs to be made in this connection is that most ideologies attempt to condition their future adherents during the years prior to maturation. Having been raised on a body of dogma, the individual is much less likely to question its premises, or even realize its effect on his thinking. This is particularly true when the individual is raised in a community in which the ideology is universally accepted since the likelihood of exposure to criticism is in this case small.

Two other techniques are used by ideological groups to seduce the intellectuals attracted to the movement. First, the leaders of the ideology may admit, in private, that their ideological principles are nonsense, and justify their behavior by stressing the value to society of their own accession to power. A second method is to allow full and free criticism by the elite in the movement, while restricting public criticism that would reach the masses who are expected to agree blindly. The first method is not often met in politics, though it is proximate to the position of the political personage who must submit to the vagaries of mass elections, and admits in private that the arguments used to cozen the masses are not really a true statement of his own position. This attitude is usually justified by asserting that such practice is necessary to prevent the inevitable election of the unscrupulous, or that the genuine political intentions of the candidate are too complex to include in an electoral program. This devastating criticism of a mass electoral system is not usually recognized as such.

The dual system, involving one standard of discussion for the elite and another for the masses, is a commonplace in social organization. Briefly, the elite is permitted full and free discussion, and even differences of opinion as to the true meaning of the symbols of the ideology, while the masses are expected to make the requisite responses and not concern themselves too much about meanings. The Catholic Church and the Soviet Communist party are classic examples of this method, and the Catholic Church in particular has developed this system to a high degree of perfection. There is a lack of knowledge, interest, and even ability to read on the part of the masses which operates as a natural selecting process. Writings that dispute the views of the church are interdicted for all those who might be contaminated, an ancient version of the modern security system. The use of Latin acts as a discreet reinforcement for the whole process. Consequently, most of the great theological disputes have been fought among the elites, with the masses supporting the various parties to the conflict for reasons not often directly related to the actual dispute. The usual corollary to the process is firm insistence that internal disputes must not be aired; a sort of "collective responsibility," such as that found in the British cabinet system, prevails. Internal discussion is permitted, but public controversy is decried as detrimental to the ideology, which of course it is.

This dual system becomes rather more reasonable when the construction of ideological beliefs is examined. The hard core of an ideology is a group of fundamental principles, properly symbolized, which are taken as absolutely true. There are usually a number of negative principles in the central core of the doctrine, also suitably symbolized. The former are used to arouse enthusiasm and support among the followers of the ideology; the latter to elicit unfavorable responses. If an ideology is visualized as a series of concentric circles, these positive and negative principles occupy the innermost circle. The principles are broad and vague, not precise. Agreement to this group of fundamentals is the *sine qua non* of becoming a supporter of the ideology. Moving away from this central group, each succeeding level finds the principles becoming more and more concrete—they become action principles rather than fundamentals—more fully delineated, and therefore less likely to command the support of every adherent to the ideology. At the extreme periphery of the body of thought contained in the ideology are the highly individual interpretations of the doctrine which are scarcely more than idiosyncrasies, with little numerical support even within the ideology, and perhaps not even officially sanctioned by the ideology.

The key symbol in most ideologies is usually the proper name of the ideology or the proper name of the social organization from which it springs as in modern nationalism. Such symbols are open to great diversity of interpretation, and of course command universal support within the ideology. These name symbols are always "good," i.e., they elicit favorable responses; other "good" symbols usually include the names of the prophets and disciples and entities or conditions which the ideology views with favor. In the Soviet ideology, for example, communism, socialism, Marx, Lenin, people's democracy and similar terms would all be viewed with approval. The symbols seldom change once they have been adopted, although their meaning may undergo substantial revision from one generation to the next. In Britain, for example, socialism was almost synonymous with nationalization and the welfare state in the first half of the twentieth century. After 1950, the welfare state was a fact and the future of nationalization of industry was being seriously questioned by some of the party leaders. The meaning of socialism was deprived of content in a very short period of time, and the support built upon half a century of unremitting propaganda had to be converted to a new and as yet undeveloped concept. This problem has not yet been solved and socialism, while it remains a "good" word, has no single meaning, even for the elite. The best parallel to this sort of term is probably the emotion-laden concepts like "mother," "home" and so on. These words produce remarkably similar responses within a given culture though no one would argue that they connote identical experiences. Instead an elaborate social myth, which is part of the ideology of the society, helps to exert sufficient pressure on the individual to conform to the expected behavior response.

The negative ideological symbols, usually derived from the chief enemies of the ideology, really appear to be more important than the positive or "good" symbols. Every ideology has its "bogeyman," whose sinister purpose it is to ruin the work of the ideology, and who must be resisted at all costs. It is a very convenient scapegoat. The communists make use of the capitalists for this purpose; Christians the antichrist; socialists, like Shakespeare's Mercutio lay a curse on both the house of capitalism and the house of communism, though the latter became a serious bogey only after 1948, while the former has had a long run of popularity. In essence, this is the "we" feeling of the closed group, directly against the outsiders—"they." The reason why ideologies make so much use of negative symbolism lies in the field of psychology rather than politics. Perhaps dislike and hatred are more potent social forces than liking and the desire to achieve some social goal. Possibly it is easier to formulate negative programs than positive programs. Certainly fear plays an important part in the entire process. Whatever the reason, the sample group used in this discussion certainly relied much more heavily upon negative attitudes than on positive proposals, though both are usually equally ill-defined.

This brief summation of the consequences of seeking mass support for an ideology can hardly be encouraging to anyone who entertains some regard for the future of rational politics. The tendency to oversimplify complex political issues, and resolve questions of political value into animalistic responses to meaningless symbolism is hardly conducive to rational thought, let alone empirical investigation. The distortion of facts that must follow any attempt to fit the stream of events into the procrustean bed of ideological absolutes is deplorable. Reason gives way, in effect, to reflexes, and political behavior becomes the consequence of a skilled manipulation of symbols by the leaders of ideological groups.

We cannot, however, stop even at this point. For if ideologies must have mass support, they must have social organization. The strength of the organization depends in part upon its size and in part upon the amount of social cohesion which it proves capable of developing. Social cohesion, the "we feeling" that develops within social groups, depends in turn upon the size of the group, its past history, the type of relationship that obtains (face to face, impersonal, remote etc.), the purpose of the group, relations with other groups, and numerous similar factors. Large groups are naturally less easily welded into a unified whole; small groups are less powerful in societies where mass voting is the means to power. For the political scientist, the important aspect of social cohesion is the type of behavior it produces, rather than the factors which increase or decrease its intensity. Among the more important of these types of behavior are fear, suspicion, or even hatred of other groups, and a concomitant feeling of friendliness and uncritical acceptance of members of one's own group. Basically, what develops is a clear separation between "we" and "they," and the more clearly the separation exists the stronger the bond between group members. These social pressures produce group values and behavior patterns, or in sociological terms, expectations of behavior, which may be far removed from the behavior of the individual outside the group. Groups further tend to produce recognized leaders, rules, procedures for rule-making, and means of enforcement. Closed groups, in fact, tend to develop into miniature societies, complete with all the paraphernalia of government and law enforcement. In most cases, groups produce recognizable trends toward authoritarian control by group leaders.

Historically, there seems every justification for assuming that ideology in fact produces authoritarianism. Calvin's Geneva, the Puritan towns of New England, Communist Russia, Nationalist and Communist China, Nazi Germany, Fascist Italy, all were ruled by authoritarian regimes. Most known religions are authoritarian in the regulation of their internal affairs. Modern nationalism, on careful observation but without adequate detailed research, appears to show signs of developing in this same direction. The structure of the modern national state tends to place authority in relatively fewer hands with the passage of time. In terms of state control of individual behavior, the increase in authority has been startling. The individual peasant farmer in absolutist France was far less governed than the farmer in modern, democratic Britain. It may be argued that the modern farmer has gained thereby, but that is really beside the point.

The crucial question, however, is not whether history shows authoritarian tendencies in ideological groups, but whether this is necessary because of the nature of ideology or whether the tendency is due to some other cause. The attitude taken here is that ideology must adopt an authoritarian organization or concede the possibility of its own demise. The need for unity, cohesion, and discipline for the reduction of internal strife, which is particularly important to ideologies, seems to demand unified authority. The struggle to unify authority leads to the repression of alternative leadership, whether in the personal interests of the contestant, or in the future interest of the ideology one cannot tell in every case, though the latter argument is always cited. The inclusive nature of ideological groups, the active suspicion of nonmembers, materially strengthens the position of the leaders. The fact that even factual data coming from without the group are subject to scrutiny, usually by the leaders of the group, before such data are accepted by the group, further strengthens this trend. In societies where the ideological leaders control the political government as well, alternative sources of information may be completely stilled, and information media almost totally controlled. Nationalism, for example, seems to be going in this direction as it renders the social consequences of deviation from the accepted viewpoint more and more severe. The question which is asked first is no longer "is it right?" but "who said it?"

This brief summary of the salient characteristics of ideology does not pretend to be complete; its purpose is to provide a framework within which the chief question posed for the study can be considered: How does ideology affect the opinions and beliefs of an individual in relation to international affairs? Clearly, the content of the ideology will play a major part in the answer to the question how one specific ideology affects individual attitudes or

opinions.   Again, I must state that this is not the question considered here.   We are interested in the influence of ideology *as*
ideology; with the general consequences of any ideology and not
with the effects of the specific tenets of a particular ideology.

Most of the great political ideologies of our time are primarily
concerned with domestic questions and only incidentally with the
relation between political societies.   The great exception to this
generalization is, of course, nationalism, which is the ideology
common to an entire political society and which operates most
effectively in the field of international affairs.   Nevertheless, most
political ideologies have been forced to deal with international
affairs once they become significantly involved in national problems.

The field of international affairs is peculiarly amenable to the
influence of ideology.   The extent of public knowledge of the facts
of international relations is limited, and interest in these questions
is slight, although it has increased considerably in recent years.
The data of international affairs are usually imprecise and in-
complete, leaving a substantial area for interpretation.   Most of
the data are processed through national agencies before they are
made available to the public; this process provides ample opportunity for the injection of ideological symbolism calculated to
produce a desired attitude toward the data.   The complexity of
the subject, which has reached such proportions that specialists
working in limited fields experience considerable difficulty in
keeping abreast of current developments, also works in favor of
the increased influence of ideologies.

It is sometimes assumed that a fact, like an elephant, stands
clear and precise for all to see and agree. Here the ancient
fable of the four blind men and the elephant is instructive. Uncritical observation, or observation which uses biased instruments,
cannot guarantee accuracy.   Ideology acts to limit the reliability
of the critical apparatus of the observer just as partial destruction
of the optic nerve causes a deterioration in the usefulness of the
eye.   Ideology restricts the number of facts that are used as a
basis for judgment by assuming contamination of certain types of
sources, and by rejecting outright data emanating from groups or
persons hostile to it. Ideology reduces the number of alternatives
which may be considered by condemning certain alternatives
which conflict with the ideology.   Ideology strongly influences the
actual conclusions reached by making certain conclusions more
satisfactory emotionally, or more desirable, than others.   It can
even lead, as we shall see below, to the substitution of completely
new, and unfounded, data when existing materials are all considered ideologically unsatisfactory.

For illustration, assume an event "A" occurs and stipulate that "A" is a true and exact version of that event. No one would be greatly surprised if an authoritarian political regime permitted only one version of that event to appear in the information media available to that society even though the version might be that "C" occurred. This type of behavior is universally recognized, and nearly universally decried so long as the society in which it occurs is external to the person rendering judgment. But all ideologies produce precisely this same general effect in all societies. In a free society, where every opinion is accorded the right to circulate, a number of versions of the event taken for illustration may appear, including, perhaps, the true description of the event as "A." But if the ideology of a particular individual makes it impossible for him to accept "A" as a true version of events, or impossible to accept anything but version "C" as a description of that event, then freedom of information is wasted upon that person. Consider the case of a British communist, who lives in a society in which information may circulate freely. The "enemy" press—the *Times, Guardian,* or *Telegraph,*— he would either ignore or refuse to believe. His "own" press, the *Daily Worker* would, in case of conflict, be the source which he would by definition be most likely to believe. Thus the source of information becomes more important than the validity of the information.

Finally, the influence of ideology is such that even where the facts of international affairs are agreed upon there is no guarantee that the value judgment made will take such facts into consideration. Ideology seems in practice to create a dual system of values: it shifts the basis of moral judgment from the facts of the event to the ideological convictions of the participants. The action that is condemned in an enemy is condoned in a friend, and Polemarchus's definition of justice is carried to its logical conclusions. Even the force of nationalism can be overridden by ideological conviction, leading to the application of the standard usually reserved for enemies to the actions of the citizens' own government. Faced with this type of behavior, facts are an encumbrance and judgment a mechanical process, devoid of ethical or moral content. Ultimately, we arrive at the nefarious doctrine that any means justify the end when the end is an absolute postulated by the ideology.

II

THE BRITISH LEFT WING

The political group that will be used to illustrate the influence of ideology upon thought regarding international affairs is known to British politics as the Left Wing. Common usage has produced in the term a useful concept, but one that is not easily defined with precision. The boundaries of the Left Wing are vague. There is no single organization which contains the Left Wing and nothing more, though everyone who is part of the Left Wing is also part of the British Labour movement, and most belong to the British Labour party. There is no formal procedure for gaining entry to the Left Wing, and the most common means of becoming a recognized member of the Left Wing seems to be self-election or a unilateral declaration by the individual.

In a general sense the term is sometimes applied to the critics of the official leadership of the Labour party. But whatever the theoretical usage, the composition of the Left Wing is reasonably well agreed upon. The group might better be termed the "extreme left" if this did not have the unfortunate connotation of membership in the Communist party and more. There is an element of "fellow-traveling" in Left Wing thought, and some measure of Marxian doctrine, but British socialism is unquestionably the least Marxist socialist movement in Europe, and these influences are not important. Avowed members of the British Communist party have been wholly excluded from the group.

The question whether or not the Left Wing really was, or is, "to the left" in British politics—whatever that term may mean—simply cannot be answered. Members of the Left Wing certainly assumed that this was the case, but the meaning of the phrase is too obscure to permit a valid judgment. Some members of the Left Wing, for example, considered the Communist party as "right wing" and condemned it for that reason. Others felt that men like Ernest Bevin were far to the right within the movement, yet Bevin would certainly have repudiated this contention and pointed to his own youthful participation in the Social Democratic Federation as evidence of his personal preferences.

There are literally dozens of groups, and thousands of individuals in Britain who either claim membership in the Left Wing, or are accorded membership by common usage. It is manifestly impossible to deal with each one separately, yet it is essential that every major viewpoint be given a hearing. Since selection is essential, the criteria used for selecting must be stated. First, those elements of the Left Wing with national significance and some national following were given preference. Second, all known members of the British Communist party were excluded from the discussion on the assumption that their opinions about international affairs could justly be said to be the views of an agency external to British politics. Third, members of the two postwar Labour Governments were excluded so long as they remained in office because of the well-known constitutional principle limiting their freedom to express individual views.

Since the study is concerned essentially with opinion, and opinion must be expressed to be known, the materials on which the study is based derive from the vocal element of the population of the total group. As noted previously, one cannot really say how far such opinions represent the views of the mute majority. Voting in general elections and at Labour party conferences, opinion polls, and other devices for quantifying political support may provide an indication of the extent to which the masses respond to particular appeals. But the process is complicated and the results seem uncertain. Do the voters choose the lesser of two evils? Should the casual voter be counted equally with the rabid supporter? Certainly not in terms of effectiveness within a political movement. These and similar questions arise to plague the quantifier, and it is doubtful that present techniques are really capable of measuring a single factor in the complicated process of political choice. The presumption is strong that the British Left Wing commands substantial support from the rank and file of the Labour movement for reasons that will be delineated below, but it remains only a presumption and should be treated with caution.

To facilitate the organization and presentation of the material, the sources of Left Wing opinion can be grouped into three major areas: the Left Wing press, which includes the leading journals customarily expounding a viewpoint that is recognizably part of Left Wing thought; the Left Wing in Parliament, which includes all M.P.'s who are usually considered part of the Left Wing; and the non-parliamentary Left Wing, containing leading spokesmen for the Left Wing point of view who are not Members of Parliament. This grouping is nothing more than an academic convenience and no significance should be attached to it. In practice, the Left Wing must be explained in terms of very small groups, and even of individuals. But it is not really possible to gather together the separate threads of a hundred opinions without some framework. Framework can, however, mean the loss of nuance which is the essence of politics, and I have tried to preserve it by indicating in some detail the areas of agreement and disagreement on vital issues.

The Left Wing press included in the study has been severely limited. The British people are exposed to the largest and most diversified body of published materials of any society on earth. More than four thousand newspapers and periodicals appear annually, and several dozen of them could be included in the Left Wing press. But if national significance is taken as the chief criterion, three weekly journals, one Sunday newspaper, and two publishing agencies qualify for the study. The three weekly journals are the *New Statesman and Nation,*[1] *Tribune,* and *Forward.* The Sunday newspaper is the co-operatively-owned *Reynolds News.* The two publishing agencies are the Fabian Society and the National Peace Council.

The *New Statesman* is published weekly in London, and was edited, throughout the period covered by the study, by Mr. Kingsley Martin. In 1946, it had a circulation of 83,571[2] and it seems reasonable to assume that this figure increased with the passage of time and with the availability of ample supplies of newsprint. The assistant editor of the *New Statesman* was Richard Crossman, who won a seat in the House of Commons in the General Election of 1945 and played a leading role in the Left Wing in Parliament. The *New Statesman* is primarily a political organ, though it has earned something of a reputation for the quality of its art criticism. The Royal Commission on the Press classified the journal as, "One of six weekly journals of opinion, which in providing a forum for informed discussion of political affairs, are in some respects the successors of the highly political newspapers of the last century."[3] Editorial opinion is, of course, pro-socialist and the *New Statesman* was perhaps the chief vehicle for Left Wing opinion in Britain throughout the period 1945-1951.

Two features of the editorial policy followed in the *New Statesman* make it particularly useful for this study: first, it devoted a substantial portion of its editorial comment to international affairs; second, it usually published statements of opinion and commentary on news events rather than "straight" factual news accounts such as those found on the press wires. This does not mean that items in the *New Statesman* had no relation whatever to fact, though this relation at times appeared very tenuous. It does imply that editorials and leaders were usually "interpretations" of current events rather than simple enumerations of facts. The relation between the factual data, which can usually be established with a fair degree of accuracy, and the interpretation of events found in the *New Statesman* offers a useful index to the amount of refraction imparted to fact by ideological preconception.

Although R. H. S. Crossman was closely associated with the *New Statesman,* editorial policy from 1945 until 1951 remained independent of the views expressed in the House of Commons by Crossman and those associated with him. The differences between Kingsley Martin and the parliamentary Left Wing were often no more than a matter of emphasis and shading, but on a number of fundamental questions they were poles apart. On the conscription issue, for example, the fact that Kingsley Martin was a professed pacifist made agreement with Crossman, who was not, out of the question.

Tribune, the second major source of Left Wing opinion in Britain, was also classified by the Royal Commission as a "journal of opinion," though it might better be called a propaganda vehicle. It originated in 1937 as an organ of the Socialist League, which was then the spearhead of the Left Wing and an important influence in the "unity campaign" taking place at that time. The key figures behind the new weekly were Aneurin Bevan, Stafford Cripps (later Sir Stafford Cripps), William Mellor, and George R. Strauss. Cripps and Mellor severed connections with *Tribune* before World War II began. George R. Strauss and Aneurin Bevan later handed over their interests in the journal to their respective wives. By 1945, policy was determined by an editorial board consisting of Jennie Lee (Mrs. Bevan), Mrs. Pat Strauss, Michael Foot, Ian Mikardo, and Jon Kimche. Jon Kimche was the editor of *Tribune* until 1948. Ian Mikardo resigned from the editorial board in 1949 following a dispute with other board members over British foreign policy.

There are no definite circulation figures available for *Tribune,* although the circulation was estimated at 40,000 in 1947.[4] If this estimate is substantially correct, a very considerable increase must have occurred by 1950 when prominent figures on the *Tribune* staff were involved in a hot dispute with the leaders of the parliamentary Labour party over foreign affairs. Individual pamphlets published by *Tribune* sold nearly 100,000 copies in one instance and nearly 250,000 copies in another.[5] Since the distribution was at least partly "tied" to regular sales, the indications are that circulation was well above the estimate cited.

In contrast to the *New Statesman,* which stood somewhat aloof from the parliamentary Left Wing, *Tribune* was primarily significant by virtue of its close association with the views of a strong element of the Left Wing in Parliament. Michael Foot, Jennie Lee,

Ian Mikardo, J. P. W. Mallalieu, Aneurin Bevan and various others interested in or associated with *Tribune* gained seats in the 1945 General Election. For them, *Tribune* was a means by which parliamentary debate could be continued in the wider context of the entire Labour movement in Britain, and without the repressive influence of the Speaker of the House of Commons, who took a rather dim view of comment that tended to be too personal and perhaps unwarranted by events.

Forward, the third member of the weekly Left Wing press, is certainly the least influential member of the trio. While circulation data are not published, *Forward* reaches many fewer readers than either of the other two journals. Nevertheless, *Forward* is the custodian of one of the best loved traditions in British socialism, the pacifistic, fervent, almost religious passion for social justice—however ill defined—that was so characteristic of Labour propaganda in the early part of the twentieth century. The editor, Emrys Hughes, is related through marriage to one of the founding fathers of the British Labour party, Keir Hardie. Hughes retains much of the old monastic fervour, and is accorded a respectful hearing even when his views are not popular.

Reynolds News, owned and published by the British Co-operative movement, appears each Sunday. It had a "pegged" or fixed circulation of 720,000 in 1947, which is large as compared to the weekly journals, but small compared to the remainder of the popular Sunday press.[6] Labour supporters often complained of both the lack of support for the movement in *Reynolds News* and of the nonpolitical character of its editorials. A portion of its circulation was undoubtedly due to the sensational nature of its leading articles. Editorial comment was usually brief, and international affairs figured infrequently in the editorial columns. Nevertheless, the paper did have a national circulation, and it did take a Left Wing viewpoint, and it merits inclusion in the study on this basis.

The Fabian Society and the National Peace Council are not, properly speaking, publications, nor are they important for the views which they expressed. They are essentially propaganda societies. Their value lies in the channel which they provided for others to express their views, and since both function in much the same manner, they can be considered together. Neither body maintained a corporate opinion, though their administrative officers took an active part in Labour propaganda activities. By arranging meetings and by publishing speeches and pamphlets by prominent socialists, they provided a valuable means of reaching an influential public. A substantial portion of their output from 1945 to 1951 concerned international affairs, and the Left Wing made a significant contribution to this body of literature. There are no circulation figures available, though each issue probably reaches fewer than 10,000 persons. On the other hand, an important element of the British Labour movement takes part in the work of the Fabian Society, and its influence reaches well beyond these simple statistics.[7]

In addition to these primary sources of editorial opinion, a great many additional journals, press releases, clippings, etc. were culled for information. They are far too numerous to list separately, and suitable acknowledgement will be made wherever necessary.

The Left Wing press plays a vital part in the opinion forming process in the British Labour movement, a part that was somewhat obscured after 1945 by the prominence achieved by members of the parliamentary Left Wing. Parliament is not always in session, and individual members, however prominent, can only speak occasionally in the House, even when it is sitting. The main burden of providing a continuous flow of information, comment, and guidance to the rank and file of the movement thus devolves upon the press. The element of continuity which the press provides is its most important contribution to Labour thought, particularly after 1945 when Labour was in power and the official machinery of the party was geared to support the Government's policies. The powerful and often acute commentary found in the Left Wing press, carefully phrased to accord with existing Labour prejudices, seems to have been far more appealing to the rank and file than the cautious voice of the "official" sources of news. Since the Left Wing press concentrated on international affairs, and provided a continuous source of "socialist" opinion not to be found elsewhere, its message to British Labour had a substantially greater impact, I feel, than might have been the case had Labour remained in opposition.

The General Election of 1945 created a completely new situation for the British Labour party. Before World War II, Labour representation in the House of Commons was small, and the dominant voice was undoubtedly that of the trade unions. Suddenly, the leading figures of the Left Wing found themselves massed inside the House of Commons, and parliamentary debates became the most important single sounding board for Left Wing opinion available in the country. This unexpected windfall was augmented by the amount of publicity given to Left Wing criticisms of the Government, even by the opposition press, particularly when conflict over international affairs began in 1946. Left Wing attacks on the Government made "good copy" and the Left Wing was given a "good press." This situation was used to good advantage.

There had been a few influential Left Wing spokesmen in Parliament even before 1945, and these were returned to the House without exception in the General Election of 1945. From this group some of the outstanding critics of the Coalition Government's policies were taken into Prime Minister Attlee's first Government, thus removing them from the study, at least temporarily. This influx of Left Wing spokesmen into government office was due in part to the genuine need for experienced parliamentarians and, undoubtedly, in part to the time honored British custom of silencing potential opposition with office. The lion does not roar with a mouthful of meat. It would be invidious, even if it were possible, to choose the decisive factor in any particular case. But a quick survey of the leading figures so treated—Aneurin Bevan, Stafford Cripps, Emmanuel Shinwell, Ellis Smith, George R. Strauss, and John Strachey,—reveals a substantial number of alumni of the defunct Socialist League.

Other Left Wing M.P.'s returned to the 1945 House of Commons and not included in Attlee's Government were Francis Bowles, Tom Driberg, Seymour Cocks, Dr. Haden Guest, Richard Stokes, and the three remaining stalwarts from the nearly expired Independent Labour party (ILP), James Maxton, the Reverend Campbell Stephen, and John McGovern. These men continued to urge more radical policies upon the Government throughout the life of the Parliament, except James Maxton, who died in 1946, and took with him the little driving force remaining in the ILP. The Reverend Stephen followed a highly individualistic and completely pacifistic line of his own. John McGovern, whether swayed by his personal religious views or by his experience with the "unity" campaigns of the 1930's one cannot say, became an ardent critic of the Soviet Union and its policies.

Since the number of Labour M.P.s entering the House of Commons for the first time in 1945 was very large, and substantial numbers of them fall into the Left Wing, it would be tedious, and indeed hardly useful, to indulge in a seriatim recitation of their individual backgrounds. Accordingly, they are grouped below into four broad categories, based upon their personal background, and the opinions and associations that they developed during the life of the Parliament. The categories used are not indicative of any genuine organization, or even of close association; they indicate the main lines of opinion on international affairs encountered in the House during these years.

The first category includes the Left Wing journalists, usually associated with one or another of the publications included in the Left Wing press. Closely associated with these journalists were a number of writers, lecturers, and journalists not directly associated with the Left Wing press but who tended to support the same general policy line. The second category comprises a fairly large body of ex-servicemen who were elected to Parliament for the first time in 1945. Many of them had spent some years abroad in one of the armed services, and returned to Britain with a keen interest in international affairs, plus some first hand knowledge of one or more particular areas. They were accorded an interested hearing by the House, and contributed substantially to Labour Party discussion of international affairs. The use of this terminology does not imply that other Labour M.P.'s did not have military service. It only indicates that military experience plays an important part in the formation of the opinions of this particular group.

The third category includes the pacifists of various sorts, who were relatively few in numbers but enormously strong in tradition. Officially, the British Labour party rejected pacifism in 1935, somewhat half-heartedly it is true, but clearly enough. The 1945 election manifesto, "Let Us Face the Future," firmly repudiated pacifism as a means of preventing war. But the fruits of a half century of propaganda are not dissipated by mere manifestos, and pacifism continued to enjoy the respect and admiration of the Labour movement, even from those who felt the attitude to be totally unrealistic. The final category contains the fellow travelers, distinguished primarily by an utter inability to accept any criticism of the Soviet Union and a complete unwillingness to refrain from making excuses for Soviet behavior, particularly in Eastern Europe.

The M.P.'s in each of these four categories exhibited certain distinguishing characteristics. The Left Wing journalists and their followers were well informed and very capable writers and publicists. They took an extremely active interest in international affairs after 1945, and became, generally speaking, the leading element in the British Left Wing, both inside and outside the House of Commons. The returning servicemen, as a body, were a striking contrast to the veterans who returned to Britain from the first world war—a group that would include Clement Attlee. World War I produced disillusionment, hatred of war, a strong tendency toward pacifism, and a disinclination to discuss strategic or military questions in any terms other than total abolition of all such matters. The new generation was quite a different breed, and hence much more influential. Military strategy and tactics played an important part in their thinking, and they were not in the least awed by the resounding tones of the Brigadiers and Generals on the Conservative side of the House. They strengthened the position of the Labour party in Parliament very much by their contributions to debates on these matters. Eventually, some of them took issue with their own government on the manner in which strategic assumptions should govern policy and some of them became severe critics of the government on that score.

The fellow travelers began the Parliament with their influence at its zenith, but this influence gradually declined as East-West relations worsened. They performed an important office for the Left Wing, and even for the whole Labour movement, in that they provided the "plausible excuse" that enabled British socialists to continue to affirm their traditional sympathy for the "great socialist experiment" being conducted in the Soviet Union long after that country had forfeited its right to such support by behavior which British socialists could hardly condone. British Labour had supported the Soviet effort from the time of its establishment, but the degree of labour support varied with the political composition of the faction expressing its views. The trade unions had offered, for the most part, cautious support; the Left Wing, on the other hand, had been and continued to be enthusiastic and uncritical. In general, the Soviet struggle with Germany, coming as it did at a time when Britain was substantially aided thereby, bolstered this sympathetic attitude and spread it throughout the whole of Britain, whatever the political affiliations of the individual.

On the Left Wing, the Soviet-German *rapproachement*, the invasion of Poland and Finland, and the absorption of the Baltic States were speedily forgotten. Soviet prestige stood high everywhere in 1945, and nowhere higher than with the Left Wing. The fellow travelers, then, spoke to a receptive audience, for the alternative to accepting their views was suspicion of Soviet intentions and doubt regarding the validity of Labour's own past views of Soviet policy. This was ideologically distasteful and practically uncomfortable, for the alternative to peaceful agreement was distinctly unpleasant. In sum, the fellow travelers labored in fertile ground, and exerted substantially more influence in the early post war years than they might otherwise have done.

The more prominent of the Left Wing journalists were R. H.S. Crossman from the *New Statesman,* Michael Foot, Ian Mikardo, Geoffrey Bing, Benn Levy, J. P. W. Mallalieu, and Jennie Lee from *Tribune,* and T. E. N. Driberg from *Reynolds News.* Associated with them were writers and lecturers like Mrs. Barbara Castle, Francis Bowles, Maurice Edelman, R. G. W. Mackay, and Leslie Hale. Crossman, Foot, and Mikardo stand out as the leaders of this group, and Crossman was, for a time, the acknowledged leader of the parliamentary Left Wing. All three men were closely associated with the production of "Keep Left," a pamphlet published by the *New Statesman* in May, 1947, outlining the Left Wing's criticisms of the Government's foreign policy. Most of the group specialized in some aspect of international affairs, and their contributions to parliamentary debates, or to the Left Wing journals, were most frequently concerned with that subject.

The more influential pacifists in the 1945 Parliament were Emrys Hughes, Rhys Davies, Reginald Sorenson, Rev. Campbell Stephen, James Maxton (until his death in 1946), W. G. Cove, James Hudson, and Victor Yates. Emrys Hughes, Rhys Davies and Reginald Sorenson were most frequently heard in parliamentary debates and they are most frequently mentioned here, but the remainder of the pacifists tended to support the same general policy line, and the pacifists as a group usually voted or abstained together. The Standing Orders of the parliamentary Labour party permit abstention on matters of conscience, though they do not allow an adverse vote. But it was hardly possible to enforce severe discipline on the pacifists in any event, even though they sometimes did vote against the Government. Labour had a very large majority, and the pacifists' votes did not really matter much; further, the strength of traditional respect for pacifism could hardly be ignored under the circumstances.

The General Election of 1945 also proved fruitful for the fellow travelers, and S. O. Davies, J. D. Mack, John Platts-Mills, D. N. Pritt, Sydney Silverman, Leslie Solley, William Warbey, and Konni Zilliacus, all of whom took particular interest in international affairs, were seated in the House of Commons. As Soviet-Western relations worsened, pressure was exerted on the fellow travelers to exact conformity to party policy, and several lost their membership in the Labour party. D. N. Pritt had already been expelled in 1940 and gained a seat in 1945 as an independent.[8] John Platts-Mills was expelled from the party in 1948.[9] Leslie Solley and Konni Zilliacus were expelled in 1949.[10] William Warbey lost his seat at Luton in the General Election of 1950.

The fellow travelers were few in number, but very active both in Parliament and in the press. Konni Zilliacus was particularly well known for his work in international affairs. During the interwar years, he was employed by the League of Nations, concurrently serving as a Labour party expert on foreign affairs. In 1935, he collaborated in a highly successful attack on the Conservative Government's foreign policy, published on the eve of the General Election.[11] He was widely known and quoted in the Labour movement, and many considered him to be nothing more than an eccentric and quite harmless individualist. Other students of British politics, including the writer, do not share this view. The position taken here is that Zilliacus was very influential and definitely harmful to Labour's interests during the immediate postwar years.

A number of Left Wing M.P.'s completely defy classification and must be considered as individuals outside the scope of these four categories. Seymour Cocks, for example, had long been a critic of British foreign policy, Conservative or Labour, and he continued his criticisms through the life of the 1945 Parliament. Richard Stokes, an independent-minded businessman, had applied socialist principles to the management of his affairs and claimed singular success in so doing. Like Cocks, he took an active interest in international affairs. Others will be encountered from time to time and considered separately.

The Left Wing outside Parliament includes a number of nationally prominent figures who were often but not always active in Labour party affairs. For the most part, they were capable and influential writers, publicists, educators, and propagandists, who performed a valuable service for the British Labour movement. Men like Professor Harold J. Laski of the London School of Economics, Professor G. D. H. Cole of Oxford University, publisher Victor Gollancz, and writers Fenner Brockway, Leonard Woolf, and Sydney D. Bailey fall into this general category. Usually it was not possible to obtain a continuous flow of opinion from these sources because politics was only one facet of their many activities. Professor Laski became for a time a regular contributor to *Forward* and his views for that period are available in some detail. For the remainder, data are sporadic and limited; the occasional book or pamphlet, details of a speech appearing in the press, these are the substance of the materials at hand. Such sources cannot be counted too heavily in any extended survey. Yet these men are important, if only because of their close association with British education and the unquestioned influence they exerted on the younger generation of British socialists who attended their lectures at the universities and elsewhere.

The British Left Wing as enumerated constituted a formidable aggregation of political talent, including some of the finest debaters and propagandists in Britain. Although we are not concerned with the extent of Left Wing influence on Labour policy in international affairs, but rather with the nature of that influence whatever its extent, it is worth noting that the actual influence of the Left Wing has hardly reached the level that might be expected at first sight. The Left Wing cannot be dismissed as unimportant, but it did not and does not at the time of this writing enjoy the measure of influence over day-to-day policy that might be presumed from the measure of its abilities. Fundamentally, this seems traceable to the lack of organization which is characteristic of the Left Wing.

There are three power centers in British Labour: a well organized trade union movement; a political party with a national organization; and a parliamentary Labour party, whose exact relationship to the other two bodies is a matter of some constitutional interest. These three power centers are not distinct entities, and there is much overlapping of membership. Furthermore, neither national party nor union nor parliamentary party are monolithic structures; they represent a balance of interests and there are sharp areas of disagreement within each body and among the three bodies. Acting in concert, coalitions of leaders emerged in the past which were able to exert a dominant influence on Labour policies for considerable time periods. But the political reality that lies beneath the surface is a shifting series of combinations which depended for their strength on the timing, personality, and circumstances involved in the solution of a particular issue.

In the past, the Left Wing has drawn much of its strength from its consistent approach to political questions. There has always been some measure of support for Left Wing policies within the various trade unions, though it has been suppressed in the past by a coalition of powerful and relatively conservative union leaders from the larger unions. This was particularly true in the 1930's. Much the same situation existed within the Labour party and in Parliament. By oversimplification of issues, persistence, and highly emotionalized argument, sometimes making use of data that must have been known to be incorrect, the Left Wing often gained acceptance for its point of view, although not always in time to gain its point in the actual policy decision. Thus the version of international affairs during the interwar years that is commonly accepted within the Labour movement today is that which originated on the Left Wing, and not that which the Labour movement actually acted upon at the time. We shall see examples of this in the chapter that follows.

On day-to-day issues, the Left Wing has not often been very influential. There appear to be two main factors which led to this singular lack of success: first, the absence of unity within the Left Wing, and a concurrent lack of that solidly based organization which makes for strength in mass movements; second, the fierce hostility of a group of powerful trade union leaders. The lack of unity is little more than an open manifestation of the very real differences of opinion that divide the Left Wing into tiny splinters on any particular issue. For the Left Wing, despite its firm support for collectivist theories, has been far and away the most individualistic element in the British Labour movement. As the course of events brought new issues to the fore, the alliances of Left Wing leaders and their supporters have shifted and there has seldom been complete agreement on a specific policy, and even then, as with disarmament, agreement was not based on the same reasoning.

This lack of organization and unity, which has paralyzed Left Wing efforts to influence Labour policies, has not escaped notice among Left Wing spokesmen and leaders. A number of efforts have been made to form an effective Left Wing organization. The Socialist League formed in 1931 had this goal. The "Keep Left" group formed in 1947 and the "Bevanite" group formed in 1951 also had as their purpose the extension of Left Wing influence. The Socialist League was held in check, and then forced to dissolve, by a combination of trade unionists including Ernest Bevin, Walter Citrine and Charles Dukes, all supported by the great general unions. The apparent solidarity of the trade union movement after 1930 was often due to the agreement among this small group and their recognized eminence in trade union circles. Beneath this apparent agreement there were individual unions violently opposed to the policies which the T.U.C. was following at the time under the influence of these men. It is worth noting that the generation of union leaders who dominated the 1930's had largely passed away by 1950. Of the twenty largest unions in Britain, ninety per cent changed leadership after 1940, while only one changed leadership during the decade after 1930.

Following the General Election of 1945, the main arena for Labour politics became the House of Commons, where the influence of the unions was not dominant, particularly after the election took place. Only four M.P.'s usually considered to belong to the Left Wing were supported by a trade union during the 1945 election: Fred Lee, Tom Williams, Walter Padley, and Aneurin Bevan. The leading figures in both postwar Labour Governments were not trade union men. Clement Attlee, Hugh Dalton, Herbert Morrison, Stafford Cripps, Emmanuel Shinwell, Chuter Ede, Hugh Gaitskell, Philip Noel-Baker, Edith Summerskill, Kenneth Younger, the leading figures in Attlee's two Governments, were all constituency-sponsored. Trade union-sponsored members declined from 50 per cent of the total in 1931 to 35 per cent of a much larger total in 1945.[12] In 1951 the potential influence of the Left Wing seemed much greater than it had been at any time in the past, given the ability to settle differences and abide by a single policy.

III

THE LEFT WING IDEOLOGY

The British Left Wing is a part of the contemporary British socialist movement, and as such it shares with other British socialists the basic tenets of its ideology. The Left Wing differs from the bulk of the British Labour movement in the stress which it places upon particular aspects of socialist doctrines, for example in the amount of emphasis which it places on the class struggle. The Left Wing also differs from other British socialists in the rigor with which it attempts to apply its principles to current affairs; it is far more dogmatic in its approach to politics than more moderate elements of British socialism, and in this respect tends to resemble more closely the socialist groups on the European continent.

Fundamentally, British socialism is committed to gradualism, and to the use of parliamentary methods to achieve political power. It relies upon mass organization and the democratic voting process, rather than direct action and the carefully disciplined revolutionary elite. In the tradition of British socialism, Karl Marx counts for but little; he is seldom quoted and almost never used as an authority for a particular line of policy. Radicalism, nonconformism, and the social doctrines of the Established Church seem to count for a great deal more in British socialist thought than the works of the classical Marxists. British socialism is reasonably tolerant of religious groups and their beliefs, though the Left Wing is inclined to anticlericalism. It seems a typical compromise between the extremes of unfettered individualism and disciplined collectivism.

Within the British socialist movement, however, there are individuals and groups who take a much more dogmatic view of politics than either of these two—the Left Wing is one such group. The strong feeling of anticlericalism, the dogmatic assumptions about the historical development of capitalism, and the degree of emphasis placed upon the class struggle, among other factors, mark off the Left Wing from the remainder of the Labour movement in Britain, and bring it into closer harmony with continental socialism.

These differences underscore the need for extreme caution in any broad generalization about British socialism. The British socialist movement is not in the least monolithic, but an aggregation of individuals and groups who are in broad agreement upon certain general principles, which are themselves very broad and vague, and who disagree fundamentally on many particular questions. This is neither strange nor unique. Any mass political movement operating in a free society will attract to its ranks a wide variety of persons, ranging from the casually interested and lightly involved to the rabid and dogmatic partisan. British socialism is not, as a body, comparable to the various communist parties, which are not really mass parties at all, but cadre parties that are rigidly and tightly controlled. The doctrines of communism are relatively precise when compared to the doctrines of British socialism. The latter consist primarily of a set of ethical assumptions which are not very clearly defined, and a set of means, consisting chiefly of nationalization, about which there are serious differences of opinion.

The Left Wing ideology, then, is taken from British socialism but remains differentiated by the individual accents given the various parts of the belief pattern. In practice, these differences of emphasis cannot really be resolved until we reach the level of the individual or very small group. Some individuals who are part of the Left Wing have been very consistent in the application of their principles over extended time periods; the pacifists are an excellent example of such consistency. But not every member of the Left Wing arrives at the same conclusions when current affairs are discussed, and even those who do arrive at the same point often do so via arguments which differ considerably. This may be slightly repetitive, but the point is essential.

The meaning of socialism in Britain is far from clear. Many socialists begin with the doctrine that the resources of production ought to be used for the common benefit and not for the benefit of a particular social class.[1] But this principle is clearly derived from some prior social principle which is usually left unstated. In many cases, socialism is considered synonymous with nationalization of the principal industries in Britain. Again, there must be some premise on which such action is justified, but this is not supplied directly in most cases. Most British socialists are strong proponents of free and equal education and of democratic processes, but these concepts, when examined carefully, prove nearly devoid of genuine content. Nearly every British socialist espouses the need for "social justice," whatever that may mean.

In brief, British socialism is based essentially upon a series of ethical maxims which are in large measure derived from past propaganda against existing social evils. It is a value system, and in many ways an admirable value system, for the regulation of social affairs. It is directed primarily, and almost solely, toward internal social problems and not toward international affairs. British socialism makes contact with the latter field in a very tenuous manner via its conception of the fraternity of man, often modified to include only the working man, and more often advocated as a set of principles than practiced as a working doctrine for international relations. In theory, this sense of fraternity with all other members of the human race dissolves national frontiers, and among the more radical members of the socialist movement in Britain an honest effort has been made to put the theory into practice. The bulk of the British socialist movement has, however, usually dropped this principle when it conflicted with nationalist sentiment. It is readily apparent that this conception of socialism is quite broad, reasonably undogmatic, and subject to considerable latitude in interpretation. In the application of these principles to specific cases, particularly in reference to domestic problems, very serious clashes arise and agreement is more difficult to reach.

Socialism is thus essentially a vehicle of protest against the injustices conceived to flow from the excesses of the capitalistic system. The fundamental antithesis between capitalism and socialism is central to the socialist ideology and provides both the chief positive symbol and the chief negative symbol of the creed. Capitalism, never clearly defined and usually used in an archaic sense, is the mortal foe in both internal and external affairs. Socialism, an equally amorphous term, appears as the knight in shining armor determined to save the common people from persecution or destruction. The predetermined end is conversion of all existing systems to socialism, or as it is more often put, the ultimate victory of socialism over the forces of reaction. Moderate socialists consider this an end which is devoutly to be wished; more dogmatic members of the movement view the end as historically determined and in some sense inevitable.

Oddly enough, in modern labour propaganda the class struggle is not really identified with social classes, but is embodied in the more generalized struggle between two systems. This may be due in part to the vast extension of the meaning of ''worker'' that occurred when the Labour party was formed, and when Sidney Webb's definition of workers by hand, brain, etc. was adopted. Whether the triumph of socialism is viewed deterministically or hopefully, socialism comes to be identified with order and progress, capitalism with injustice and disorder and even anarchy.

In domestic affairs the class struggle becomes a mortal combat between these two forces, and is identified with the political battle between the Labour party and the Conservative party; internationally, the same application is possible if socialist states are substituted for the socialist parties of internal politics.

The chief goal in international politics for most British socialists is peace. This sounds mundane, but actually is not, for peace is used in a very special sense which makes it literally identical with the triumph of socialism. In domestic politics, peace is considered impossible until socialism has triumphed over the enemy; for a capitalistic victory leads only to the rule of naked force and a continuation of class strife. A socialist victory, on the other hand, would end the class struggle, although the consequences of a subsequent victory by capitalism are not really considered. International peace will likewise be achieved only with the ultimate triumph of socialism, for the mere absence of war is not peace. Peace, in these terms, is a condition in which enlightened co-operation and interdependence among nations are clearly recognized as essential. The triumph of world socialism becomes an article of faith for British socialists fully as much as for any continental socialist group, and it is particularly important in the ideology of the British Left Wing.

From this fundamental postulate, the Left Wing derived two of its most important principles of international affairs: first, that the immediate goal of British socialism must be the overthrow of the capitalistic system in Britain, by peaceful means usually, and the substitution of a socialist state; second, that the most useful contribution to world peace possible for British socialists was to speed up the process as much as possible, meanwhile assisting the struggling masses in other nations to achieve *their* social revolution with such resources as remained from the domestic conflict. This goal has been agreed upon for more than half a century, though it was argued, until 1926, that bloody revolution might be needed to accomplish the task in Britain.

Faith in socialism thus can be and is elevated into a complete if somewhat vague system of domestic and international politics. The process has the effect of concentrating attention upon the negative side of socialist thought, the opposition to what are conceived to be the consequences of capitalism. This is one of the most striking features of Left Wing propaganda. Capitalism is of course held responsible for the continuation of the class struggle in Britain and elsewhere. In its extreme form of imperialism, capitalism is responsible for colonialism and war, particularly the latter, which was due, in the eyes of the socialists, to the struggle among the great capitalist powers for control of the world's resources and markets. Most British socialists, and especially the Left Wing, oppose nationalism because socialism is "international." They oppose militarism because it is only another manifestation of the evil influence of capitalism. While these views were particularly strong in the early part of the twentieth century, they were still present in sufficient force to require an elaborate justification of Labour party support for an "imperialist war" as late as 1940. In a more positive vein, any interpretation of events, domestic or international, which showed the forces of progress—the socialists—gaining on the forces of reaction, was much favored. This led, naturally enough, to strong socialist support for the only "socialist" nation extant, the Soviet Union.

These general principles constituted the inner core of socialist belief during the interwar years and beyond. To illustrate their application, as well as some of the corollaries which appeared from time to time, the remainder of this chapter will attempt to summarize the main trends of socialist thought about international affairs during the interwar years and to a lesser extent during World War II, and relate these broad principles to the more specific doctrines commonly held by members of the Left Wing. Two fundamental issues—the disarmament question and the attitude to be taken toward the Soviet Union—can serve as the focal points of the summary.

The Left Wing, or parts of it at least, proved remarkably consistent in its approach to international affairs during the early part of this century, much more so, certainly, than did the main body of the Labour movement. The "imperialistic" policies of the British Government during the Boer War and World War I were consistently opposed by the Left Wing.[2] It is significant that it was a man usually considered to be primarily a trade union leader, Arthur Henderson, who represented Labour in the Asquith and Lloyd George cabinets. The elected leader of the Labour party, Ramsay MacDonald, stayed aloof and consistently opposed the Government. The trade unions, generally, proved more amenable to the influence of nationalism than did the Left Wing. In general, though with many exceptions, the British trade union leadership proved much more pragmatic about the application of "socialist principles" to international affairs than did the political side of the Labour movement, and certainly much more so than was the case with the Left Wing.

After World War I, the entire Labour movement began to drift toward the attitude adopted by the more radical elements of the Left Wing, particularly in regard to international affairs. This attitude was an admixture of support for the Soviet Union, for war resistance and for disarmament, and opposition to the peace settlement made at Versailles. The Treaty of Versailles was assailed by the Left Wing even before it was published.[3] The victorious powers, imperialists all to the Left Wing, were scorned and derided for imposing a severe peace upon Germany (called imperialism in a new form), for attacking the new socialist state in Russia, and for saddling Germany with the blame for a war which was nothing but an inevitable expression of the capitalistic system. Assiduous cultivation of this viewpoint by Left Wing spokesmen soon produced a "myth" around the Treaty of Versailles which paralleled that found in Germany, little related to facts, but accepted without question in most Labour circles.[4]

The new League of Nations, on the other hand, had a mixed reception. Most of the Left Wing denounced it as a "League of Capitalists" which was worth nothing. Other elements of British socialism supported the League, though there were many misgivings about the sanctions clause. The whole socialist movement was united in support of the "great social experiment" taking place in Russia, and western interventions were roundly denounced. The Left Wing took a characteristically extreme view, however, and remained consistent to the principle long after other elements of British socialism had lost some of their ardor for Soviet policy.

The critical year for the British Labour party, and perhaps for the whole of Europe, was 1931. In Britain, the economic crisis which led to the collapse of the MacDonald Government and the National Coalition Government that followed, proved a traumatic experience from which the Left Wing has not yet recovered.[5] The Independent Labour party, which had been quarrelling with the Labour party for some time, now disaffiliated itself. The General Election of 1931 proved disastrous for Labour's fortunes, nearly wiping out Labour representation in the House of Commons, and placing leadership of the parliamentary Labour party in the hands of an ageing pacifist, George Lansbury, who proved utterly unable to resolve the contradiction between his personal convictions and the growing international tensions brought about by Hitler. The loss of the old party leadership produced a period of near anarchy within the Labour movement as forces regrouped and prepared once again for future electoral battles.

During periods of crisis, when direction is uncertain, those whose aims are clear often exert a degree of influence out of all proportion to their numerical strength. This proved to be the case within the Labour movement for a time after 1931. The I.L.P. took up its cudgels against the Labour party from the outside; within the party, the Left Wing opened an intensified campaign in favor of its own policies. The Socialist League was established in 1931 to act as a "ginger group" within the party and help chart the new course which the party would take. The official policy of the Labour party moved steadily toward unilateral disarmament and war resistance. The Left Wing demand for a resolution favoring unilateral British disarmament was defeated at the 1932 Labour party Conference mainly because Arthur Henderson was opposed. But the Conference did pass a resolution expressing its "unalterable opposition" to the rearmament of any country, including Britain, in any circumstances.[6]

The following year, the Conference instructed the National Executive Committee of the Party to: "Pledge itself to take no part in war and to resist it with the whole force of the Labour Movement, and to seek consultation with the Trade Union and Cooperative Movements with a view to deciding and announcing what steps, including the general strike, are to be taken to organize opposition of the organized working class movement in the event of war or threat of war, and urges the National Joint Council to make immediate approaches to endeavor to secure international action by the workers on the same lines."[7]   Embodied here are the ideals of international working-class action to prevent war which were prevalent in Left Wing circles during the period. The resolution, which was accepted by the National Executive Committee of the Party without argument, was passed unanimously. It marks the zenith of Left Wing influence on Labour's foreign policy during the 1930's.

To this point, the British trade unions had been concentrating their attention upon domestic policy, and paying little attention to international affairs. The advent of Hitler, and his successful suppression of what had been the most powerful and well organized trade union movement in Europe within a few months, prompted action by British trade union leaders. An investigation of European totalitarianism was sponsored by this group, and the results were embodied in a report that was approved by the T.U.C. and the British Labour party Conference, in 1933.[8]   The report was vigorously attacked by the Left Wing because it included a firm denunciation of the Soviet Union, along with the other totalitarian states in Europe, but the bloc votes of the great unions easily carried the day in both conferences. Although the report did not advocate British rearmament, it was a clear sign that the drift toward war resistance and unilateral disarmament would henceforth be resisted by some of the more influential leaders of British unionism. This might have settled the issue had not the Labour party won a bye-election at Fulham in October, 1933, and then a series of additional bye-elections, as it appeared at the time simply by taking a pacifistic line.[9] The natural antipathy of the Left Wing to rearmament was henceforth strengthened by the unwillingness of the leaders of Labour's political organization to relinquish a potent political weapon. Not until 1937 did the leaders of the trade unions and the political party reach forthright agreement on the armament issue.

Germany began to rearm in 1934, hastening the work of those who were busy framing a new Labour approach to international affairs. A special report entitled "War and Peace" was prepared and submitted to the T.U.C. and the Labour party Conference in 1934.[10] It rendered the resolution passed by the party Conference in 1933 null and void, and gently but firmly replaced control of the general strike in trade union hands. Labour could not, it stated, oppose war indiscriminately; not all wars were to be opposed, but only those which were unjust. Sanctions, which were denounced by most of the Left Wing, were supported in "all risks and consequences," though it must be said that this support was limited to economic sanctions and did not contemplate military action.

The report, firmly supported by Ernest Bevin and Walter Citrine, then the key figures in the T.U.C., was easily paced through both T.U.C. and Labour party Conference in 1934. But the leaders of the parliamentary Labour party and the Left Wing continued to support a policy totally at odds with the policy contained in "War and Peace." Clement Attlee, for example, produced the so-called "Attlee formula" which really allowed no rearmament whatever, since, "The League of Nations does not say that you must keep a force of this or that size. The League of Nations was founded on the idea of the reduction of armaments and not the increase of armaments."[11] The Left Wing simply ignored the report completely. This attitude was much resented by the union leaders concerned, particularly Ernest Bevin. At the Labour party Conference in 1935, Bevin launched a slashing attack on George Lansbury which led to his resignation as Leader of the parliamentary Labour party.

International affairs figured prominently in the General Election of 1935, and Labour urgently demanded sanctions against Mussolini, though again they were careful to insist only upon economic sanctions. The Conservative argument, that Britain was not willing to risk military sanctions and that economic sanctions without military support were useless, was bypassed. In any event, the sanctions question soon lost its force as Hitler marched his troops into the Rhineland, in defiance of the Treaty of Versailles, and precipitated another real crisis. The Left Wing, which had loudly demanded sanctions against Mussolini, now denounced the Anglo-French staff conversations with equal vehemence. Labour was totally opposed to any action against Germany that might eventuate in war.

In July, 1936, an important side issue developed when the Spanish Civil War broke out, followed by a storm of indignation from Labour in general and the Left Wing in particular. Bevin and other trade union leaders cautioned against an oversimplification of the issue and supported the neutrality policy followed by Britain. The Left Wing simply denounced the Civil War as a treacherous attack on the "democratic Spanish Left Wing" by a "fascist right wing" supported by Germany, Italy, and the Church. Even the stand taken by the Soviet Union failed to move the extremists, and their version of events was pressed again and again upon the Labour movement. At every Labour party Conference, at least one Left Wing spokesman managed to include in his speech a denunciation of Franco, and we shall meet with the continuation of that attitude after 1945. Without discussing the details of the case, the technique employed by the Left Wing is instructive. Constant repetition, carried on long after the event lost significance, led to a gradual assimilation of their viewpoint by most of the Labour movement. By 1945, few bothered to inquire into the details of the Spanish Civil War, and the Left Wing version of events became a commonplace in Labour circles.

Meanwhile, the armament issue remained unsettled. The Labour party Conference of 1935 vacillated. In 1936, Ernest Bevin, speaking, he said, for a large group of unions, announced that they had been "double crossed" and demanded a showdown on the issue. But Clement Attlee and Herbert Morrison managed to avoid a vote on the question, staving off the final settlement until 1937, when the Labour party finally passed a resolution stating that: "A Labour Government will unhesitatingly maintain such armed forces as are necessary to defend our country and fulfill our obligations as a member of the British Commonwealth and the League of Nations."[12] This removed the "Attlee conditions," and reconciled the leaders of the Parliamentary Labour party and the leaders of the trade union movement.

The Left Wing, however, remained unconvinced. Aneurin Bevan, then a prominent Left Wing spokesman, proposed the following very shortly after the resolution quoted above was passed by the 1937 Conference: "We should conduct throughout the country such a campaign against the National Government, against its armament policy and against its foreign policy as will make our position quite clear: We should say to the country that we are prepared to make whatever sacrifices are necessary to give whatever arms are necessary to fight fascist powers. . .but we are not going to put a sword into the hands of our enemies (the Conservative party)."[13] Here the ideological bias is clearly shown. The greatest enemy is not fascism, but the internal enemy, conservativism, or more specifically, British capitalism. Failing a change in government, the Left Wing was prepared to rely upon international working-class action to maintain international peace. On this question, their attitude in 1937 was precisely what it had been in 1921, and indeed in 1900.

As an adjunct to their policy of opposing armaments, a number of prominent figures on the Left Wing had been pressing strongly for unity with the British Communist party. In January, 1937, the Labour party warned a number of these men—particularly Professor Harold Laski, Aneurin Bevan, Stafford Cripps, Tom Horabin, H. N. Brailsford, and John Strachey—to cease their activities in the "unity campaign." A few days afterward, the Socialist League was disaffiliated from the Labour party. Finally, Stafford Cripps, G. R. Strauss, Aneurin Bevan, and Commander G. R. Young were expelled from the party for failing to heed the warnings. The disruption of the Socialist League took away much of the driving force behind the unity campaign.

A more subtle form of propaganda remained in Left Wing hands in the form of the Left Book Club, organized in 1936 to publish important socialist works and promote discussion groups. At its peak, the organization numbered nearly 700 discussion groups, and perhaps 50,000 members. The selection committee of the club comprised the more Marxian elements of British socialism, including Harold Laski, Victor Gollancz, and John Strachey. The list of publications reflects this alignment, and many standard Marxist works were published and distributed. The Club exerted a very substantial influence on Labour opinion during the late 1930's and the early war years.

The Labour party's official policy changed radically after 1937. British agreement to the partition of Czechoslovakia was denounced, though not so roundly as Labour supporters later assumed. The British guarantee of Poland's frontiers was welcomed by most of the Labour movement, but strongly denounced by the Left Wing. What in fact seems to have occurred was a shift in Labour policy, while the attitude of the Left Wing remained unchanged, particularly on the basic issues of armament of Britain and co-operation with British capitalism in a defense effort. Clement Attlee described the situation extremely well in his book on the Labour party:

> The Party is agreed in its rejection of the policy of balance of power and of the use of force as an instrument of policy. It is agreed on the objective of a world co-operative commonwealth. It aims at the subordination of national sovereignty to world loyalty, the reduction of all national armaments to the lowest possible level by

international agreement, and to the substitution of arbitration for war. All agree on the need for removing private profit in the manufacture of and trade in arms. Equally, there is no difference of opinion as to the vital necessity of removing the economic causes of war, and basing the new world order on firm economic foundations as well as on political institutions. The differences of opinion arise over two questions—the use of force and the extent of the possible cooperation with capitalistic states and non-Socialists.[14]

These two areas of difference, of course, have a profound influence on the conduct of international policy. Although this was written in 1937, it remained a true description of Labour opinion until well into the second World War.

The outbreak of war in 1939 found only the pacifists, the remnants of the Independent Labour party, and part of the Socialist League opposed to British participation. Those opposed were soon joined by the British Communist party, which contrived a remarkable *volte-face* when the Soviet Union joined with Germany and denounced the British war effort. Labour supported the war, offically, though its leaders refused to join Neville Chamberlain in a coalition government. Following the initial attack on Poland, there was a hiatus, called the "phony war" period, when no decisive action took place. Discussion of a negotiated peace became popular in Labour circles, and the nature of the discussion revealed the gap between ostensible policy and the fundamental precepts on which Labour depended.

The Left Wing, in many cases, demanded immediate withdrawal from a war which was considered imperialistic and not worth supporting. The ideal of international working-class action was still very much alive, and not only in Left Wing minds. As late as November, 1939, Clement Attlee declared that once Germany made restitution to Poland, Czechoslovakia, and Austria, a negotiated peace was quite possible, and Attlee clearly felt that the German people might yet rise and throw Hitler out.[15] In February, 1940, the National Executive Committee of the Labour party issued a statement which said, in part: "Victory for democracy must be achieved, either by arms or economic pressure, or better still by a victory of the German people over the Hitler regime, resulting in the birth of a new Germany."[16] This rather naive faith in the German people dissipated rapidly after the British armies were ejected summarily from Europe to the resounding cheers of the "German people." By 1941, Labour stood for "total victory, refusing all negotiation."[17]

Undoubtedly, much of the opposition to the "imperialist war" came from the British Communist party following its sudden shift in attitude at the beginning of the war. But it also stemmed from the indeterminate influence of Marxism, from a friendly attitude toward the Soviet Union, and from the work of organizations like the Left Book Club, all of which were a vital influence on Left Wing opinion. Opposition to the war gained considerable headway late in 1939, and Professor Harold Laski, strangely enough, was called upon to produce an argument against this attitude. Strangely, because Laski himself took this attitude. Laski duly produced a pamphlet which made no attempt to deny that the war was an imperialist war, but did set forth extenuating circumstances which would permit British socialists to support the war in any case.[18]

Laski argued that British imperialism was past its zenith and waning rapidly; German imperialism was now at the virulent and expansive stage. Both nations were imperialists, and therefore the war was an imperialist war. Nevertheless, British socialists should support British imperialism in opposition to German imperialism since socialism was still possible under British rule, but completely impossible under German rule. There were no ethical arguments involved in the pamphlet; only the question of how far the ideology could benefit from the choice of actions available. In June, 1941, the mainspring of the "anti-imperialist" bloc suddenly, and unwillingly, changed sides and became an ally of British imperialism. Nothing further was heard of the issue.

The British defeat in Europe, symbolized by Dunkirk and the fall of France, removed any remaining illusions about negotiated peace, and Labour took what constituted a very serious step and joined the new Government formed by Winston Churchill. A political truce was arranged between the two parties, permitting each party to retain its present representation in the House of Commons without opposition from the other, and the 1940 Labour party Conference approved the decision after the fact.[19]

The Left Wing was, from the beginning, opposed to the truce. One portion of the Left Wing, led by Sir Richard Acland, formed the Commonwealth party and gained a few seats by opposing Conservative candidates in constituencies supposedly covered by the truce. By 1942, Left Wing hostility to the truce had reached the point of attacking Labour party leaders for remaining in the Coalition Government, and Clement Attlee had to defend his position at the 1942 party Conference.[20] By the date of the following Conference, opposition was so fierce that Attlee devoted the whole of his lone speech to the 1943 conference to the subject.[21] In December, 1944, with the war in Europe as yet unsettled, the party agreed to end the Coalition as soon as the European War was finished, without waiting for the end of the war in the Far East as had originally been planned.

This sequence of events is an important indication of the extent of Left Wing preoccupation with political matters even at the most dubious stages of the war, and perhaps more important, its unremitting hostility to any association with the "capitalist" elements in Britain. Very probably, the memories of the disaster of 1931 were still strong, and the parallel is frequently mentioned though it had little or no relevance to the new situation. Interestingly enough, this hated association with the Tories was usually laid at the doorstep of the union leaders, and Ernest Bevin in particular, and not attributed to Clement Attlee or Herbert Morrison, though Bevin was guilty, in public at least, of nothing more than defending the need for a Coalition Government during the emergency, a position which Attlee and Morrison carefully avoided.

Turning to the second major item of Left Wing interest during the interwar years—the relation of Britain to the Soviet Union— we find a most instructive example of the attitude which the Left Wing could be expected to adopt when its ideological beliefs conflicted with another set of principles, in this case the most fundamental tenets of the western political tradition. A bifurcation of views in regard to the Soviet Union had appeared within the Labour movement as early as 1921. The trade unions were universally sympathetic to the demand of the Soviet leaders for the right to work out their own destiny without outside interference. But the unions found themselves increasingly irritated by the activities of the British Communist party, and the efforts of British communists to infiltrate the ranks of the unions. The "unity" campaign of the 1930's was roundly denounced by most union leaders, although a few radical unions did support the program. The nonunion members of the socialist movement, and in particular the Left Wing, consistently and actively supported both the Soviet demand for freedom from interference and the communist proposal for "working class unity." One cannot truly say of the trade unions that they were hostile to the U.S.S.R. in the 1930's, but they were far more critical of Soviet behavior than the Left Wing, or even than the political leaders of the Labour Party.

The Soviet-German Nonaggression Pact of August, 1939, came as a great shock to British Labour since it clearly opened the way for German aggression in the West. Officially, the Labour party condemned the Soviets for a totally unscrupulous action. The Left Wing, however, remained loyal to its idol, though the antics of the British Communist party did disgust a few spokesmen from the left.[22] The Left Wing press either refused to comment on the pact (Forward), refused to condemn the action, though recognizing that it created some difficulties, as was the case with the *New Statesman,* or openly supported the pact, as did *Tribune,* which even managed to call it a ". . .great reinforcement for peace in Eastern Europe."[23]

Later, the *New Statesman* published an apologia which concentrated on the fact that Soviet interference in Poland would not affect the outcome of the conflict, while it would reduce the size of the rump state remaining in German hands. In *Tribune,* Stafford Cripps went far beyond this attitude to warn the British Government not to construe its guarantee of the Polish frontiers to include Soviet encroachment, and to state that Russia would remain in Poland only until the war ended, ". . . for her own protection, and to assist and encourage the Polish people in their struggle against the landlord class."[24] This position was somewhat weakened by an article in the same issue, written by Konni Zilliacus, which argued that Russia was only taking back what had been stolen from her previously. Only the *New Statesman* (October 1, 1939) of the Left Wing press took notice of the Soviet assimilation of the Baltic states, and this journal merely noted that it placed the Baltic states in the same position vis-à-vis Russia as Egypt then stood in relation to Britain. Thus the Left Wing weathered the initial stages of Soviet aggressiveness in Eastern Europe without much difficulty.

The Soviet invasion of Finland created rather more strain on Left Wing loyalty to Russia and brought a strong manifesto from the Labour party denouncing its actions: "We condemned the clumsiness of the British Government, in its earlier relations with the Soviet Union; but that cannot excuse the Russian Government's Pact with the Nazis on the eve of the war, much less its unprovoked attack on Finland in shameless imitation of the Nazi technique in foreign policy."[25] Despite the pressure, the Left Wing continued to seek, and find, excuses for the Soviet Union's policies. It was possible, in the first instance, to blame the western powers for driving Russia into a position of bitter frustration by refusing to enter into an alliance with her, and treating her like a social pariah. But the central argument, best illustrated by a special leader published in *Tribune* (December 8, 1939), used as its basic justification of Soviet policy her need to establish a firm base against the coming capitalist attack. It was widely believed, or at least stated, by Left Wing spokesmen, that the western capitalists might band together and launch a joint attack on Russia as a condition of peace. *Tribune* itself claimed that the Soviet Union had originated this charge, but accepted it nonetheless.

Harold Laski frequently used the argument, most prominently, perhaps, in the pamphlet supporting the "imperialist war" already cited, wherein he claimed that a "palace revolution" could occur which would lead to a *rapproachement* between the western nations, and a combined attack on Russia led by "French and British capitalism." Aneurin Bevan used this same thesis in the House of Commons in November, 1940, when he attacked the British Government for failing to make a suitable agreement with Russia in 1939 because of pressure from American and British capitalists, because, as he said: ". . .powerful though the help of America may be, the Soviet Union could bring this war to a conclusion in one week."[26] It need hardly be said that this line of reasoning proved untenable after June, 1941.

In the winter of 1939-1940, then, the Left Wing evaluation of the Soviet Union came into conflict with some of the more powerful social forces in modern times and survived, apparently undiminished. Loyalty to party, national sentiment, and even virulent hatred of Hitler all pointed to condemnation of the Soviet Union; none of these influences carried sufficient weight with the Left Wing to override its faith in its own tradition.

When Germany invaded Russia, bringing that country into an unwanted alliance with Britain, the Left Wing stood completely vindicated, in its own view. Without a pause for self-congratulation, it sprang to attack the British Government for failing to assist the Soviets to the fullest extent of which it was capable. Aneurin Bevan, for example, rose in the House of Commons on June 24, 1940, two days after the German invasion of Russia began, and only one year after the British Expeditionary Force departed from Dunkirk without most of its baggage, to express his fear that British domestic stability might be endangered by the absence of a second land front, since the British people would believe that: ". . .the Government is pulling their punches in assisting Russia because it is Russia. . .I am afraid a very large number of people who ought to be going all out will be subconsciously inhibited by the fact that the Soviet Union is now an ally of ours and that belief in the inhibition will become so widespread that very many people will cease to believe in the sincerity and earnestness of the Government's war effort."[27] This is tantamount to an accusation of treason against Bevan's political opponents, based solely on ideological grounds.

Beginning with the attitude described above, the Left Wing naturally followed the course of the war with great care, searching for signs of latent hostility toward Russia which might result in failure to assist her against Germany. They spotted their first quarry in the so-called "second front" issue. Russia had demanded that the allies open a land front against Germany on the European continent as soon as possible. Taking its cue, the Left Wing pressed its own government to fulfill that demand as speedily as possible. Perhaps one example, again taken from the speeches of Aneurin Bevan, will illustrate the line of reasoning which the Left Wing was following at the time:

> The reason why the Germans have not been beaten is that the Government have not had the guts to do it. . .If that (the second front) is not done, and if Stalingrad falls, and the Russians are driven behind the Urals, the working class people in this country will be asking why. It will be no use for the Prime Minister to tell them that military considerations make it impossible, because unfortunately for the Prime Minister, the British people have more confidence in the sagacity of Voroshilov and Timoshenko than in that of Winston Churchill, and they know that the Russian Generals have declared that a second front is a practicable military possibility and has been for a year. . .[28]

This general attitude continued, and indeed intensified, until the invasion of Europe was launched in June, 1944, little abated by the invasion of North Africa. Suspicion of the intentions of the British Government was intense and continuous, as we shall see in the next chapter.

World War II is also important as a period in the development of Left Wing thought because of the opportunity it provided for speculation about the structure of world political and economic institutions in the postwar world. Such speculation was by no means confined to Great Britain, nor to the Left Wing in Britain, but the vision of the postwar world which the greatest part of the Labour movement in Britain came to accept as desirable was predicated very largely on the ideological beliefs of the Left Wing, and was very largely a product of Left Wing speculation. The remainder of this chapter will be spent examining the principal concepts thus evolved; the next chapter contains a detailed examination of their application to a particular problem area in Europe.

The place of the Soviet Union in the postwar world was taken for granted, though some of the Left Wing intellectuals carried their speculations rather far. Harold Laski, for example, pictured a "Sovietized Asia,"[29] and G. D. H. Cole asked rhetorically as early as 1941 if it might not be better "for Germany as well as Eastern Europe to be included in an enlarged U.S.S.R."[30] Such views derive from a fundamental assumption that was nearly universally held by Left Wing socialists in 1945, i.e., that the world in general, and Europe in particular, was "going left," and that

peace would bring the establishment of a new world order predicated upon socialism and closely aligned with the Soviet Union in
international affairs.[31] Theoretically, this assumption is deeply
rooted in socialist tradition, since socialism is committed to the
ultimate triumph of its own principles. Such an assumption appeared in Attlee's *Labour Party in Perspective,* already quoted.

By the spring of 1940, when the hope of negotiated peace had
finally been abandoned and speculation about the postwar world
increased, it soon appeared in full strength, suitably adapted to
current conditions. Perhaps the earliest statement of the principle that the postwar world would be a socialist world appears in
Labour's War Manifesto, published in September, 1939: "With the
defeat of the aggressors, there emerges the prospect of building
a better world from which the roots of economic and political
grievances have been removed."[32] The concept was clarified and
made more specific by Harold Laski early in 1940: ". . . it is
precisely the business of Socialists to see that the ideological
nature of the war becomes even more fully understood and that the
best way to do this is to see that the social question is ever more
consistently emphasized as an integral to the maintenance of that
national unity which is a condition of victory."[33]

More precisely still, the "new world order" concept appeared
in an official Labour party statement of principles issued in early
1940: "A new World Order which applies these principles (for
maintaining peace) can only be founded on Socialism and Democracy. Lasting peace depends on social justice within states no
less than on political justice between states."[34] And, in perhaps
more mundane dress, but more plainly stated was Clement Attlee's
statement in 1940: ". . .the world that must emerge from this
war will be a world attuned to our ideals."[35] This hardly leaves
room for chance developments. These illustrations are typical of
a vast number of similar arguments, and they are of course fully
consistent with Labour's past traditions. Since the beginning of the
century, and before, Labour had argued that war was due to capitalism, and that hope for a peaceful world order was identical with
the hope for a socialist world order.

The generalizations made above are not, however, adequate as
a description of the attitude of the Left Wing to the war as a potential instrument of social change. The Left Wing was far more
dogmatic, and their hopes involved a much more drastic alteration
of the existing structure of Europe. In effect, the Left Wing demanded support for the coming revolution, which would sweep
away the old regimes and establish socialist orders in their place.

By 1942, Left Wing influence, and the natural inclinations of the Labour movement, had produced a statement of policy with terrifying implications:

> The Labour Party recognizes that, as the Axis governments begin to crumble, widespread revolution is certain in countries they now dominate. It declares its view that each people is entitled to determine its own form of government, subject only to its obligation to accept and respect the four freedoms and the international implications to which they lead. It will oppose any attempt on the part of the victors at the conclusion of the war to use their military or economic power against the determination of each people to shape their own destiny, apart from the obligation to which reference has been made. It is convinced that it would be a grave dis-service to the future of the world to use the power of victory under penalty of postponement of recovery, to promote *in any country where revolution may occur,* the claims of any privileged interest, whether of class or religion or dynasty, against which the revolution is a protest.[36]

This attitude of firm support for social revolution, wherever it might occur, and for whatever reason, within the limits of the four freedoms, was swiftly transposed by the Left Wing into firm support for all revolutions, with or without the "four freedoms."

Left Wing thought during World War II, then, was comprised of two main strands which were taken directly from the interwar years, and one which was added as a result of the opportunities the war offered for social revolution. The two concepts carried over from the interwar years were bitter opposition to armaments and war as consequences of the capitalistic system, and the identification of the Soviet Union with the cause of world socialism. The third concept added to Left Wing thought was Labour's faith in the emergence of a new world order which would be based upon socialism. These strands of thought cannot be kept apart. The Soviet Union, for example, was expected to play some part in the creation of the new world order, hence there was no surprise in Left Wing circles when the U.S.S.R. proceeded to do precisely this during the liberation period. The application of these principles to the course of events did, nevertheless, produce some really startling consequences.

IV

THE LIBERATION OF GREECE

The German occupation of Europe during World War II produced a kind of political *tabula rasa* since it was quite clear that the regimes which exercised power during the period of German domination would have to be replaced, and in many instances, the regimes which had exercised power before the German conquest were discredited, and very unlikely to return. In the circumstances, a genuine struggle for power began within these occupied countries and reached its peak during the liberation process when, in many cases, the struggle for power was in fact decided. These struggles provided more scope for the projection of ideological sympathies into the international arena than any similar period in recent times, and the British Left Wing was granted an opportunity to give free rein to its hope and sympathies, which it in fact did. The record of Left Wing hopes and aspirations, its periods of exaltation and black despair as it followed the fortunes of its favorites, provides an invaluable insight into the effect of its ideological convictions on its attitude toward international affairs.

The extent and duration of the German occupation nearly severed relations between continental territories and the pre-1939 regimes in exile. Inside the occupied territories, in some cases, strong resistance movements developed which came to exercise quasi-governmental authority in regions where German control was slender. While these resistance movements were opposed to the occupation, they were in many cases even more strongly committed to support a completely new regime in the postwar period. Very frequently, the local communist party provided the hard core of the resistance as the communists were generally trained to operate underground, and to make use of nationalistic aspirations for their own ends. By 1945, even the noncommunist elements of the resistance in France and Greece and other occupied areas were strongly imbued with socialist doctrines. Harsh antagonism appeared between the leaders of the resistance and the leaders of the various governments in exile. Within the resistance too there were dissonances caused by differences of opinion about the nature of the postwar political settlement in the territory concerned.

These resistance movements figured prominently in Left Wing thought. Clearly, they were the element in occupied Europe most likely to determine the political and economic structure of the continent, if the great powers could be prevented from enforcing a settlement, hence the Labour manifesto cited in the last chapter. The pre-1939 regimes in much of Europe had been illiberal and autocratic, and opposed to communism and socialism alike. Many had taken a friendly view of Hitler's avowed purpose of destroying communism root and branch. If the British Left Wing was at times unfamiliar with the nature of the leaders of the resistance movements, it was all too familiar with the hostile character of the pre-1939 rulers and unalterably opposed to their return. In these circumstances, it is not surprising that the British Labour movement, and the Left Wing in particular, took a very favorable view of the resistance without inquiring too closely into its principles. For the Left Wing, the resistance became a "good" symbol, and the old regimes a "bad" symbol and, as in the case of the Civil War in Spain, events were fitted into the preconceived pattern which such symbols should follow. Criticism of any resistance movement, for any reason, became a sign of "black reaction" with little or no regard for the facts that may or may not have warranted such criticisms.

Along with this profound respect and admiration for the resistance movements on the Continent, there went a profound mistrust of the intentions of the British and American governments, and particularly of the former; this mistrust was not alleviated by the presence of Labour representatives in the Coalition cabinet. The Left Wing believed that the capitalistic British Government would attempt to use its power to suppress the coming revolution(s) in Europe, and watched its behavior during the liberation period with a suspicious eye. When the British Government tried to honor its commitments to the exiled governments of pre-war Europe, it brought upon itself a torrent of abuse from the Left Wing.

The first such incident came during the occupation of North Africa when the American Commander, General Eisenhower, made use of pro-Vichy French military leaders, notably Admiral Darlan, a move that was politically stupid, though it may have been militarily necessary. Though this action was only later endorsed by the British and American governments, the Left Wing saw in the incident a predetermined plan for returning "reactionary" French interests to power in the area, thus threatening the new world order concept seriously. The Left Wing poured out a scathing denunciation on the parties concerned, and particularly on the British Government, which in truth played little part in the entire affair.

When Allied forces failed to arrive in Italy in time to prevent the German reoccupation of the country and save the "Italian revolutionaries" from the "forces of reaction" represented by Marshal Badoglio, another Left Wing attack followed. Even Soviet recognition of the Badoglio Government left the Left Wing unmoved, though parts of the Left Press expressed profound disappointment with Soviet behavior.[1]

Against this background of rather impassioned antagonism and hostility, events in Greece began to make an imprint in Britain late in 1943, and finally erupted into the headlines in December, 1944, when the Greek communists essayed a *coup d'état* and failed because of British interference. For a clear picture of this rather confusing episode, three facts must be established clearly: first, the extent to which the British Government was informed of events in Greece; second, the actual course of events; third, the interpretation made of these events by the British Left Wing. These data are set forth in this chapter.

Contemporary newspaper accounts of the Greek liberation are almost totally unreliable. Even the *London Times* succumbed to the emotions of the moment and published a number of rather surprising editorials. Fortunately, a number of first hand accounts have been published since 1945, and it is possible to reconstruct a reasonably accurate picture of the course of events. The most useful of these accounts was written by the Senior British Officer in the Military Mission to Greece, Colonel C. M. Woodhouse.[2]   The British Ambassador to Greece published his version of the revolution in 1944.[3]   A British paratrooper who jumped into occupied Greece to dynamite a railroad bridge, and made contact with the various resistance groups, has written an account of the trip.[4]   An American correspondent,[5] and a British correspondent,[6] both of whom were present during the December uprising, have published accounts of their experiences. Two British White Papers have appeared on the subject, though they are less satisfactory than might be hoped.[7] The British T.U.C. sent a delegation to Greece early in 1945, and its report has been published.[8]

Other material is available in the Report of the Supreme Commander of the Eastern Mediterranean, on file in the British War Office. Accounts which appeared subsequent to the time when this chapter was written (1954) have not altered the version presented here to any great extent. In the main, the points stated below are agreed upon by all sources. Where there is not agreement, the points at issue are noted as carefully as possible. This is not to state, however, that all questions have been solved, for they have not. Why, for example, did the Greek communists forego the opportunity to take Athens before the British arrived, only to make the attempt later under much less auspicious circumstances? There simply is no good answer to the question, and to others, at the moment.

Perhaps the best place to begin a survey of Greek affairs is on August 4, 1936, when General Ioannis Metaxas assumed dictatorial power with the compliance of the Greek monarch, who signed an act voiding certain provisions of the Greek Consititution of 1911, thereby enabling Metaxas to sieze power, and thereby violating the monarch's own constitutional oath. Metaxas ruled Greece until his death on January 29, 1941. Mussolini, eager for conquest, presented the Greeks with an ultimatum in October, 1940, which was firmly rejected. The Italian armies sent to subjugate the Greeks were repulsed in the narrow mountain passes and thrown back into Albania. Hitler, impatient with his ally, drew sufficient forces to overrun Greece from the troops massing for the invasion of Russia and sent them into the peninsula. Metaxas had steadily refused British aid, but his successor, one Korizis[9] (or Koryzis) accepted British help, and British troops entered Greece only to be overcome by superior German forces and forced back on the Island of Crete and then to the mainland of Africa. The Greek monarch returned to North Africa with the British forces, along with his Government, then headed by a Cretan named Tsouderos. The Government consisted chiefly of remnants of the old Metaxas regime, though Tsouderos was a Liberal.

With Metaxas dead, and Greece under German occupation, the Greek Government-in-exile had two problems to occupy its time: first, the Cabinet members associated with Metaxas dictatorship must be purged; second, the status of the monarch had to be clarified. Tsouderos began, very slowly, to make changes in the Government. In October, 1941, he denounced the Metaxas regime; the Greek Cabinet was then reorganized. Early in 1942, it was again reorganized to include a larger number of republicans and moved to London. By the end of 1942, the government in exile consisted of a majority of royalists, a few republicans, and no members of the Metaxas regime. The future of the King had not been settled, and though the King may have felt that he could again return to Greece and resume his position, the Cabinet had not made a formal commitment on the subject.

Inside Greece, political forces remained active despite the occupation. A collaborationist government was organized by the Germans in 1942, but it had little to say beyond the scope of German power. In the mountainous northern regions, a substantial resistance movement appeared, consisting of a number of separate bodies. In order of their size and appearance, they included: The National Liberation Front, EAM, and its military component, the National Popular Liberation Army, ELAS. This group will be referred to here as EAM/ELAS. Next in size and order of appearance was the National Republican Greek League (EDES). Minor groups included the National Social Liberation Movement, EKKA, and a few others that can safely be ignored. EAM/ELAS and EDES were the chief instruments of the resistance from the beginning.

EAM/ELAS was founded in September, 1941, and placed a guerilla force in the field for the first time in the early part of 1942. EAM/ELAS originated with, and was dominated by, the Greek Communist party (KKE).[10] EAM/ELAS amalgamated with the Popular Democratic Union (ELD), and the Socialist party of Greece (SKE) early in 1943. These diverse elements remained in EAM/ELAS until 1945, when the true character of the movement was revealed.

EDES also came into being late in 1941, led by an able and energetic military commander, General Zervas. The charter of the organization indicates its purpose, and is worth quoting in view of the controversy that arose later:

> To work for and achieve the setting-up in Greece. . . .of a democratic constitution of a popular character and Socialist in form, after a free plebiscite (on the monarchy).

> To resist with all its energy and prevent the forcible return of the King, if he wishes to attempt to return before the free expression of the will of the Greek people has been pronounced.[11]

EDES was basically a socialist organization, not necessarily republican, but certainly not committed to the monarchy. Most of EDES activity was centered in northwestern Greece, and both the group, and the territory controlled by the group, were smaller than those controlled by EAM/ELAS.

EKKA was organized in 1942, and had no military forces until 1943. It was twice attacked by EAM/ELAS and finally wiped out completely in April, 1944. The leader of EKKA, Colonel Psaros, was brutally murdered by EAM/ELAS men.[12]

The British first made contact with the Greek resistance in 1942, when the small unit intended to cut German supply lines was dropped into Greece by air.[13] Early in 1943 Colonel Woodhouse arrived in Greece as a "permanent" British representative,

with orders to contact all guerilla bands, arrange supply routes,
etc. Through British mediation, EDES and EAM/ELAS signed
the so-called "National Bands Agreement" in July, 1943, de-
lineating their respective spheres of influence and accepting the
British as mediators. Since Britain controlled most of the in-
coming supplies, she was in an excellent position to enforce her
demands for internal peace.[14]

Since there were signs of unrest within Greece, and in the
Greek Government-in-exile, the first need was clearly to bring
the two sides together and attempt a settlement. There had already been a mutiny in the Greek Brigade in Cairo in March,
1943, and this had led to a Cabinet crisis and a new reorganization.
Indications were that the gulf between the Greek Government
and the Greek people was widening rapidly while the resistance
was tightening its control over much of northern Greece. In
August, 1943, the British Government brought several leading
members of the resistance to Cairo to meet with the Greek
Cabinet. The communist leader of the delegation from Greece
immediately demanded control of three key cabinet posts, to be
exercised inside Greece, and a clear statement on the future of
the King.[15] A genuine crisis followed, since the republican members
of the Cabinet were sympathetic to the demand for a settlement of
the position of the King. The conference was a failure, and the
resistance leaders were flown back to Greece.

Back within occupied Greece, EAM/ELAS obtained a sufficient
supply of arms from the Italian surrender to furnish one complete
division and immediately attacked EDES. The British finally cut
off all supplies to EAM/ELAS and forced a truce, promptly broken
by EDES in an effort to regain lost ground. In January, 1944,
British mediation once again secured agreement on paper, this
time called the "Plaka Bridge Agreement."[16] EAM/ELAS then
turned to political action, and formed the Political Committee for
National Liberation—a familiar sequence of words after 1945—and
gave this group control of the area dominated by its forces.
Meanwhile, there was yet another mutiny in Cairo among Greek
troops stationed there, and an even more serious Cabinet crisis.
It was now clear that an agreement between the exiled government
and the resistance would have to be made very soon if civil war
were to be avoided.

The British Government therefore arranged another conference,
this time in the Lebanon, which took place from May 17 to May
20, 1944. A Government of National Unity was agreed upon and
formed, reserving places for EAM/ELAS delegates. However
EAM/ELAS refused to take part and denounced the agreement,
making further demands on the government. The British would

not allow the Greek Cabinet to meet these demands, and an impasse was reached, broken by the arrival of a Soviet delegation at EAM/ELAS headquarters on the night of July 25-26. Immediately, EAM/ELAS policy changed. On August 5, it announced that it would join the new Government, and on August 17, five EAM/ELAS representatives were sent to Cairo to meet with the Cabinet. This Government of National Unity was then moved to Caserta to prepare for the liberation of Greece. While it was located there, yet another agreement was signed, placing all guerilla forces under the control of the British Commander, and enjoining against any attempt to occupy Athens until permission was granted by the British.

Until the autumn of 1944, Greek affairs had excited little attention in Britain, quite understandably of course. The general terms of British policy in Greece were announced by the Prime Minister in November, 1943; the terms included little more than support for the Greek monarch until an election could be held.[17] In December, 1943, Anthony Eden returned from Cairo and gave the House of Commons a statement about armed groups inside Greece, ". . . in different degrees hostile to the Germans," but this statement excited little comment at the time.[18] A few comments about Greece appeared in the Left Wing press in 1943, but they were isolated and of little value, though they showed a strong antimonarchical bias and some hostility to the British Ambassador, Reginald Leeper.

The Prime Minister returned to Greek affairs in an extensive war statement made in February, 1944, in which he made the following statement about Greek politics: "There is also present the idea that powerful elements among the (Greek) guerillas are thinking less of driving out the foreign enemy than of seizing the title deeds of their country and establishing themselves as the dominant party irrespective of the views of the masses of the nation after the war is over."[19] This was received in silence, and brought no comment in the Left Wing press. Anthony Eden broached the subject once again in August, 1944, following the Lebanon Conference: "His Majesty's Government do not consider that at the present time any Greek political party which has the interests of Greece at heart can justify a refusal to join the National Government, or make conditions of the nature of those put forward by EAM."[20] Again, the Government's statement was allowed to pass without comment.

Nevertheless, the Left Wing in Britain had begun to take some interest in Greek matters. The state of Greek affairs was in fact quite well known. The Lebanon Conference and its results were well publicized.[21] Much surprise was engendered by the arrival of the Soviet delegation,[22] and the subsequent EAM/ELAS announcement that it would take part in the coalition government. The mutinies in the Greek forces in Cairo were used as an excuse for denouncing the British Government's policy in the Middle East.[23] The EAM/ELAS attack on EDES was also known, though not really believed.[24] In the House of Commons, Aneurin Bevan, Seymour Cocks, Tom Driberg, and others did attack the British Government in August, 1944, for supporting a decadent monarchy in Greece against the expressed wishes of the people, but they ignored the policy statements made by the Government during the debate.[25] Thus, the Left Wing was generally aware of events in Greece, supported the resistance without knowing too much about its characteristics, and opposed British policy without any clear understanding of the data on which the policy was based. There was little detailed comment, however, from the time of the brief outburst of interest in August, 1944, until the fighting began in Athens in December, 1944.

The Greek Government of National Unity returned to Greece on October 18, 1944, without incident, although nothing could have prevented the occupation of Athens by EAM/ELAS had they made the attempt. It faced an enormously complicated food problem, since the economy was at a standstill, and a complicated security problem, since armed bands of guerillas roamed the countryside at will. The coalition foundered on the attempt to solve the security problem. The Greek Brigade that had mutinied in Cairo was brought into Athens on the advice of the British Government, although against the advice of Colonel Woodhouse. The EAM/ELAS representatives in the Cabinet were given the task of drawing up a plan for disarming all irregular forces. They completed the draft on November 28, but repudiated it the following day. On December 1, the plan went into effect, and the EAM/ELAS ministers resigned in protest when the Cabinet met without them. EAM/ELAS had scheduled a vast demonstration in Athens for December 3 and had received permission to hold it; this permission was now withdrawn, but the demonstration went ahead as scheduled. Electricity supplies in the city were cut off, and firing broke out around noon on December 3. The cause of the firing was much disputed and remains unsettled.

The following day, December 4, EAM/ELAS launched a major attack on the city, and by midnight controlled most of Athens. In the early hours of December 5, the British forces were ordered to intervene and stop the fighting. For some ten days, the issue hung in balance until British reserves arrived from Cairo. Winston Churchill flew to Athens on Christmas Day, and secured the appointment of a Regent, Archbishop Damaskinos, when he returned to London. On January 11, EAM/ELAS sued for peace, and a truce was arranged on January 15. A final agreement was signed at Varkiza on February 15, 1945. There were tales of terrorism, hostage-taking, mass reprisals, and really serious repression by EAM/ELAS during the fighting, many of which were later verified by reliable sources. This brief resume of the conflict is far from complete, but it provides an adequate framework for assessing the attitude of the British Left Wing.

The House of Commons in London was engaged in a debate on the Reply to the King's Speech during the first days of December 1944. Sir Richard Acland and Hugh Lawson of the Commonwealth party had tabled an Amendment to the Reply that condemned the British Government for supporting "reactionary" rather than "genuine people's" movements in liberated Europe.[26] They were joined by Aneurin Bevan and George Strauss in the debate, but events in Greece were not at this stage part of the argument. Fighting began in Greece on a Saturday, and the Sunday press was filled with lurid tales of fascist Greek police shooting down innocent Greek citizens in the streets of Athens. When Parliament resumed on Monday, the Prime Minister, in reply to a Private Notice Question, made a careful limited statement in which he stated that the origin of the fighting was obscure, but that the British Government was determined to prevent the imposition of a minority dictatorship on the Greek people by a group of armed communists.[27] This was not considered satisfactory by the Left Wing, and an attempt was made to move the adjournment on a matter of immediate importance, but this the Speaker would not accept. The critics were advised to table another Amendment to the Reply.

On December 8, the following amendment was moved by Seymour Cocks: "But humbly regret that the Gracious Speech contains no assurance that His Majesty's forces will not be used to disarm the friends of democracy in Greece and other parts of Europe, or to suppress those popular movements which have so valorously assisted in the defeat of the enemy, and upon whose success we must rely for future friendly co-operation with Europe."[28] This amendment was later subjected to postnatal criticism for its "unrepresentative" character, but it collected thirty votes in the Division that followed debate, and caused something more than one hundred abstentions, which is scarcely "unrepresentative."

It may appear, at first glance, that the amendment has little direct relation to the course of events in Greece, and in one sense this is true; that is, the amendment is worded in terms of the meaning of events in Greece to the British Left Wing rather than as a detailed examination of British policy in Greece. The antecedents of the amendment are clear. It is simply a statement of the belief that Europe was going "left," that the instrument of this change would be national resistance movements, and that it was the task of British socialism to assist these revolutions wherever possible. The arguments advanced by the supporters of the amendment had very little to do with the facts of the case; they were concerned with establishing broad lines on which British policy might be criticized, and the Greek EAM/ELAS movement supported. In fairness, there is no reason to suppose that the British Left Wing really knew very much about the EAM/ELAS organization, in more than general terms. What concerns us most is the effort made to fit events into the pattern which the preconceived goal demanded, and the actions which were necessary to do so.

The opening argument in the House of Commons, made by Seymour Cocks, attempted to show that the British Government was supporting a reactionary monarchy in Greece against the representatives of the people. Cocks denied that EAM/ELAS was a communist organization, though he agreed that it might have a communist core, a point which other Left Wing spokesmen were not willing to concede. He demanded a coalition government for Greece in which all parties would be represented in accordance with the wishes of the Greek people. Other speakers from the Left Wing expressed the same general sentiments, with an occasional touch of the macabre, as in this excerpt from a speech by T. Driberg: "To my mind it is a war between the bulk of the Greek population on one side, and a few quislings and Royalists on the other, backed by British bayonets."[29] The Government spokesman, Anthony Eden, answered all of the factual questions raised in the debate, but convinced no one on the Left Wing. Thirty M.P.'s voted against the government, and a very substantial number of Labour M.P.'s abstained. No Labour Minister spoke during the debate. In fact, only forty-seven of one hundred and sixty-five Labour M.P.'s registered a vote. Twenty-three of these voted with the Government, including Stafford Cripps.

The Left Wing press showed substantially the same reaction as that which appeared in the House of Commons, though the first issues in December appeared before the crisis in Greece broke out. In the first edition of Left Wing journals to appear following the crisis, the pattern was set by *Tribune* which devoted the whole of its first leader to an electoral campaign tactics feature by Aneurin Bevan (December 8, 1944). The Greek Civil War was outlined briefly, and fantastically, in a column of shorter notes. "British intervention in the internal affairs of Greece has provoked a major crisis." It had led to the resignation of the

EAM/ELAS ministers, who had already agreed to demobilize their troops. Ambassador Leeper had prevented this demobilization and the British Commander had very conveniently "discovered" a plot against the Greek Government. But aside from this brief mention, the matter attracted little attention. The *New Statesman* (December 9, 1944) published a summary of events, noting with approval the strong response to the call for a general strike, but the Left Wing was not really interested. They were concentrating, at the moment, on the coming Labour party Conference, and their demand for an end to the Coalition Government in Britain. The *New Statesman,* in fact, coupled its story of events in Greece with a demand that Labour members of the Government resign. Thus the Left Wing tended to deal with policy in Greece as part of a broader general policy of using the opportunity offered by the war to gain political advantage, and this accounts in part for the generalized nature of its arguments, although the arguments might refer to the specific question of Britain's Greek policy.

The 1944 Labour party Conference, which met in mid-December, also illustrates this tendency to generalize. The basic resolution dealing with European liberation, moved by Arthur Greenwood, the Leader of the Labour party in opposition in the House of Commons, spoke directly of Greece but contained broader sentiments applicable to all of the liberated areas:

> This Conference deeply regrets the tragic situation which has arisen in Greece and calls upon the British Government most urgently to take all necessary steps to facilitate an armistice without delay, and to secure the resumption of conversations between all sections of the people who have resisted the Fascist and Nazi invaders with a view to the establishment of a provisional National Government which should proceed to a free and fair General Election as soon as practicable in order that the will of the Greek people may be expressed.[30]

Both the resolution and Greenwood's supporting speech give evidence of the confusion about factual data that existed in the Labour movement at the time. Greenwood was not aware that a national government had already been formed in Greece, nor that EAM/ELAS had been asked to disarm and refused, since both points played a prominent part in his demands on the British Government.

The Government's policy was supported by the General Secretary of the powerful National Union of General and Municipal Workers, and by Ernest Bevin, who gave a strong personal endorsement of the policy followed in Greece. But the Left Wing reply, when it came, swept these arguments into the discard. Aneurin Bevan, in a speech typical of those opposed to British policy in Greece, used this technique to support his own point of view: "Mr. Bevin has described what has been happening in Greece. I have no time to answer him. But there is one complete answer to him. Only three bodies of public opinion in the world have gone on record in his support, namely Fascist Spain, Fascist Portugal, and the majority of the Tories in the House of Commons."[31] Bevan went on to speak in general terms of the need to support the socialist movements in Europe during the liberation. Other speakers were genuinely concerned with Greek events, but unable to arrive at a solution which would avoid the inference that the sacred representatives of the resistance had in some way done something wrong. The debate, in the last analysis, was inconclusive.

An indication of the extent of the confusion, and the attitude which Labour in general and the Left Wing particularly tended to support, is found in the following resolution, passed unanimously by the Conference almost immediately after the debate on Greece terminated: "This Conference expresses its admiration of the resistance movements which have proved their value to the allied cause. It demands that the Government shall give an immediate pledge that, as territories are cleared of the enemy, their administration shall be left to the democratic control of their own inhabitants with no attempts at interference or dictation by outside forces, political or military."[32] This is precisely the same as the argument applied to the Greek issue by the Left Wing, stated in general terms. This is illustrative of the tenacity with which the Left Wing maintained its position in the face of controversial facts.

The same approach to the problem of liberation appears in the brief debate on Greek affairs in the House of Commons that followed the Labour party Conference by a week. Aneurin Bevan brushed aside the argument that an attempt to seize power had been foiled by the British Government: "My hon and gallant friend, like a good many others, has been pretending that we are endeavoring to suppress an attempt by EAM at dictatorship. There is not the slightest evidence of that. . .on the contrary, all the evidence is against it. EAM would never have succeeded if they had been so bungling as they appear to be. . . .There is no evidence whatsoever that this was a military coup d'état."[33] Yet Bevan's own journal, *Tribune* (December 22, 1944) published a special leader a few days later which argued that communist leadership in Greece was essential as a condition of successful revolution. Other issues were treated in the same manner. When news of EAM atrocities first reached the British press, they were denied by the Left Wing press, and justified by the needs of the moment, sometimes in the same issue.[34] When the Prime Minister, armed with documentary evidence of EAM/ELAS atrocities, lashed out at his critics in the House of Commons, the Government was, in one case, denounced for its failure to prevent these very atrocities.

Discussion of Greek affairs ended in January, 1945, on a very unhealthy note. The Government felt that its policies had been justified by events; the Left Wing remained completely unconvinced, and the great bulk of the Labour movement probably felt that some sort of injustice had been done to the Greek resistance movement. Within six months, the Left Wing returned to the attack, this time against its own government, with its position unchanged. Several aspects of this affair merit attention.

First, and perhaps most important, the Left Wing never established a clear-cut position that could be attacked with empirical data. They took their stand on the general principle that resistance movements were good, and opposition to them was reactionary, and refused to accept any data that did not present this picture of events. Their interpretation of events depended solely upon the character of the participants and not their behavior, and in fact really depended upon an assumed character in the participants which was clearly derived from ideological conviction. This disregard for fact is perhaps the most striking aspect of the Left Wing reaction to the Greek Civil War.

The second factor that strikes the observer is the unwillingness of the leaders of the Labour party, with the notable exception of Ernest Bevin, to take a firm position on the Greek question and attempt to explode the Left Wing version of British policy. In the nature of things, criticism of the Left Wing by nonsocialist sources, which was plentiful at the time, is utterly meaningless within an ideological group like the Labour movement. When, at a later date, the British Labour Government was forced to pay the price for this vacillation by sustained attack from the back benches of its own party, it is difficult to muster sympathy for the men who were in a very real sense responsible for their own predicament. Thus the Greek issue illustrates a second aspect of ideological groups and their relation to politics, i.e., the serious need for responsible leadership within the ideology.

Finally, the assumptions that lay behind the Left Wing case against the British Government bear closer scrutiny. These were very clearly stated in a special leader in *Tribune* published on December 29, 1944. What, the writer inquired, were the conditions of democracy that are required in eastern Europe at this time? For Tories and Liberals, he replied, the question can be answered very simply. Democracy means free elections within a constitutional framework of law and order, and this was generally agreed among these groups to be the best solution to the problem of re-establishing political control in Europe.

But for socialists, the writer went on, this was not really adequate. Suppose that the guardians of law and order in Europe were really the enemies of democracy? This, he thought, was certainly the case in Italy, in Greece, in Belgium, and save for Tito in Yugoslavia, everywhere else in Europe. Here, the Liberal and Tory solution was not adequate. First, the antidemocratic ruling groups must be overthrown; bullets must clear the way before ballots can do their work.

> The first condition of democracy in Europe is the revolutionary overthrow of anti-democratic ruling groups, and the smashing of anti-democratic state machines. That is the main driving force behind the struggle of the resistance movements in all the liberated countries.

> The second condition of democracy in Europe is a firm broadly-based alliance of the democratic forces in each country, inspired by the will to preserve their free cooperation after the victory over the forces of reaction has been won.[35]

The forces of reaction, and the nondemocratic ruling groups are of course the nonsocialists and noncommunists. The leader is a frank appeal for support for those socialist or communist groups which combine to seize power by the use of armed force in the liberated continental countries.

In the light of these principles, the Left Wing attitude toward the Greek Civil War is perfectly understandable, and even logically necessary. Further, the Left Wing attitude toward the establishment of communist-dominated regimes in Eastern Europe is predictable along these guide lines. It might be said that this shows a singular lack of faith in the ability of socialism to appeal to the instincts or reason of a free electorate under free conditions despite the frequent use of the word "democratic" in Left Wing argument. But much more important, this attitude certainly implies a dogmatic assertion that one particular segment of the political community *should* hold power, and that any action which that segment might take to assume this power is fully justified in advance. This, clearly, is the greatest peril in any dogmatic ideology which presumes to know the end of man as a political animal.

V

DISINTEGRATION OF THE GRAND ALLIANCE

The British General Election of 1945 resulted in a substantial—and surprising—victory for the Labour party. This created a completely new domestic political situation in Britain, and thus becomes the ideal point of departure for a study of political opinion in the country. The Left Wing of the Labour movement, as we have seen, had pressed very hard for an early election, even though a Labour victory seemed quite unlikely, and had played an important part in the final decision to proceed with the election before the end of the Pacific war. Undoubtedly, fear of a repetition of the events of 1931 played a substantial part in the Left Wing desire for haste, since they almost invariably showed a pathological hatred of coalition government after that date. Whatever the motive, the outcome of the election created an urgent need for the development of a new Left Wing attitude toward government policies; it could not be expected to continue opposing a Labour Government as it had opposed the Conservative Government and the wartime Coalition Government.

When election excitement abated, the Left Wing was already looking forward with confidence to a new order of things in the field of domestic politics, and of course in international affairs as well. In fact, the Left Wing expressed far more interest in international politics than did any other element of the Labour party during the 1945 Election. A survey of the formal election addresses, which are filed in the library at Transport House, indicates this emphasis very clearly. In Britain, every candidate is allowed to prepare and mail to each of his prospective constituents a brief statement of principles. The Labour party provides a rather innocuous "standard form" which can be used by less inventive, or more conservative party candidates. Almost without exception, recognized Left Wing candidates improvised broadly on the principles to be followed in foreign relations, and placed their improvisations in conspicuous places on the broadsheets. Most

66

moderate candidates, including the leading members of the parliamentary Labour party, kept international affairs discreetly in the background, contenting themselves with a simple, formal statement on Labour's intended policy.

The Left Wing made considerable use of two major theses regarding international affairs during the election campaign. The first thesis, which originated with Dr. Hugh Dalton, stated that the natural affinity between Labour and the Soviet Union would give a Labour Government a decided advantage in its dealings with that country as against the position of a Conservative Government. The second, which originated in Left Wing opposition to the policies of the wartime coalition, was a demand for an end to "continuity" in foreign policy, that is, a statement of the view that a Labour Government could not possibly continue the foreign policies laid down by a Conservative Government, assuming that the policies of the wartime coalition were, in fact, Conservative policies despite the fact that the Cabinet contained leading members of the Labour party. Both of these theses were to play a crucial part in Left Wing propaganda during the next two years.

The best illustration of the first thesis is found in the statement made by Hugh Dalton at the 1945 Labour party Conference:

> Given that Anglo-Soviet relations are clouded from time to time by suspicion and misunderstanding, I most emphatically hold that a British Labour Government is far more likely to remove these suspicions than a British Tory Government. . . One of the great arguments we should address to the electorate at large is that a British Labour Government would be far more likely to create a state of confidence and mutual trust between London and Moscow than any alternative Government in the Country. [1]

This is partly a variation on the "warmongering" charge that is traditionally hurled against the Conservative party during British elections, and partly a restatement of the old socialist suspicion of Conservative hatred of the Soviet Union. By 1950, when close affinity and fellowship with the Soviet Union had lost its electoral value, the Labour party turned full circle and began to stress the traditional antagonism between socialists and communists, but this is only natural in political propaganda, and it does not imply that the statement was not sincerely meant.

The Left Wing demand for an end to "continuity" in foreign policy stemmed from the *prima facie* assumption made by leading Left Wing spokesmen that there must be some difference between a Labour policy and a Conservative policy, or more frequently, between a socialist policy and a nonsocialist policy. The leaders of the Labour party were rather loathe to adopt this argument and concentrate on international affairs, since the unchallenged leader of Britain in external matters was Winston Churchill, and the Conservative party had been using this argument during the election campaign. Instead, the official policy of the Labour party placed international affairs "above party," hoping, perhaps, to offset some of the Conservative advantage in the field.[2] In truth, the question never really became an issue during the election.

It must also be said that the Left Wing on no occasion provided the public with a clear statement of the new direction British foreign policy might take under the direction of a Labour majority in the House of Commons. In context, it appears that a "socialist" foreign policy meant some measure of support for "progressive" elements in other countries, an extension of the opinions expressed during the Greek Civil War. Britain was asked to cease championing "out of date fascism" and join Russia in expressing the aspirations of the "common people" of Europe.[3] Another spokesman suggested "support, protection, and assistance" for the European socialist revolution, "wherever it appears" as a suitable basis for British policy.[4] One of the leading pacifists in the Labour party asked that Britain abandon her interests in the Mediterranean area and withdraw completely from the region.[5] More commonly, a new policy was demanded in Greece, Spain, and in Poland. These views are reasonably representative of Left Wing opinions prior to the General Election of 1945.[6]

When the outcome of the election was announced and Labour realized that it had won a very substantial majority in the House of Commons the Left Wing was understandably jubilant. Hopeful expressions, and somewhat guarded requests for change turned suddenly into firm demands, and some extremely confident predictions. Harold Laski, writing in *La Tribune Économique,* told his French readers without qualification that the British Government would soon drive Franco from power in Spain.[7] The *New Statesman* (August 18, 1945) also announced the imminent downfall of Franco, while Kingsley Martin, in a special leader, further predicted a complete renovation of the Greek Government. Other Left Wing spokesmen expressed similar views. It seems clear that the Left Wing really felt, in the first flush of success, that a change in the ideology of the rulers of Britain would bring definite changes in foreign policy just as it was expected to bring a change in domestic policy. The General Election thus had the effect of raising Left Wing hopes very high, and the sequence of events that followed frustrated these hopes with remarkable consistency. In the process, the Left Wing was driven to engage its own government in parliamentary combat because of the depth of its ideological convictions.

It can be argued, of course, that the Left Wing had no reasonable grounds for allowing its expectations to run so high. Certainly two crucial points were overlooked. First, the behavior of the Soviet Union already boded ill for Left Wing hopes of a settlement through the mediation of a Labour Government, and the chief target of Soviet hostility was clearly Great Britain—at this time—and not the United States. Second, the new British Foreign Secretary was Ernest Bevin, the only member of the Coalition Government to support its international policies openly, a traditional antagonist of Left Wing policies, and openly hostile to communist efforts to infiltrate his own Transport and General Workers' Union. It was nearly absurd to expect that Bevin would suddenly repudiate his past views and adopt the Left Wing view of what British foreign policy ought to be.

This chapter covers the period from the General Election of 1945 through the Labour party Conference of 1946. It opens on a Left Wing that is confident and looking forward to happier days; it closes in failure as the Left Wing proved far too weak to influence the Labour Government's foreign policy through the party conference. It contains a period of extreme frustration for the Left Wing. The Conference of Foreign Ministers met in London in September and failed miserably. The United Nations Organization began its meetings in London early in 1946, and ended in heated argument, particularly between Britain and Russia. Soviet policy in Eastern Europe, the crisis in Iran, and other trouble spots clearly revealed the weakness of the Grand Alliance. In the spring of 1946, Winston Churchill, already convinced of the futility of further attempts to reach agreement with the Soviet Union, aired a proposal for an Anglo-American alliance in a speech at Fulton, Missouri; the Left Wing response shows how little its attitude had changed since the European war ended. Although there were few decisions made during the period, great power relations worsened steadily and Left Wing apprehensions grew as the tension mounted. The Left Wing then demanded a change in order to halt the deterioration of international co-operation, and this demand is examined in detail in the chapter which follows.

The new Parliament met for the first time early in August, 1945, and adjourned immediately until August 16. During this brief recess, the Left Wing had an opportunity to clarify the general line of policy it had adopted toward great power relations. It also had time to absorb the news of the first use of atomic weapons and ponder its significance. The immediate reaction was suspicion of American intentions. The new bomb was American-developed and American-controlled, and the Soviet-oriented portions of the Left Wing found much to reflect upon when it was realized that the Soviet Union had not had any knowledge of the development of the weapon. The general reaction of the Left Wing was a decided suspicion of the United States, and the suggestion that control of the process be discussed among the great powers. Meanwhile, the process should be shared equally among all the allied powers.[8] *Tribune* alone proposed a comprehensive program for controlling the weapon, including the establishment of an international agency, an internationalized territory, facilities for use of the international organization vested with such control, and a program of international inspection. Perhaps some of the hostility to the United States encountered at this time stemmed from the ill will created in Britain by the abrupt termination of the Lend Lease program, which the Left Wing assumed as a matter of course to be an overt act of hostility in protest against the outcome of the British General Election.[9]

For the Left Wing, the capitalistic United States was now the supreme ideological enemy, and this natural antipathy was substantially bolstered by the end of Lend Lease and the American policy of retaining control of the atomic bomb pending the establishment of an international inspection system. In the early autumn of 1945 a caricature of the United States began to appear in the Left Wing press that was decidedly unflattering. The United States was pictured as an irresponsible, prodigously powerful economic giant, controlled by a capitalist-dominated, reactionary Congress much influenced by military leaders. By November, 1945, this caricature had been so strongly disseminated that Clement Attlee was hailed as the "savior of civilization" when he returned from the United States with an agreement to discuss the question of controlling atomic energy in the new international organization. In the long run, the stand taken by the Left Wing in 1945 was not carried through. Left Wing criticism of United States policy in the Atomic Energy Commission constantly shifted ground, and the crux of the control system proposed—international inspection—was never clearly defined. Further, the final report of the committee was completely ignored when it appeared in 1948. For a time, however, the issue was used by Left Wing spokesmen as a "justification" for Soviet hostility.

On August 16, 1945, the new House of Commons met, observed the traditional formalities, heard the King's speech, and began to debate the Reply to the Throne. The former Prime Minister, Winston Churchill, freed now from the responsibilities of office, and doubtless smarting from a sharp political reverse, followed the usual chaste and uncontroversial mover and seconder.[10]

Churchill produced a lengthy speech, which included a sharp castigation of Professor Harold Laski and his role in the previous election and some comment on the current state of international affairs. He was followed by the new Prime Minister, who exchanged political barbs with Churchill, meanwhile carefully avoiding all questions relating to foreign affairs; these were left to the new Foreign Secretary.

On August 20, 1945, Ernest Bevin made his first appearance as Foreign Secretary and delivered a long, tedious, and careful speech to the House of Commons. Bevin never really learned to feel at home in Parliament; he was much more in his element at a Labour party Conference or a meeting of the T.U.C. where his personal prestige and oratorical skill produced truly remarkable results. In the House, he tended to stick close to his brief. Bevin's survey of external affairs had been awaited with considerable trepidation on all sides. In the making, the speech spread dismay through the Left Wing, and a very considerable measure of relief among the Conservatives and Liberals present. It spelled the end for Left Wing hopes of a new direction in British policy that would end "continuity" and embark Britain on a "socialist" policy. For Bevin clearly and firmly repudiated the view that ideology was an adequate basis for British external policy; instead, he accepted the policies followed by the wartime Coalition Government with few changes. The present government in Greece—much maligned by the Left Wing—would continue to receive British support. The government of Spain was a matter for the Spanish people to decide. Britain was very much dissatisfied with the present regimes in Eastern Europe which had been installed by the Soviet Union and did not represent the wishes of the people in these countries. In sum, there were no significant changes in policy; Anthony Eden might well have made precisely the same speech, though more gracefully.

In the debate that followed Bevin's presentation, the spokesmen for the Left Wing tended to ignore the content of Bevin's statement and concentrate on their own hopes and fears in international affairs. Only Michael Foot, a prominent figure in the group associated with *Tribune,* attacked Bevin directly for denouncing the communist-dominated police states in Eastern Europe, and even Foot did not challenge Bevin's factual data.[11] The Greek Government was strongly attacked by a number of speakers from the Left Wing.[12] The pacifists immediately began an impassioned appeal for an end to peacetime conscription.[13] The United States came in for some criticism of its policy for dealing with atomic energy, and particularly for refusing to share the "secret" with the Soviet Union. Strong pleas were heard from nearly every Left

Wing speaker for an end to "continuity" in foreign policy, though Bevin had just completely repudiated any radical changes and refused to accept the need for basing policy on ideology.[14] Clearly, the Left Wing was not in agreement with Bevin on several important questions, but the length and complexity of Bevin's statement made it quite impossible to produce effective criticism within the scope of a single debate.

British political interests, "right" and "left," had awaited Bevin's statement with considerable misgivings. A general survey of the reaction to the speech in the British press is very instructive and helps establish the climate of opinion of the times more plainly. The *London Times* (August 21, 1945) blandly pursued its traditional policy of supporting all governments with a noncomittal resume of the speech which noted that there had been no surprises, and it apparently expected none. The conservative *Daily Telegraph* (August 21, 1945) was frankly delighted with Bevin's "vigorous and sagacious" effort, noting with some enjoyment the areas of agreement between Churchill and Bevin. *Time and Tide* (August 25, 1945), not to be outdone, called the speech one of the most balanced, well informed, and comprehensive efforts made by any British Foreign Minister in the past ten years, which is strong praise indeed for a Labour Minister from a conservative weekly. The *Tablet* (August 25, 1945), Catholic and violently anti-Soviet, had reservations about Bevin's policy in Eastern Europe, which had not appeared sufficiently vigorous to please, though it expressed pleasure with the main body of Bevin's effort. The *Manchester Guardian* (August 21, 1945) chief organ of the Liberal press, was likewise pleased with the speech. Thus the Conservative and Liberal press, in general, expressed considerable satisfaction with their new Foreign Secretary on the occasion of his first major policy speech. This contributed substantially to the displeasure of the Left Wing, which felt that there was something fundamentally wrong when a policy speech from a Labour Minister met with such hearty applause from the Opposition benches.

The Labour press, if we include all of the newspapers that normally supported Labour, was a trifle less certain of the proper attitude to take. The *News Chronicle* (August 21, 1945) noted that Bevin's policy was based firmly on Coalition policy, and "continuity" was thus established, but made no further comment. The *Daily Herald* (August 21, 1945), official organ of the Labour party, took a snipe at Churchill's "strangely sympathetic" remarks about General Franco, and made much of Bevin's casual reference to the favorable view the British Government would take of a change of government in Spain, though this was merely an aside in the speech. The *Daily Worker* (August 21, 1945) naturally singled out the reference to "police states" in Eastern Europe for severe criticism, and heaped praise upon Lyall Wilkes for his attack on the Greek Government. Obviously, there was some Labour disappointment in the foreign policy statement, but the lines of criticism were not yet clear.

Within a week, however, the Left Wing press was in full cry against Ernest Bevin. The "Letters to the Editor" columns were filled with messages from dismayed Labour supporters, chiefly from the Left Wing, who were aghast that Bevin had failed to repudiate "continuity" and adopt a "socialist" foreign policy, particularly in reference to Greece and Spain. Others took issue with Bevin's attitude toward the "revolutionary democracies" in Eastern Europe.[15] Several prominent pacifists expressed the belief that Bevin's policy would almost certainly lead to further armaments (as it did) and that the price of such military expenditures would be the loss of the social services program at home. The pacifist alternative was usually framed in terms of complete abandonment of existing commitments and concentration on the problem of socializing the British economy.

Thus the first official contact between the new Foreign Secretary and his own supporters provided little hope for peaceful cooperation in the future. Bevin's statement was forthright and unmistakable. The Left Wing hedged for a few days then launched forth against the statement in quite hostile terms. The most striking aspect of the controversy, certainly, was the relative unimportance of the issues which the Left Wing raised. British policy in Greece, and the character of the Spanish Government, however large they may have loomed to the Left Wing, were peripheral to the Foreign Secretary's task. In the context of great power relations, Franco and the Greek King were minor figures, and concentration upon them by the British Government could almost be deemed frivolous. Apparently, the Left Wing wished to see some sort of gesture without realizing that the British Government was in no position at that time to waste its energy in useless posturing.

The truth is that if the Left Wing approach to international affairs is viewed in broad terms one finds that they really ignored the central problem facing the British Foreign Secretary—the relationship between Britain, Russia and the United States. Even when the question was approached by the Left Wing, it did so in an oblique manner. Yet the Left Wing was acutely conscious of the problem. The dilemma arose from the increasing difficulty the Left Wing encountered in its effort to maintain ideological affinity with the U.S.S.R. as the facts of international affairs conflicted

more and more with the theoretical framework laid down by the
Left Wing ideology. The Left Wing would not relinquish its theory
nor would it accept the facts at face value. It remained, in effect,
on the perimeter of events, watching with horror as great power
relations debilitated steadily, but concealed the crucial issue as
the Puritans concealed and suppressed sin, hoping, perhaps, that
the problem would solve itself or go away. In these terms, the
crux of the argument between the Labour Government and its Left
Wing followers was the inability of the Government of a great
power to procrastinate to the same extent as an irresponsible
political faction.

In the confusion that ensued when the facts and theories of international relations clashed, the fellow-travelers, who had faced
the problem of great power relations and decided in favor of the
U.S.S.R., played a vital role. For a time, they were the bellwether
of the Left Wing, setting international data in a context which not
only made it possible for convinced Left Wing socialists to support the Soviet Union, but in fact made it very difficult for them to
do anything else. One of the more proficient members of the fellow traveler group, Konni Zilliacus, demonstrated the technique
required for this sort of leadership on the occasion of his first
speech in the 1945 Parliament.[16] He began with the obviously true
assertion that world peace could be maintained easily if the great
powers remained unified. Unity, he then contended, could only be
maintained if suspicions did not arise among these great powers.
Suspicions, on the other hand, were certain to arise unless possession of atomic weapons was shared equally. If this were not
done, suspicion would lead to an arms race, and "arms races invariably lead to war." Secrecy was clearly the responsibility of
the United States, therefore the United States bore the burden of
guilt for any arms race that might occur, while Winston Churchill
shared the guilt since he had agreed to this policy while he was
Prime Minister of the wartime Coalition. Bevin had taken this
policy from the Coalition Government, and it was essential that he
realize what had occurred and change direction.

The speech is a masterpiece of socialist propaganda. Every
member of the Labour movement in Britain could find something
to applaud. The pacifist could join in the denunciation of arms
races; the anti-American could blame the United States for deteriorating great power relations; the pro-Soviet socialist found
his own prejudices carefully fed. This type of speech was produced very often indeed by the more prominent of Britain's fellow travelers.

The storm raised by Bevin's initial speech had scarcely subsided when the failure of the London Conference of Foreign

Ministers threw another bombshell into world opinion. Parliament had recessed, but the Left Wing press reacted violently, and in the process demonstrated the extent to which the Left Wing is itself a highly individualistic group. As soon as it was clear that the conference had indeed failed, the pacifists dropped the entire question. The *New Statesman* urged Britain to adopt an attitude of strict impartiality and neutrality, cultivating her European neighbors and dissociating herself from both Russia and the United States. *Tribune* claimed that Russia was merely seeking security and had committed a "diplomatic blunder." *Reynolds News*, which was following a definitely fellow-traveling line at the time, placed the blame for the failure of the conference on the United States, which had caused the difficulty by demanding strategic bases in the Far East, and which was hindering the social revolution taking place in Europe in every way possible.

In the initial phase of the discussion that followed the Conference, there was no tendency to associate the failure with the United States' atomic energy policy. It was generally felt, in the British press, that western protests against Soviet policy in Eastern Europe were responsible for much of the friction and the Left Wing press usually added that American "imperialism" in the Far East was heightening Soviet fears of a capitalistic attack. The possibility that the Soviet Union had expansive intentions was dismissed as ridiculous; the argument was usually substantiated by the statement that Russia had no economic reason to be expansive. Expansion was a characteristic of capitalistic imperialism, not socialism.[17] It is difficult to convey to the reader the magnificent assurance with which these assumptions were stated. The Soviet Union was a socialist nation, and socialist nations were not expansive, and that was that. The tenor of the argument is most reminiscent of the indomitable dogmatism of the scholastics.

Early in October, 1945, the American President announced that his Government would not divulge the processes used to manufacture atomic weapons until adequate safeguards had been devised against their misuse. The Left Wing immediately pounced upon the statement and tied it to Soviet "suspicions" of American intentions to produce an interpretation of current world tensions which included the beginning of a new arms race, the economic collapse of Britain, and eventually full scale warfare. Left Wing writers now had no doubts whatever that the Foreign Ministers Conference had collapsed because of Soviet fears of an atomic attack by the United States.[18]

After a curious lapse of some weeks, the atomic energy issue was introduced into current affairs once again and debated energetically for the remainder of 1945. The suggestions made were numerous. Some, like fellow traveler Konni Zilliacus, suggested openly that Britain share such information as she possessed with the Soviets immediately. Others, like Harold Laski, did not go quite so far but demanded unequivocally that this "fantastic secrecy" be dropped, and argued that once this was accomplished agreement would be possible. When Winston Churchill announced his support for the American proposal it gave Left Wing suspicions an additional fillip, and added partisan fuel to the fires of controversy.[19] Even Lord Beaverbrook's *Daily Express* (November 8, 1945) expressed the hope that data might be shared with Russia if it would ease international tensions. Churchill was roundly denounced by the Labour press,[20] supported by the *Daily Mail*, and *Daily Telegraph*, supported with reservations by the *Liberal Manchester Guardian*, opposed by the *London Times*, and of course firmly scourged by the Left Wing press.

The Left Wing was by now fully convinced that the Soviet Union lived in mortal dread of an American atomic attack, and criticism of the United States increased measurably in Left Wing organs of opinion. The pacifist *Forward*, in a very defeatist tone, now asked that Britain unilaterally withdraw from Europe and the Mediterranean Sea region, and announce that she would in no circumstances go to war with any other country. Readers who have forgotten the antecedent for this request should consult the Labour party resolution of 1935 cited in Chapter III.

In this atmosphere, one would expect an international agreement to discuss controls to be greeted with considerable enthusiasm, yet the British-Canadian-American agreement was debated in the House of Commons in surprisingly mild terms.[21] There is, of course, a tendency for M.P.'s to speak to the matter which interests them most on those few opportunities which present themselves to catch the Speaker's eye, but the hue and cry raised over atomic energy seems all out of proportion to the attitude taken by the Left Wing during the debate. Fellow traveler J. D. Mack extolled the virtues of "progressive society" in Eastern Europe. Henry Usborne entered a strong plea for his favorite subject, world government. Leah Manning asked for Yugoslavian control of Trieste. Others wandered equally far from the Three-Power Statement on Control of Atomic Energy which was the nominal subject of debate. In fact, this debate virtually ended discussion of atomic energy and speculation about Soviet fear of atomic war. The agreement was coldly received in the Left Wing press, and the whole issue was allowed to lapse speedily.

When the Moscow Conference of Foreign Ministers agreed to sponsor a United Nations Commission for Atomic Energy, the Left Wing took a distant and disinterested view of the entire affair.

In fairness, the announcement was made when excitement over the coming meeting of the United Nations Organization was growing, but it certainly did come as an anticlimax after long and heated discussion. The truth seems to be that the Left Wing position became untenable after the three-power agreement was signed, and the issue was simply side-stepped.

The debate on the agreement however, coming late in November of 1945, produced four basic Left Wing assumptions about international affairs. The debate can thus function as a useful stopping point for a review of Left Wing opinion. The four general attitudes, which appeared to command widespread support from the Left Wing during the course of the debate, all relate directly or indirectly to the great power conflict then in progress; together they provide a basis upon which a coherent interpretation of Left Wing opinion can be constructed. The first point is the strong conviction that appears in the speeches of various M.P.'s, Labour, Conservative, and Liberal alike, that the behavior of the Soviet Union could best be explained by her fear and suspicion of the West rather than any intrinsic hostility on her part. This view was expressed by speakers as widely separated politically as Anthony Eden, Clement Davies, the Leader of the Liberal party, and Clement Attlee, as well as by most speakers representing the Left Wing, *e.g.*, Fred Lee, Leslie Lipson, Seymour Cocks, Leah Manning, and the Communist M.P., William Gallacher. The Left Wing was alone in assuming that this fear was grounded, and even well grounded, in the attitudes of the United States.

A second assumption, not shared by nonsocialists but common on the Left Wing, was best stated by Seymour Cocks: "It seems to me absurd that the United States should demand bases in the Pacific Islands, and claim that she is virtually the only country to decide on the future of Japan, and then that she should interfere in Rumania and Bulgaria. Just as we recognize the Monroe Doctrine in the West, so should the same or a similar doctrine be recognized in Eastern Europe. We should concentrate chiefly upon cultivating our own garden, which in some ways is the richest and most promising of all."[22]

This practice of "equating" Soviet policy with some western policy became very common in Left Wing opinion, as did the neutralism and the implied concentration upon domestic policy, ignoring the international power struggle.

A third viewpoint commonly expressed by Left Wing sources at this time was an extension of the doctrine stated by Hugh Dalton at the 1945 Labour party Conference, i.e., that the ideological affinity between Russia and British socialists would make peaceful cooperation easier. In fact, of course, Britain had been the chief target for attack by the Soviet Union in the months immediately following the war. But the theory was not abandoned. Instead, the Left Wing assumed that Russia simply did not yet realize that British socialists were sincere, and once she was convinced of this sincerity she would open her arms to her British neighbors. The means suggested for convincing the Soviet leaders was the traditional proposal that Britain proceed as speedily as possible to socialize her own economy.

Finally, there appeared on the Left Wing a line of reasoning which proved to have a remarkable capacity for survival. It originated, apparently, with the British fellow travelers, and the first clear statement of the principle was made by Konni Zilliacus. It was meant, almost certainly, to shore up one of the weakest points in the armory of those who sought to justify the behavior of the Soviet Union, particularly in Eastern Europe:

> I want to warn the Government against the danger of slipping into the position of marking down Communism as the new enemy in Europe because it is fatally easy to do so on the ground that one totalitarianism is very much like another. The catch is that Communism today is inseparable from the resistance movement in Europe. The resistance movement is inseparable from the working class. The working class is inseparable from the socialist revolution in which we, as Socialists, have taken one side and the hon. gentlemen on the other side have taken another . . . Until we reach agreement (with Russia) it is hopeless to attempt to go forward with the U.N.O. or with the organization of peace.[23]

This is one of the plainest statements available which shows the price some members of the Left Wing were quite willing to pay to obtain the social revolution which they felt to be desirable as an ideological end. For although the concept seems to have originated with the fellow travelers, it is nonetheless based upon Left Wing tradition, and it appealed very strongly to the leaders of the post war Left Wing. This argument reappeared whenever Soviet policy in Eastern Europe came up for discussion.

At the beginning of 1946, the outlook for great power agreement was considerably more sanguine than it had been in October, 1945. The Moscow Conference of Foreign Ministers had seemingly broken the impasse, though in actuality only at the price of substantial western concessions. The real disagreement in the Control Council in Germany had been masked to some degree by French recalcitrance. The United Nations had not yet met, and the familiar quarrels in the Security Council were still in the future. Left Wing hopes for a new order in Europe remained strong, and developments in eastern Europe, instead of causing dismay, actually bolstered the confidence of the Left Wing. There was at this time no question in the minds of the leaders of the Left Wing of a choice between alliance with the United States and alliance with the Soviet Union; in fact, Winston Churchill was severely criticized for stating that such a choice was required. Though the British Government had not been able to reach an amicable settlement of existing problems with the Soviets, there was as yet no open hostility between the two countries. The prime objective of the Left Wing remained the accomplishment of the European "social revolution," and it devoted far more attention to this problem than to great power relations. Anti-American sentiment had already appeared in some strength, partly as a normal consequence of socialist suspicion of the arch-capitalist state; partly because of the flurry over atomic energy and the termination of Lend Lease. British pacifists steadily pursued their own goals in their own way, particularly the abolition of conscription, reduction of armaments, reduction of Britain's overseas commitments, and withdrawal, unilateral if necessary, from areas in which a conflict of interest was likely to arise with the Soviet Union.

This hopeful attitude was dissipated, month by month, throughout 1946. Soviet actions in Eastern Europe, and at the various international conferences that were held, soon alienated western opinion and forced the chief governmental leaders in the West to re-evaluate their own policy objectives in a drastic manner. In Britain, the worsening of British-Soviet relations led to a worsening of relations between Ernest Bevin and his own back benches. Bevin's interpretation of Soviet policy was impugned; government statements of Soviet action were denied outright in a manner reminiscent of the Left Wing reaction to the Greek Civil War. Each Soviet move was balanced against some real or imagined western "threat" to the U.S.S.R. and each western charge against Russia was met with a *tu quoque*. By the autumn of 1946, the Left Wing had failed in its effort to convince the government that its assumptions about the Soviet Union were in error, using in this case the party Conference as a medium, and the Left Wing was also having much difficulty in maintaining its support for its own party and the Soviet Union simultaneously.

The first of a series of bad moments for the Grand Alliance was the Iranian crisis in 1946, which was brought to the attention of the Security Council in January, 1946, by the Iranian Government. The crisis had been brewing for some months. Britain and Russia had occupied Iran jointly in 1941, agreeing beforehand to withdraw their troops six months after hostilities ended. In October, 1944, the Soviets had demanded an oil concession from Iran, and when the request was refused (on British and American advice), launched a vicious propaganda campaign against the Iranian Government, even calling upon the people of Iran to rise and overthrow it. Once the war ended, the United States, which was not a party to the agreement, departed speedily and urged both of the occupying powers to do likewise. This left Britain in a rather vulnerable position, for the Soviets refused to withdraw early when this was suggested, and a revolt broke out in the Soviet-controlled territory of Azerbaijan which Soviet troops refused to allow the Iranian Government to quell. After repeated attempts to gain entry to the area, the Iranian Government brought the matter to the Security Council. In retaliation, British policy in Greece was also denounced to the Security Council, and the stage was set for an acrimonious beginning to the Security Council's work.

The initial reaction of the Left Wing to these charges and counter charges was one of skepticism. It was doubted, at first, that a revolution had really occurred in Iran, and once this was obvious, the Left Wing shifted its emphasis to the "reactionary" character of the Iranian Government, ignoring the issue of Soviet troops being withdrawn from the area.[24] The pacifist *Forward* immediately resumed its demand for unilateral British withdrawal from the area, without regard to the facts of the dispute. On the other hand, Soviet charges against British policy in Greece were welcomed and "heartily endorsed" because they clarified the position there for all the world to see.[25]

Once the discussions in the Security Council began, Andre Vyshinsky and Ernest Bevin exchanged pleasantries in language that was only barely diplomatic, and it was generally conceded that Bevin carried off the honors. He remained a prophet without honor in the Left Wing of his own party, however, for his actions were almost universally subjected to severe criticism. Even the lordly *Economist* (February 9, 1946) did not feel that his approach to the debate was conducive to good relations. Only one Left Wing writer, Michael Foot, heartily endorsed Bevin's stand and vigorously denounced the Soviet Union's policies.[26] The remainder of the Left Wing press either ignored the proceedings, or chided Bevin for being overly aggressive. The discussion of Greek affairs, on the other hand, was fully reported, and considerable regret was expressed that the Soviet Union had failed to present the "real problem" in Greece, which centered upon the "reactionary" character of the Greek regime and not upon the points which were raised in the Security Council.[27]

Criticism of Bevin's conduct in the United Nations Security

Council appeared in both the Left Wing press and in the House of Commons debate on the United Nations meeting which began on February 21, just one week after the Security Council adjourned. The grounds for the criticism, however, were tenuous, as in this excerpt from a speech by Lester Hutchinson: "It is felt that when our policy meets with such hearty approval from the Opposition, there must be something wrong with it. It is felt that if the Tories applaud it cannot be a Socialist foreign policy."[28] This feeling was very widespread on the Left Wing. A similar situation might arise, perhaps, if the American Secretary of State were suddenly to find his policies heartily endorsed by the Soviet Government. This type of argument, which is really based on the failure of events to adapt themselves to a theoretical model, produces a vague feeling of uneasiness in the reader after a time, for the precise arguments which were used to attack the Foreign Secretary were not really clear. In fact, there is a curious absence of comment on the factual data involved in the Greek crisis and the Iranian crisis which seems to be a product of the Left Wing tendency to discuss events in general terms without specific reference to a given body of data. This form of argument is extremely difficult to evaluate.

Once the Security Council adjourned, and there was time for second thoughts, some elements of the Left Wing began to retract their previous positions on Greek and Iranian affairs. *Tribune* (February 15, 1946) now noted carefully that the criticisms it had made of Ernest Bevin were very different from those which Vyshinsky had made in the Security Council. It conceded that Bevin had acted correctly when he resisted the Soviet accusation, though it was not willing to concede that British policy in the Middle East did not require re-evaluation and change. Harold Laski, writing in *Forward* (February 16, 1946) likewise recanted, though he too asked that Ernest Bevin make a new approach to Moscow and try to find some basis for friendly agreement. The *New Statesman* was more resourceful than this, however, and merely shifted ground. It now argued that Russia had been difficult at the United Nations meeting because the United States had refused to grant her an extensive rehabilitation credit. Whatever the circumstances, Bevin should have modified his approach to meet Soviet suspicions, since it was "certain" that Russia desired only peace, and nothing would be gained by attacking her in public. On this note, the immediate issue closed, but the Left Wing continued to press for a change in British policy toward Greece.

The remainder of the spring of 1946 brought little easement in international affairs. The Canadian "spy trials" which involved personnel of the Soviet Embassy in Canada were avoided by the

Left Wing press. In the March defense debate, an alliance of fellow travelers and pacifists—notably Emrys Hughes, Rhys Davies, and Konni Zilliacus—attacked the defense estimates and demanded a reduction in armaments. The Left Wing then discovered in the permanent officials at the Foreign Office a potential source of anti-Soviet bias because of their class affiliations which allegedly made the officials unsympathetic to the cause of international socialism and there followed a period of criticism of civil servants which was almost unprecedented in recent British history. Again, it was the fellow travelers who led the Left Wing into a muddle of emotionalized behavior. On January 12, 1946, Konni Zilliacus published an article in the *Daily Worker,* followed by a similar article in the *New Statesman* published early the following February, both of which attacked the high-level civil servants in the Foreign Office. The question was then taken to the House of Commons by fellow traveler William Warbey and used to oppose the nomination of Alexander Cadogan (later Sir Alexander Cadogan) as Permanent British Representative to the United Nations.[29] On On February 23, Warbey and R. H. S. Crossman raised the issue again in letters to the *New Statesman.* By March, the Left Wing was up in arms over the question, demanding a new policy which would consider class background in the appointment of civil servants. This enterprise bore fruit at the 1946 Labour Party Conference in the form of a substantial number of resolutions asking for action, and a fairly sharp debate on the subject.

It is not possible to determine, until the records are available, the precise point at which the leaders of the western nations decided that agreement with the Soviet Union was not possible without concessions that were too great to consider. Certainly the general public in both America and Britain remained largely ignorant of the true state of affairs. A few prominent persons had gone on record in Britain as early as the autumn of 1945 stating that the Soviet Union was fundamentally hostile to the West, and that genuine agreement was unlikely.[30] The first important political figure in Britain to take this position was Winston Churchill. He had publicly expressed serious concern about Soviet intentions early in the life of the 1945 Parliament, then he supported the American decision to retain sole possession of the processes used to manufacture atomic weapons; and finally, in the spring of 1946, he proclaimed publicly the need for a completely new approach to the Soviet Union by the western powers. The speech in which this proclamation was made, and an Anglo-American alliance was proposed, was delivered at Fulton, Missouri, in the presence of the President of the United States. It threw a bombshell into the Left Wing in Britain, and in fact elicited comment throughout the world.

The Fulton speech was in the nature of a massive review of wartime and postwar international politics, and a suggested method for dealing with the problems which remained outstanding.[31] Churchill outlined those aspects of Soviet behavior which appeared to him to justify the assumption that the Soviet Union had expansive intentions, and he suggested that Russia in fact posed a real threat to the western nations. He urged that the West retain its military armaments until the United Nations Organization was strong enough to ensure peace and security. He felt that the United States should retain control of atomic weapons at least temporarily. The two chief problems of the age, he thought, were poverty and tyranny, and the first could not be dealt with so long as the second remained alive. The best hope for an end to tyranny he found in a close association between Britain and the United States, including military staff conferences, common use of facilities, and eventually joint citizenship. War was not inevitable, he felt, since Russia desired only the fruits of war, and not war itself, but he believed that Russia would continue to advance until she was opposed by a strong deterrent force. These were the essential features of a rather long and complex speech; it is necessary to state these essentials to have a basis for evaluating the subsequent criticisms of the speech made by the Left Wing in Britain.

Perhaps a year later, the Fulton speech would have commanded ready assent among the leaders of western governments and roused little comment in the press. Coming as it did at a time when the chief concern of the western people was the search for a means of reaching agreement with Russia, it went far beyond that stage of public opinion which had been reached in most western countries. There are two aspects to the speech: first, the estimate of Soviet intentions; second, the proposals suggested to meet the presumed threat. The "quality" press in Britain tended to agree with the first of these assumptions but felt that the policy suggestions which Churchill made were not entirely suitable. The *London Times* (March 8, 1946) for example, agreed that anxiety was warranted, but preferred collaboration with Europe and the Commonwealth to becoming an American "satellite." The *Manchester Guardian* (March 8, 1946) also agreed with Churchill's evaluation, but felt that his solution was futile unless the United States was prepared to give active support to such a program, and it was inclined to doubt the willingness of the American Government to adopt such a policy. Labour's official organ, the *Daily Herald* (March 8, 1946) likewise accepted the estimate of trends in Soviet policy, but stoutly resisted what it called a policy of "ganging up" on Russia.

If the quality press was unwilling to follow Churchill in the direction he proposed to move, the Left Wing and its press were unwilling even to look in that direction. In fact, Churchill's speech produced what can only be described as mass hysteria on the Left Wing. The parliamentary Left Wing, led by T. E. N. Driberg and William Warbey, demanded that the Government repudiate the speech, and, when the Prime Minister refused, a motion of censure against Churchill was tabled by Warbey and signed by 105 Labour M.P.'s.[32] The motion, which did not reach the floor of the House, read as follows:

> World Peace and Security: That this House considers the proposals for a military alliance between the British Commonwealth and the United States for the purpose of combatting the spread of Communism, such as were put forward by (Churchill) . . . are calculated to do injury to good relations between Great Britain, the United States, and the U.S.S.R., and are inimical to the cause of world peace, and affirms its view that world peace and security can be maintained not by sectional alliances but by progressively strengthening the power and authority of the United Nations Organization to the point where it becomes capable of exercising in respect to world law, order, and justice, the functions of world government.[33]

The motion of course repudiates the conception of regional alliances under the United Nations Charter on which later western associations were built. It also injects into the proposal a conception of ideological warfare which, in all fairness, Churchill did not assume. The original speech opposed the spread of Soviet *power,* but said nothing of the spread of communism. In fact, communism —as an ideology—had little influence in Europe outside France and Italy except in those areas dominated by the real or implied threat of Soviet military power. The danger which concerned Churchill was the danger of Soviet influence fostered by military pressure, not the danger of spreading communism. By introducing the ideological theme, the Left Wing was able to argue, and did argue at great length, that it was unsound to oppose military force to the spread of ideas. No one would disagree, though there may be limits even to this truism. But this was not really the question at issue, nor had it been an issue in international affairs since 1945; expansion of an ideology and expansion based upon physical pressure are two quite different matters.

The moderate press in Britain had tended to agree with Churchill's estimate of the world situation, though they did not concur with his conclusions. The Left Wing press, excepting

Tribune, vehemently denied even this assumption, and there is every reason to suppose that most Labour party supporters agreed. The attack on Churchill was formidable. *Reynolds News* (March 10, 1946) claimed that Churchill was trying to bring Britain under "Wall Street" domination, whereas British socialists felt that the Soviet Union was best suited to help Britain carry out its social revolution. Charges of Soviet imperialism were dismissed as sheer nonsense, since Russia had no economic reason to expand. Others denounced the speech as a "sellout to American capitalism, the deadliest foe of European socialism," and as an example of Churchill's "war-mongering" activity, based upon latent hostility to the Soviet Union, or, in some few cases, once again claimed that the Soviet Union had committed "diplomatic blunders" which Churchill was trying to capitalize upon for political gain.[34] Perhaps the best general summary of the Left Wing reaction to Churchill's speech came from Harold Laski. In a special article in *Forward* (March 16, 1946) Laski argued that Britain was as yet unwilling to choose between Russia and the United States, for an alliance with the United States would lead to "Wall Street" pressure to abandon socialism. Churchill could not be accepted, since he was a well-known anti-Soviet spokesman and a "black reactionary." Soviet imperialism was impossible, for there was no economic reason for Russia to seek other territories. This brief article contains the gist of most of the arguments used against the Fulton speech.

Typically, none of Churchill's data were refuted, or even seriously mentioned. His conclusions were attacked a priori and without supporting evidence. In fact, a regular "myth" grew up around the Fulton speech, and the Government's failure to repudiate the speech was used as a club to beat the party leaders in the autumn of 1946. Oddly enough, however, those who made use of the club did not sign the censure motion, if the Conservative Centre copy of the motion and its signatories is correct.

While the Left Wing was protesting the charges of Soviet imperialism, the Soviets themselves were adding new grounds for the accusation by their behavior in Iran, thus increasing the difficulty of the Left Wing position. Russian troops were to withdraw from Iran on March 2, 1946, but the day prior to the scheduled withdrawal, the U.S.S.R. announced that the arrangement could not be met. The elections in Iran scheduled for March 4, were cancelled immediately and on March 15, the Iranian Government announced that the situation would once again be taken to the Security Council. On March 19, another protest was lodged against the U.S.S.R. though Russia stated that she would withdraw within six weeks. When Andrei Gromyko failed to obtain a postponement of the discussion, he withdrew from the Security Council meeting, leaving his colleagues in a somewhat uncertain position. On April 15, a joint Iranian-Soviet communiqué stated that Russia would withdraw her troops in the near future, but the Iranian representative at the United Nations continued to press charges in the Security Council. On April 25, 1946, the Government of Iran withdrew its charges, though the matter was left on the Security Council agenda. Late in May, 1946, Soviet troops left Iran, and the Iranian representative at the United Nations was relieved of his duties. In the end, Russia withdrew, leaving in her wake considerable alarm and a great many unanswered questions.

During this second Iranian crisis, the Left Wing made use of two techniques to justify the Soviet position: one, which we have met before, was the equating of a western action with a Soviet action, apparently in the belief that one offset the other, although the parallel is sometimes difficult to find; second, the "reactionary" character of the Iranian Government was assumed to justify the peculiar actions of the Soviet Government, apparently because the Soviets were attempting to produce a "social revolution" in Iran. These procedures raised considerable problems for the Left Wing, as can best be seen when events are taken in sequence.

In the first week of the crisis, *Tribune* (March 8, 1946) urged Britain not to take a "holier than thou" attitude toward Russia so long as her own troops remained in southern Iran, and particularly because this would mean an alliance with the "reactionary" government at Teheran, which was unthinkable for a socialist government. The solution, it felt, was a new Iranian Government which was more representative of the people. The *New Statesman* (March 9, 1946) simply denied that there was any reason to assume that the Soviet Union would remain in Iran, but stated, *obiter dictum*, that there would be ample reason for her to do so as the Iranian Government was "very reactionary." The following week, when the facts were more clear, *Tribune* (March 15, 1946) shifted ground and asked that the deplorable social and economic conditions in Iran be alleviated by Great Power intervention, while the *New Statesman* (March 16, 1946) returned to the argument that Russia was extending her frontiers out of fear of a western attack. *Forward* then entered the lists with a restatement of its previous appeal for a complete withdrawal from the Middle East, and the *New Statesman* (March 30, 1946), in the last analysis, blamed the United States for forcing Iran into the crisis. The Left Wing press thus managed to show amazing consistency over a period of time, though we cannot, of course, attach too much importance to the weekly shifts in opinion in political journals.

Toward the end of March, 1946, the Left Wing press began to

mount a concerted attack against the growing charges of Soviet imperialism, chiefly by taking a broader view of Soviet policy that ignored day to day events. This development is of considerably greater significance than a simple reaction to daily affairs since it appears to represent a thought-out policy rather than an immediate response to a specific situation. The initial statement of this attitude was published by the *New Statesman* (March 23, 1946) in a special, unsigned, leader. The writer explained at considerable length that comparisons between Hitler and Stalin were particularly dangerous, since Stalin "unquestionably" wanted and needed peace. He also stated that ideological conflict between Russia and the West was not in any case "fundamental" and was therefore unlikely to cause serious difficulty. The regular editorial columns of the *New Statesman* took a similar line in the following issue.

In *Reynolds News* (March 30, 1946), the point of departure taken for the new trend was the failure of the Soviet Union's leaders to grasp the western conception of democracy. The chief point of the article was a denunciation of the concept of Soviet imperialism; it was claimed that Soviet actions which were being construed as imperialism were really due to fear of the West. Harold Laski, in *Forward* (April 4, 1946) added that the Soviet Union had as much right to oil concessions from Iran as had the western powers, and since it was obvious that the Soviet Union desired peace and had no expansive intentions, Soviet imperialism was not even possible. The only reasonable explanation of Soviet behavior was, therefore, her fear of the West, which should be attributed to the American refusal to share possession of atomic secrets. These broader approaches to Soviet policy, for such they were, show the same elements that made for consistency in day to day opinion on the Left Wing of the Labour movement.

In May of 1946, international affairs were only lightly discussed by the Left Wing as the Labour party prepared for the annual Conference, which was to be held in July. There was one brief debate in the House of Commons early in June, in which the Foreign Secretary made an important statement about British policy in Germany, making it clear that Britain would have to make "different arrangements" if a settlement could not be made in the near future.[35] Most of the Left Wing M.P.'s who followed Bevin concerned themselves primarily with the question, Is Britain following a Socialist foreign policy? The reply given was uniformly negative, and British policy in Greece and Spain was cited most frequently as justification for this conclusion. This is quite interesting, in a way, since the Government of Poland did propose that the Security Council examine the position of the Spanish Government and determine whether it constituted a threat to the peace, and the Left Wing press responded in a very lukewarm manner. *Tribune* doubted that a case could be made for international action; *Reynolds News* favored severing diplomatic relations only; the *New Statesman* was willing to go as far as economic sanctions. Only Harold Laski, among prominent party members, took an extreme view and favored sanctions, nonrecognition of Franco, and recognition of the Government-in-Exile. Despite this attitude, Ernest Bevin was firmly denounced when the British Government failed to support the Polish Government's proposal in the Security Council. It is very difficult to see precisely what was wanted, except, perhaps, as stated before, some sort of "grand gesture."

The 1946 Labour party Conference met at Bournemouth early in July, with Professor Harold Laski in the Chair. The preliminary agenda, containing some 500 resolutions, showed the predominance of Left Wing influence by the number of resolutions regarding international affairs which were worded in terms of Left Wing goals. About ten per cent of the resolutions dealt with some aspect of foreign policy: four resolutions concerned Spain; nineteen dealt with general foreign policy; five with British-Soviet relations; seventeen with Foreign Office appointments; eleven with conscription. With a few exceptions, all were severely critical of the government's past record.

The most important resolution on foreign affairs was tabled by the powerful National Union of General and Municipal Workers, and later adopted by the Conference. As might be expected, it pledged hearty support for its old trade union comrade, Ernest Bevin. The other extreme was succinctly stated by the resolution proposed by the Salford, West, Divisional Labor party: "This Conference views with grave concern the continuance of a Tory foreign policy by a Socialist Government."[36] Other criticism of British foreign policy included the view that Britain could, if she were willing, materially improve the state of Anglo-Soviet relations; that Britain should break off diplomatic relations with Spain; that the staff of the British Foreign Office was traditionally Conservative and therefore unable to carry out a socialist foreign policy. It would be interesting and valuable to trace the genesis of one of the Divisional Labour party resolutions to their source, but this proved impossible. The writer talked with various members of some of the London Divisional parties, and it seems likely that the Left Wing journals like *Tribune* and the *New Statesman* were a paramount influence at this level, but the evidence is too flimsy to allow more than speculation.

Chairman Harold Laski opened the Conference with a speech that in its allocation of praise conspicuously ignored the work of the Foreign Secretary. Laski disliked Bevin personally in any case, and this may have influenced his judgment. But the statement which he made on international affairs is worth quoting at some length since, as was often the case, Laski produced a fine summary of the attitudes of the Left Wing:

> Let us admit, as I am sure that the Foreign Secretary would be the first to admit, that the international problems before the Government are grave and intricate. As a Socialist Party, we must regard it as a tragedy in which our responsibility is grave, that Spain is still crushed beneath the ugly tyranny of Franco. Nothing would persuade us to regard a revival of the monarchist traditions embodied in a Vatican-sponsored Bourbon as relevant to the liberation of a tortured people. What is true of Spain is also true of Greece. For us, as Socialists, the return of the King would be a sorry end to the brave struggle of a nation which first taught the world the significance of freedom. And I desire to say with blunt emphasis that we should place no confidence in a regime led by a King who has not only already broken the Constitution he was pledged to observe, but behind whom, also, crouch old and evil vested interests whose sole concern is to equate their private enrichment with the public welfare.
>
> I add here what I believe is necessary, if painful to affirm. No small part of the responsibility for Russian suspicions must be borne by those who have decided upon secrecy in relation to the atomic bomb. [37]

This speech, which shows Laski's remarkable consistency, was not debated.

The foreign affairs debate, in which the Left Wing was vitally interested, was opened by Philip Noel-Baker, who moved the NUGMW resolution expressing approval of Bevin's policies. The opposition then moved the following resolution: "This Conference, recognizing that the only hope of lasting peace lies in the international adoption of Socialism, and regretting the Government's apparent continuation of a traditional Conservative Party policy of power politics abroad, urges a return to the Labour Party foreign policy of support for Socialist and anti-Imperialist forces throughout the world." [38] The mover, J. W. Kagan, spoke as a "bewildered" member of the rank and file of the party, who believed that Ernest Bevin was favoring the United States over the Soviet Union, though the former was the last stronghold of capitalism and the

natural enemy of all socialists. Following Laski, he placed the
blame for deteriorating relations upon American atomic policy.
His seconder suggested rather pointedly that he would prefer to
see Bevin's applause coming from his own supporters rather than
from the Opposition benches. The influence of the Left Wing
seems reasonably clear.

The momentum acquired by the Left Wing attack on the civil
servants in the Foreign Office is demonstrated by the second
resolution moved at the Conference in opposition to official policy:

> This conference calls upon the Government to undertake
> a drastic revision of the existing methods of recruitment
> for the Foreign Service. Further, in order to ensure that
> the execution of a Socialist foreign policy is entrusted to
> men who believe in it, rather than to those whose whole
> background and tradition have rendered them incapable of
> understanding the first principles of such a policy, it calls
> upon the Government to make the fullest use of its powers
> of retirement on generous terms, without stigma, of
> public servants whose capacity for useful service is ex-
> hausted and their replacement by persons in accord with
> the progressive attitude of the British public as shown in
> their decision at the last General Election. [39]

The attack on the Foreign Office found expression in one of the
most amazing proposals made in British politics in some years.

The "traditional" attack upon the Spanish Government was also
moved from the floor of the Conference: "This conference is of
the opinion that the continued existence of the Fascist Franco
regime in Spain constitutes a threat to world peace and security.
It therefore calls upon the Government to break off diplomatic relations with Franco and to appoint a representative to the Pro-
visional Spanish Republican Government." [40] Finally, a large composite resolution was moved from the floor, which contains the
essence of a number of resolutions put forward by Divisional Labour parties, and small trade unions, in the preliminary agenda.
Such composite resolutions are worked out off the Conference
floor by agreement among those who sponsored the resolutions
which are compiled together. This one contained resolutions on
the need for support for "progressive" forces, the need for close
relations with the Soviet Union, and the need to repudiate the
Fulton speech:

> This Conference is of the opinion that world peace can
> only be based on a British policy directed to ensure firm

friendship and co-operation with the progressive forces throughout the world, and in particular with the U.S.S.R., and that such a policy should over-ride British imperial interests. The Conference re-affirms the pledges made by Conferences of the Labour Party in the past to respect, co-operate with, and assist in every way possible the struggles of the working-class movements in all countries toward Socialism and of colonial peoples toward liberation.

This Conference recognizes that to this end every endeavor should be made to eradicate the remnants of Fascism throughout the world. The Conference therefore calls upon the Government:

a. To maintain and foster an attitude of sympathy and friendship toward the Soviet Union and do all in its power to establish the interchange of trade and cultural relations with the U.S.S.R., including the interchange of weekly broadcasts on the lines of the B.B.C. American commentary.

b. To repudiate Mr. Churchill's defeatist proposal to make the British Commonwealth a mere satellite of American Monopoly Capitalism which will inevitably lead to our being aligned in a partnership of hostility to Russia.[41]

The mover supported the resolution with a strong, anti-American speech, emphasizing the need for world socialists to unite and oppose capitalistic nations like the United States and refrain from close association with them, therefore avoiding the inevitable collapse that followed the "bust" of the capitalist system.

The general debate that followed these resolutions once again demonstrated the tendency for the Left Wing to discuss events in generalized terms without reference to specific incidents or data. The arguments employed were seldom factual, and they depended far more upon ideological cliches and emotional appeals to the past than upon reliable evidence. The facts of American-British-Soviet relations were never really stated; the possible need for an alliance with one side or the other was never verbalized. Thus Francis Noel-Baker confessed his "shame" because the Labour party had been unable to do more in Spain since it achieved power, but never stated what might really be done. Richard Acland and William Warbey spoke on the question of Foreign Office appointments along the lines laid down in the resolution quoted above.

Konni Zilliacus produced another of his major efforts to sway the audience by denouncing the "Churchillian" policies of the Labour Government.

The resolutions which criticized Government policy, and the arguments used in debate, considered on their merits and with due regard for the relative importance of their subject matter, hardly seem a suitable basis for a serious disagreement between the Labour Government and its supporters. The position of the Left Wing is reasonable only on ideological grounds, that is, their criticisms become important within an ideological framework, or at least acquire significance in such a framework. The sincerity of some elements of the Left Wing may be questioned, but there was widespread agreement on many of these points, and the behavior of the Left Wing is really quite consistent with its initial premises and thus provides little ground on which sincerity can be questioned. The Left Wing came to the Labour party Conference seriously disturbed with the course international affairs was taking, and, I believe, they genuinely felt that their suggestions should be considered seriously by the Government. Within the framework of the ideology, their arguments are in fact quite powerful, inadequate though they may seem to an outsider. Their hope of influencing Government policy was disappointed completely. The afternoon session on foreign affairs began, and ended, with a speech by Ernest Bevin, who demonstrated beyond doubt that his technique for handling Labour party Conferences was much superior to his command of House of Commons procedure. Those resolutions which Bevin accepted, notably the NUGMW resolution, were passed by the Conference; those resolutions he opposed were roundly defeated or withdrawn with suitable apologies. The Conference ended with the Government, and its Foreign Secretary, enjoying the formal endorsement of the overwhelming majority of those attending the sessions. It also ended with a disgruntled and unconvinced Left Wing, now prepared for more drastic action to arouse Labour sentiment in favor of its own proposals.

VI

THE LEFT WING REVOLT
IN PARLIAMENT

The best argument in favor of the sincerity of the British Left Wing is undoubtedly its behavior in the autumn of 1946. Leading figures in the Left Wing may have supported the same policy for different reasons, but there can be no doubt that their intentions were sincere, however misguided they may appear in retrospect. The attempt to convince the leaders of the Labour Government that a change in foreign policy was essential had failed at the Labour party Conference. Great power relations continued to deteriorate through the summer of 1946 as the Paris Peace Conference made little headway, the Foreign Ministers' meetings produced few concrete results, and the economic situation in Germany worsened. Convinced that the situation had grown so serious that desperate measures were required, and perhaps assuming rather egotistically that their own position was sound, the leading figures on the Left Wing in the House of Commons decided to challenge the Labour Government by tabling an Amendment to the Reply to the Throne criticizing the Government's foreign policy. No better indication could be given of the reality of Left Wing concern than a step as serious as this.

By American standards, party discipline in the House of Commons is strict, and it is a very serious matter indeed to challenge party policy on the floor of the House. There are regular weekly meetings of the Labour party at which policy can be discussed in private, and members are expected to support the decisions reached in these meetings. Abstention is, of course, permitted on matters of conscience but the Standing Orders of the Labour party do not allow an adverse vote. The Left Wing decision to take this step was made after the party Conference in July. Of course there was no intention on the part of the "rebels" to bring down the Government, for the mover asked leave to withdraw when the debate ended, and a Division was forced by the members of the

Independent Labour party who could command only the two necessary Tellers. The Amendment was rejected by a vote of 353 to 0,
with most of the "rebels" abstaining. The leaders of the Left
Wing group which rebelled were R. H. S. Crossman, Michael Foot,
and Ian Mikardo. It should be noted that this was not a pacifist-led
movement. The pacifists in fact moved another Amendment to the
Reply which was rejected by 320 to 53, and in this case Crossman
and his friends voted with the Government.

Undoubtedly, the chief motive for the "revolt" was the extreme
sense of frustration generated by the Labour party Conference,
though other factors very probably contributed to the general sense
of alarm and concern. Certainly the Left Wing press reflected
this sense of frustration very strongly in the weeks immediately
after the Conference ended. There was some harsh criticism of
the leaders of the Labour party for their behavior at the Conference, where they were accused of consuming too much conference
time. There was also a great deal of criticism of the structure of
the party, which the Left Wing claimed permitted the great trade
unions to dominate the policy-making process by the use of their
bloc vote. Both of these criticisms had been heard before from the
Left Wing, particularly in the late 1930's, but the vigor with which
they were pressed was unusual. The Conference was universally
condemned by the Left Wing as a complete failure—no valid criticism of party policy had been permitted to develop. As matters
stood, the Left Wing felt the party Conference was little more than
a "rubber stamp." Further, the "conservative" unions would not
permit ginger groups to form and advocate "more Socialist" programs, without interfering. Ernest Bevin, as a person, as a Minister, and as a trade union leader, came in for a particularly large
dose of criticism. The Left Wing press claimed he had shown a
complete "lack of concern for the views of the rank and file."
This is understandable, since Bevin more than any other single
member of the Government stood precisely and clearly in the way
of success for Left Wing principles in foreign policy. Finally,
there were the usual mutterings about "abdication of Socialist
principles" directed against the Government, the parliamentary
Labour party, the Conference, and the trade unions. This bitter
and futile resentment of the manner in which their views had been
treated at the party Conference was undoubtedly a key factor in
the Left Wing decision to take the issue to the floor of the House of
Commons, whatever the price.

A second factor that contributed substantially to the increasing
dissatisfaction of the Left Wing was the disastrous failure at the
polls of the socialist parties of Europe in 1946. By early summer, it was apparent that Left Wing hopes for a socialist Europe

were founded on sand as one country after another rejected socialist leadership, often in favor of one of the Catholic parties. As
the possibility of a new world order declined, the Left Wing felt
that the Labour Government must bear some responsibility for the
failure of continental socialists since it had not acted vigorously
on their behalf. The first sign of this despondency was an important but unsigned leader in *Tribune* (July 7, 1946), which began on
a melancholy note: "The Revolutionary Spring of European Liberation is over. One year after the end of the European War, when
the broad highway to Democratic Socialism seemed to lie open
before the eager young men of the resistance movements, Europe
is split into an eastern zone of Communist domination and a western zone which is rapidly turning into an anti-communist reaction." It noted that Catholic parties had emerged as the dominant
force in European politics and that they were now in a position to
form a real anti-communist bloc "under the aegis of the Papacy."
The passive attitude which the British Government had adopted
toward the Franco regime in Spain and the Salazar dictatorship in
Portugal, together with British toleration of a very reactionary
regime in Greece, had served as a pretext for Soviet encroachment in Eastern Europe. The Labour Government had been unable
to break this vicious circle and this was its greatest failure. The
Soviet Union, for its part, was merely continuing its wartime
policy of "compartmentalizing" Europe; the western nations had
adopted the same policy in response to Soviet encroachment. All
of this had very little to do with the "brave new world" for which
men had fought the war.

It was, therefore, absolutely essential that a new start be made
before it was too late. If this were not done, the division of the
world into two blocs would soon be complete and a totalitarian
Soviet system would face a hostile capitalistic system threatening
ruin for the whole world. The leader suggested, as a necessary
first step, that: "We need a positive policy of all-out practical
solidarity with Democratic Socialist forces everywhere, and a
definite and unmistakable rupture with a political tradition which
relied for support mainly on semi-fascist or semi-feudal forces of
reaction in Europe and the Middle East, and the super-capitalistic
anarchy still reigning on the other side of the Atlantic." Whereas
previous Left Wing approaches to international affairs had begun
with the assumption that the movement to the Left, in Europe and
elsewhere, was unmistakable and even inevitable, this writer be-
gins at the point where socialist influence is waning. But the
solution propounded ultimately remains the same—a "socialist"
foreign policy of supporting other socialists and opposing capitalists.

A slightly different explanation of the current crisis in international affairs, and the tensions that existed within the Labour movement about these questions, was provided by Michael Foot in this same (July 7, 1946) issue of *Tribune*, although the ideological foundations of the two arguments are clearly identical. Foot argued that certain elements in the British Labour party had planned to continue the Coalition Government after World War II, and they had insisted that the same policy lines were valid even though the Coalition had been dissolved—an obvious reference to Ernest Bevin. This attitude had led the Labour Government to "hold back" in the general denunciation of Franco Spain; it had caused the Government to follow an antisocialist policy in Greece; it had led to British support for the Dutch position in Indonesia; it had led to the appointment of foreign representatives who were wholly out of sympathy with Labour's socialist ambitions. Although the emphasis is somewhat different, the root of the trouble is still seen to lie in the failure of the Labour Government to adhere to its own ideology. Unlike some members of the Left Wing, Michael Foot was aware of Soviet pressure, and had even supported Bevin's resistance to Soviet charges in the Security Council meeting in January. Nevertheless, he felt that this pressure was not an adequate reason to abandon Labour's international program:

> The campaign which the Soviet Union conducts against us is not a reason for abandoning our Socialist objectives; it is rather a reason for pursuing them all the more boldly. If, on account of Soviet pressure, we should draw back from the great departures in policy which already have been made in India, and Egypt, if, on this same account, we should refuse to stand boldly for Socialist aims in Europe, we should only succeed at one stroke in deviling our reconstruction at home, in imperiling our moral prestige abroad, and in manufacturing more Communists in the process than were ever converted by the Cominform.

These two articles are the foundation stone on which the Left Wing built its case against the government; both, of course, are ideologically based. The principles involved were brought together and published in a series of four articles entitled "Reorientations" that appeared in the *New Statesman* during August and September, 1946.

The first "Reorientation" article appeared on August 31, 1946. It combined the growing criticism of Ernest Bevin, the fear of the power of Catholicism on the continent, the growing fear for Britain's economic future, and the possible need to abandon the domestic socialist program if military expenditures were substantially increased, then related these specific points to the general proposals already made for a new direction in British foreign policy. The end result was a Left Wing position which recognized the rapidly widening split between East and West, and proposed that Britain maintain a position of neutrality between the two behemoths. Two of the assumptions made in the first of these articles are of particular interest here, since they demonstrate the extent to which Left Wing thought is self-contained and consistent. In the first place, the writer assumed, and stated explicitly, that the Labour Government's foreign policy was a complete reversal of Labour's traditional policy. This was not really true at all, though it *was* a reversal of the traditional Left Wing policy in international affairs. The fact that the trade union leaders, and Ernest Bevin in particular, had reversed the trend in the direction of complete adoption of a Left Wing policy early in the 1930's was conveniently forgotten. The second assumption was that Labour had convinced the British electorate that it was best suited to conduct international affairs (in the General Election of 1945). This, we have already seen, was untrue of the whole Labour party, which avoided the issue, but true enough of the Left Wing, which did make an issue of foreign policy during the election. This tendency to assume that the Left Wing tradition was the true Labour tradition is commonplace in Left Wing thought, but seldom better illustrated than on this occasion.

The remaining thesis found in the first of the "Reorientation" articles was chiefly a personal denunciation of Ernest Bevin. Following the election, the writer charged, Ernest Bevin had been converted to anticommunism, and British policy was henceforth shaped by his personal likes and dislikes and not by socialist conviction. Bevin had come to lean heavily upon the antisocialist staff in the Foreign Office, and thus was led to adopt antisocialist policies. He had accepted the view that Stalin and Hitler were both totalitarians and both expansionists, and this was a fundamental error (this view apparently derives from Konni Zilliacus' first speech in Parliament, cited above). Russia could not be expansionist since she had no economic reason to expand. Since Bevin's policies were thus heavily laden with antisocialist principles, there was literally no chance whatever that they would succeed, it being taken for granted, of course, that the proper road to success could only be socialism.

The second "Reorientations" article appeared in the *New Statesman* on September 7. It recapitulated these ideas briefly, then returned to the attack on Ernest Bevin. He was now accused of propagating, since his installation in office, the "false and dangerous" view that Britain must either stand up to the Soviet Union or capitulate. This reasoning was false because Britain could not, in the last analysis, stand up to the Soviet Union at all, nor could she rely upon American assistance because the United States was not sufficiently reliable and Britain would find herself alone facing Russia across the European continent. The suggested alternative was for Britain to begin reducing her military commitments to a bearable level, and to refuse any additional commitments that would increase her military spending. Second, British vital interests should be defined carefully and Britain should remain neutral between the United States and Russia, since this was her only possible means of surviving. Finally, Britain should "play for time" and use all of her influence to help ease world tensions, but on no account should she join one or the other of the great powers in a military alliance. The best choice for Britain was probably an Anglo-French alliance, but the opportunity for this may already have been lost because of Bevin's close association with the United States.

The third article in the series appeared on September 21; it was devoted to British relations with the socialist parties in Europe immediately after World War II and the serious mistakes which had been made in this area. At the time of writing, the author did not feel that it was possible to distinguish between the American capitalist attitude toward European socialism and the British socialist attitude toward European socialism, particularly in Greece, Spain, and Italy. Bevin had assumed that he must choose between "guns and butter" and had opted for guns; this was an error, since Britain could have chosen the "middle way" of encouraging European socialism and building a socialist Europe which would provide the alternative to both communism and capitalism which was so badly needed. The final article, published September 28, attacked the instability of the United States, implying that any policy which depended upon such a vacillating body was sheer madness. With a parting thrust at Ernest Bevin, and the personnel of the British Foreign Office, the series came to a close.

The author of these four articles, intentionally or not, provided what is an almost classic example of writing intended for an ideological group. Nearly any staunch Labour supporter could find something in the four articles which he would approve. All of the good symbols "socialism," "democracy," "peace" were included in the positive proposals made in the series; on the other hand, few of the important negative symbols of Left Wing thought—

capitalist, fascist, Spain, Greece—were omitted. For the pacifists, the writer suggested a reduction in armaments, and inveighed against war; for the fellow travelers there was support for the Soviet Union and the progressive forces of Eastern Europe; for the anticapitalist, a resounding diatribe against the United States; even the Labour intellectual, searching for an alternative to Soviet communism and American capitalism, found his answer in the neutral "third way" which the writer proposed. It is significant that these identical principles were brought out and dusted off once again when the Left Wing parted company with the leaders of the Labour party in 1951. Their appeal was nearly universal. Not everyone would support every part of the series of proposals made; but the policy outlined in the four essays was certain to obtain a substantial amount of over-all support in any Labour gathering. On this broad and general ideological basis, the Left Wing went to war against its leaders.

When the House of Commons resumed on November 13, 1946, the Left Wing came prepared for battle and determined to make one last desperate effort to redirect the Government's foreign policy. Even before Richard Crossman moved the "rebel" Amendment to the Reply, Ellis Smith, William Warbey, and T.E.N. Driberg had attacked the Government's proposed alliance with the United States because of the dire consequences which they foresaw for the British economy. When the Amendment to the Reply was moved, these dissidents hastily joined forces with Crossman and his friends, though their reasons for supporting the amendment were not the same. The ideological basis of the rebellion is clearly revealed by the terms of the Amendment:

> And expressed the urgent hope that His Majesty's Government will so review and recast its conduct of international affairs as to afford the utmost encouragement to, and collaboration with all nations and groups striving to secure full Socialist planning and control of the world's resources, and thus provide a democratic and constructive Socialist alternative to the otherwise inevitable conflict between American capitalism and Soviet Communism in which all hope of world government would be destroyed.[1]

While the Conservative party sat back in a state of high amusement, the Labour Government underwent a searching analysis of its own foreign policy by its own back benches. The "rebels" had chosen their time well. The very formidable Ernest Bevin was in Washington, and the much less fearsome figure of the Prime Minister sat on the front bench, waiting to reply to the debate.

The amendment was moved by R. H. S. Crossman in a very able, though somewhat circular speech which began with a broad survey of the problems facing the government in foreign policy and contrasted the "socialist" character of Labour's domestic policy with the "unsocialist" character of its international policy. Crossman claimed that Labour had won the General Election of 1945 on a program which was based on the assumption that a Conservative victory would result in an Anglo-American bloc hostile to Russia and would result also in the division of the world into two camps. It was not surprising, therefore, that the Soviet Union took a very suspicious view of the British Government once it was clear that its policy remained identical to that followed by a Conservative-dominated Coalition. He, Crossman, was heartily opposed to communism, and he was aware of the limited degree of co-operation achieved between Russia and Britain during the war. But he felt that it was the purpose of democratic socialism to provide a suitable alternative to both communism and capitalism, and the key to this alternative was the neutral third force.

Having outlined the essentials of his argument, Crossman turned to the delineation of his points one by one, and thereby lost some of the force of a well-marshalled argument by the addition of extraneous materials. In the end, he provided the House of Commons with a well-presented mixture of slogans, ideological dogmatism, debating points, and profound insights into current international problems. The more important of his points, in the order of presentation, were:

> It is essential that Britain remain independent of both blocs, and able to propagate its own socialist solution to world tensions since this is "what everyone really wants."

> The aim of foreign policy must be to carry out at the international level the domestic policies of the Government (achieve a socialist society).

> The peoples of the world "danced in the streets" when Labour won the election in 1945, and the Government had let them down badly.

> Churchill's Fulton speech had been consistent with his past record, but this was not a socialist policy. Why had the Government failed to disavow the speech?

> America was "plainly" seeking economic domination in the Far East, particularly in China, hence her demand for strategic bases. The Chinese people wanted neither capitalism nor communism but would welcome democratic socialism.

President Roosevelt's death had disorganized the progressive forces in America, and the United States was
now controlled by the war and military departments.
Henry Wallace had clearly indicated the imperialistic
tendency of American policy.

The economic chaos which prevailed in the United States
would "inevitably" lead to severe slumps that could
wreck the British economy if the ties between the two
countries were close.[2]

On the strength of these and similar arguments, Crossman demanded three changes in Government policy: first, a complete
disavowal of the Fulton speech; second, an end to any staff conversations between Britain and the United States; third, a more
independent socialist foreign policy.

While this might appear sufficient to the needs of a back bench
M.P. for one afternoon, unlimited time in the House of Commons
is a heady wine, and Crossman launched into an analysis of world
problems and the causes of international tension. He assumed that
tension had arisen out of the Soviet propaganda attack, which in
turn arose from the Soviet view that Britain was weak and help-
less and hence the weakest link in the western chain. The Soviets
were opposed to the British Empire, since they were an anti-
imperialist power, therefore they were using this opportunity to
destroy the Empire. But the propaganda attack was having the
opposite effect; the Empire was growing stronger under Soviet
pressure. This could lead to a "perpetual armistice" which would
be unbearable over a long time period. The Soviet campaign had
meanwhile destroyed the hopes of the European "left" and was
involving Britain in a ruinous arms race. The solution, he believed, was to abandon the notion that Russia was aggressive, any
more than the United States was aggressive, and: ". . . make the
assumption that there is not going to be war for some time at
least, desist from staff conversations outside the Commonwealth,
and not subordinate policy to strategy, and put everything we have
into the Socialist policy of building Socialism and Democracy
wherever we can."[3] Crossman then resumed his seat. But his
excursion into cause and effect had demonstrated the weakness of
his position. It was not, as he claimed, Soviet propaganda, but
Soviet *behavior* which caused sleepless nights in the western
world. Further, Britain, the prime target of the Soviet offensive,
was being asked to stand aside and permit Russia to argue with
the United States. Finally, and most important, the full meaning
of a "socialist" foreign policy was never defined any further than

offering assistance to other socialists. Apparently the Labour government found that this was simply not an adequate basis for the conduct of international affairs.

All of the Left Wing speakers who followed Richard Crossman in the debate supported his general position, but the diversity that appeared among those apparently united behind a single theme demonstrates very clearly the striking individualism in which the Left Wing abounds. Almost every speaker had a personal interpretation of the meaning of the "revolt" and the intention of the Amendment. The seconder, Joseph Reeves, thought it was a protest against the "entangling alliance" proposed by Churchill in his Fulton speech. Jennie Lee, (Mrs. Aneurin Bevan) believed the question had been raised because of the danger that foreign policy might lead to serious repercussions on the domestic economy and perhaps endanger domestic socialism. Sydney Silverman, one of the more important fellow travelers in the 1945 Parliament, interpreted the "revolt" still differently: "Our complaint is that the Government's conduct of foreign affairs during the past thirteen to fifteen months has been merely a continuance of Tory foreign policy, and that the enthusiastic support which the Foreign Secretary gets, in the absence of any repudiation from the Government Front Bench, is a confirmation that this is so. I am sure that no one on the Government Front Bench believes that there ought to be no difference between a Socialist foreign policy and a Tory foreign policy."[4]

This version of the "revolt" very nearly becomes a personal attack upon Ernest Bevin, and perhaps an effort to separate Bevin from the remainder of the Cabinet. In view of Bevin's past relations with the Left Wing, some element of personal animosity may well have played a part in the attitudes of some members of the Left Wing.

Prime Minister Attlee replied to the debate very briefly, rejected the neutralist concept, and denied that foreign policy could be either "Tory" or "Labour." Britain, he said, did not attend international conferences on behalf of some "ideological abstraction." When Attlee returned to his seat, the parliamentary phase of the "revolt" was ended, although the Amendment was pressed to a division by the I. L. P.

British policy remained as before; the Left Wing alternative was once again rejected. Again, the Left Wing remained dissatisfied; their convictions unchanged. The meaning of the "revolt" was too broad to allow acrimony and criticism to cease. As one of the supporters of the "rebels" stated later:

> Our case was that the world was drifting into two great
> power blocs and that we were drifting into the American
> orbit through lack of determination to keep out of it. Our
> distrust of Russia was still so weak that we thought it
> possible to maintain a neutral, third force position be-
> tween America and Russia. . . It was a return to the
> Labour Party attitude of the 1930's toward Russia. It was
> a recurrence of the old feeling that Russia really was a
> Socialist country, and that, given a chance, she might
> develop toward democracy. We felt that she was not being
> given that chance, and America and Britain were unnec-
> essarily building military alliances against her which
> were bound to make her afraid and were bound to make
> the international situation worse. . . In short, we thought
> that collective security against Russia was more danger-
> ous than the menace of Russia herself.[5]

The writer of this description later altered his views and thus
parted company with the Left Wing. But his statement of the antecedents of the revolt is precise. It was a return to pre-war attitudes, and it was to recur again and again in the postwar years.
    The Left Wing press of course hailed the "rebels" as saviors
of the Labour movement, and immediately began the process of
"interpreting" what had in fact been said in the House of Commons, producing in the process some rather fundamental changes.
Michael Foot, who wrote at some length on the "rebel" case,
pointed out that there had been no decisive break in British foreign policy in 1945 though such a break was required a priori.[6]
He realized that part of the demand for a change in foreign policy
had originated with the communists and fellow travelers, but he
did not feel that this influence was dominant on the Left Wing.
Foot, unlike many others, accepted the thesis put forward by Jennie Lee in the House of Commons, i.e., that the British economy
could not bear the strain of its present foreign policy without
sacrificing some of the social service program. Therefore: "can
we not as swiftly as possible take the Soviet Government at its
word and discuss the details of disarmament?" This is quite different from the arguments advanced by R. H. S. Crossman, and
Tribune hastened to point out in its next issue that it was nonsense
to single out armaments as the dominant thesis of the "revolt,"
although this is precisely what Jennie Lee and Michael Foot had
already done. The truth seems to be that this aspect of the "revolt" commanded more support within the Labour movement than
any other. Pacifists of course supported the drive against armaments, and the fellow travelers leapt upon the old Labour theme
than "armaments always lead to war" almost immediately.[7]

Within a few weeks, following the vagaries of public opinion, the "revolt" began to develop along lines which its originators seem not to have really planned. The waning power of Great Britain as an international force for peace was now taken as the point of departure, and it was urged by a wide variety of Left Wing spokesmen that Britain reduce her commitments as speedily as possible else the drain on resources might interfere with the success of the socialist experiment being conducted in Britain. It is quite clear in context that the Left Wing still believed firmly that the greatest contribution to peace that Britain could make would be to socialize her own economy as quickly as possible. We find the plainest statement of this position in a pamphlet by G. D. H. Cole published in the spring of 1946 on the eve of the 1946 Labour party Conference:

> (Foreign policy should include measures which) . . . shall bring aid and comfort to those elements among other peoples which are recognizable as like-minded with itself and with the predominant forces of opinion in Great Britain, which it has a clear mandate to represent. That is, first and foremost, to its fellow Socialists. . . British policy. . . ought to be such as to strengthen the forces of liberal Socialism all over the world, but most of all in those countries which are our near neighbors and share with us, in high degree, a common tradition of Western European culture. [8]

It seems clear that one of the influences of ideology is to impart an enormous stability to purposes, for whatever the point of departure, the end seems to remain the support for the ideology and those who support the ideology, particularly at home. This had been the essence of Crossman's argument in the House of Commons.

This argument was swiftly superseded by the simpler and more potent principle of immediate disarmament, and the arguments usually advanced to support the proposal were skillfully supplemented by an implied threat to the social service program which was the pride and joy of British socialists. The conception of the neutral third force was retained, for only the fellow travelers were willing to consider close association with the Soviet Union, and no one on the Left Wing was amenable to a close association with the United States, particularly at this time. Yet when the concept of the third force is examined carefully, we find that it is still dominated by the Left Wing ideology, for it is based upon the conception of a *socialist* alliance in Europe, and not on an alliance with capitalist countries.

The Left Wing had not advanced any closer to alliance with capitalism than it had been when Clement Attlee was writing *The Labour Party in Perspective* in 1937. Even as the "revolt" was taking place, the European elections were ruling out this very possibility. The Left Wing thus began with a lost cause because the tenets of the ideology would not permit association with the types of government that in reality existed on the continent. Further, the course of events in the first six months of 1947 did nothing to add substance to the belief that the Soviet Union harbored nothing but peaceful intentions. It is difficult to see how the concept of neutrality could be tenable under any other circumstances than in a world in which Soviet aggressiveness need not be feared, and even more difficult not to see how patently aggressive the Soviet Union did appear at this time.

The British Left Wing escaped from this dilemma, but it required the use of a technique that can hardly be considered honest. The menace of American policy was consistently "played up" in the Left Wing press and in speeches by Left Wing spokesmen, while the menace of Soviet behavior was either "played down" with equal consistency, or even totally ignored. Perhaps two examples of the technique will suffice. When General George C. Marshall was appointed Secretary of State of the United States, the Left Wing greeted the appointment with a storm of apprehensive criticism of the "militarization" of American foreign policy. The elections held in Poland, on the other hand, though characterized by extreme violence and intimidation, were depicted by the Left Wing as a struggle between the "progressive" elements in Poland and the "ultra-reactionary" groups supported by the Catholic Church in which the sympathies of British socialists should lie with the former. To grasp the full extent to which this technique was employed it is perhaps necessary to read through all of the available literature in a given period. Certainly these brief examples could be multiplied many hundreds of times.

The demand for disarmament which had been stimulated by the "rebel" action in Parliament died away during the last two months of 1946, only to revive sharply when the severe economic crisis began in February, 1947. Discussion of manpower resources and the cost of maintaining great power status was widespread, and not only on the Left Wing. The pacifists of course launched another campaign against military spending; they were now joined by most of the Left Wing, and some of the more moderate elements of the Labour movement. The attack made on the military estimates in the spring of 1946 had been led by the pacifists and the fellow travelers. [9] The "rebels," for the most part, had supported the Government against the Amendment to the Reply moved by pacifist Victor Yates in the autumn of 1946, though one of the group stated that the ''rebels'' would oppose the Government's Conscription Bill in committee and demand a reduction in the length-of-service clause.[10] Through the spring of 1947, no opportunity was lost by the parliamentary Left Wing to raise the question of military expenditures and to urge a drastic reduction in British commitments and the release of manpower for the domestic economy.[11]

The seriousness of the economic crisis of 1947 forced the British Government to review its commitments and take steps to rid itself of the more onerous of them. In February, 1947, the Government informed the United States that Britain would withdraw its forces and support from the eastern Mediterranean region in the very near future, and asked the United States to assume the task of supporting Greece and Turkey by economic and military assistance. This dumped the problem of maintaining the integrity of the Middle East squarely in the American lap. Reluctantly, the Truman Administration responded and requested Congress to provide the necessary funds. In a special message, President Truman outlined the need for assistance, and stated the reasons why the United States should provide such aid, and the basis on which it should be offered. This program came to be called the Truman Doctrine and it is usually held to mark a turning point in American foreign policy after World War II, and the beginning of active American participation in international affairs.[12]

In view of the significance later attached to the Truman Doctrine by the Left Wing, the exact terms of Truman's message are worth noting. Truman pointed out that the economic consequences of the German occupation had been catastrophic, and the scarcity of goods had been further aggravated by the Greek Civil War. Further: ''The very existence of the Greek state is today threatened by the terroristic activities of several thousand armed men led by Communists who defy the Government's authority at a number of points, particularly along the northern boundaries.''[13] Thus both economic and military assistance was needed by the Greeks. Truman, while urging that assistance be granted these countries, had no illusions about the Greek Government he was trying to aid: ''The Greek Government has been operating in an atmosphere of chaos and extremism. It has made mistakes. The extension of aid by this country does not mean that the United States condones everything that the Greek Government has done or will do. We condemned in the past, and we condemn now, extremist measures of Right and Left. We have in the past advised tolerance and we advise tolerance now.'' [14]

The general principle at stake, as it appeared to Truman and his advisors, was as follows: "I believe that it must be the policy of the United States to support free peoples who are resisting attempted subjugation by armed minorities or by outside pressures. . . .I believe that our help should be primarily through economic and fiscal aid, which is essential to economic stability and orderly political progress."[15] The speech has been quoted rather extensively to ensure that the basic principles involved in the American decision to assist Greece and Turkey are clear.

It could hardly be expected that the British Left Wing would welcome American interference in Greece when it had already attacked its own socialist Government's support of the Greek Government. In fact, the Truman Doctrine became the bete noire of the Left Wing and was more often quoted as evidence of American imperialism than any other single American action. The Left Wing interpretation of the Truman Doctrine, which was virtually unanimous, held that it was "another long step" in American expansion, a phase in the struggle for control of Middle Eastern oil, and economic imperialism getting under way. As Harold Laski put it: "It must be taken, I think, as the announcement that the United States is going to use its massive power to limit the growth of Socialist influence in general and of Russian influence in particular."[16] The feeling that it was a deliberate attempt on the part of the United States government to suppress socialism in Europe was very widespread. The belief that it was a "warmongering" policy dictated by Wall Street interests also appeared, but chiefly in the writings of the fellow travelers and the pacifists.[17] The full implications of the Truman Doctrine were not discussed in April, 1947, as the Left Wing prepared for battle on the conscription issue, but it reappeared much later as a whipping boy for Left Wing antagonism to the United States.

The Left Wing united, temporarily, to oppose the Government's Conscription Bill, but there were really two quite different points of view involved. The pacifists, a few Liberals, and some of the fellow travelers were opposed on principle to any conscription at all. Other members of the Left Wing who were not pacifists and not opposed to conscription on principle still opposed the proposal to conscript for eighteen months on the grounds that this would endanger both the domestic economy and the future of the Labour program for socializing Britain's economy. This bifurcation appeared during the Second Reading of the Bill on March 31, 1947, when a Division was forced, and a substantial part of the Left Wing opposed the Government, but not the group associated with R. H. S. Crossman and his "rebels."[18] The division list shows the pacifists, the communists, the fellow travelers, and a few

Liberals voting against the Government. The group which abstained at this stage, however, opposed the Bill in Committee, threatening, of course, to add their votes to those already opposed to the Government, and secured a reduction in the length-of-service clause from eighteen to twelve months. This technique, using the principles of a large group of Labour supporters to obtain the specific demands of the smaller group, becomes increasingly important after 1947.

The Left Wing was by this time, (in the spring of 1947), almost frantically opposed to any policy that would either endanger the British economy, or involve an increase of East-West tension which would force Britain into an increased arms program without regard to the consequences for the economy. When the meeting of the Council of Foreign Ministers again adjourned with almost no progress following seven weeks of bargaining, the Left Wing was appalled. The chief point of discussion had been the German question, and reparations had been one of the chief stumbling blocks. In the anxiety to avoid a complete breakdown, which would make nonsense of Left Wing opposition to conscription, *Tribune* (April 18, 1947) seems at one stage to have favored the payment of reparations by Britain and the United States:

> The Anglo-American argument is forceful. It says that so long as Germany has to be kept alive by dollar loans to finance her surplus imports, and until she has paid occupation costs and import loans from a future export surplus, any reparations from current production amount merely to payment of reparations to Russia by the Western Powers. But it still remains true that a compromise on this question is as important to us as to Russia, and that unavoidable expenditure incurred for this purpose may in the most direct sense be an investment in nothing less than world peace.

Others, like Harold Laski, suggested long-term loans to the U.S.S.R. as a substitute for reparations. The *New Statesman* simply placed the blame for the breakdown on the Truman Doctrine. The issue was minor, in the Left Wing press, but it is an indication of the genuine anxiety of Left Wing spokesmen to avoid a complete break with Russia at all costs. The concern now, however, was not to protect the good name of the Soviets, though this principle still had its adherents, but to protect the British social service program, which was much more real and meaningful to most British socialists than the abstractions of an international ideology.

The Labour movement was once again, however, preparing for a party Conference. The group of Left Wing M.P.'s who had directed the "revolt" in the House of Commons the previous autumn had continued to meet regularly throughout the winter, and produced a new statement of principles early in May, 1947, which was published under the title "Keep Left."[19] Most of the writing seems to have been done by R. H. S. Crossman, Michael Foot, and Ian Mikardo, but a number of M.P.'s signed the finished pamphlet. Its purpose was simply to provide a basis for discussion at the coming Conference, and of course to provide a general program which would command the adherence of the Labour movement. The new emphasis upon the protection of domestic socialism is clearly revealed. Although the pamphlet does summarize the arguments used against the Government in the autumn "revolt," its chief emphasis is upon the more recently developed opposition to the Government's armament program. The men who sponsored the pamphlet were not pacifists themselves, and their opposition to armaments was based entirely upon its economic consequences and the dangerous effect it might have upon the domestic welfare program.

Thus the pamphlet began with a lengthy survey of Britain's economic ills, which were attributed primarily to the size of the armed forces which the Labour Government was maintaining. This, it was now claimed, had led the group to stage a revolt in Parliament and to oppose the Government's conscription program. The writers realized that a sharp reduction of British forces would necessitate fundamental changes in British policy abroad, but they felt the circumstances justified the needed changes. Britain must recognize the truth; she was no longer a great economic power, for: "However many men we maintain in the armed forces, and however many millions we spend on the service budgets, the British Isles are no longer defensible in a major war." This pessimistic outlook, which had been refuted specifically by *Tribune* in the autumn of 1947, became the fundamental tenet of the newly developing position of the Left Wing.

The United States, the pamphlet continued, had become militarized at the upper levels of government and had adopted Winston Churchill's Fulton policy for its own. But the American Chiefs of Staff realized that they could not maintain large American forces abroad, and they were seeking manpower to fill the forward wall of defenses in Europe. The implication is clear that the United States was pressing the British Government to increase, rather than decrease, its military forces and the British Government was not prepared to do so. "Keep Left" also maintained that American fear of Russia was predicated on a myth, since it was not possible to make valid comparisons between Hitler and Stalin, if only because Russia had no economic reason for expansion. For her part, the Soviet Union had good reason to fear the western powers. Russia had twice been invaded by western nations; the West had permitted Hitler to rearm and had tried to persuade him to attack Russia and not the West in 1939; the United States had used its financial resources to make anticommunist loans to reactionary regimes on the Soviet borders and to oppose the forces of socialism. Hence Russia could hardly be blamed if she regarded American policy as a threat to her security.

In any case, the writers of the pamphlet felt that it was a policy of despair to conclude that the gap between Russia and the western powers could not be bridged. For failure to do so would mean the destruction of Britain, the ruin of Europe, and a world-wide visitation by the full horrors of atomic warfare (though Russia had not, at this time, developed atomic weapons). Further, this view could not be equated with the terms of the United Nations Charter, which both Britain and the United States had signed. Finally, the argument against Soviet totalitarianism ignored the fact that she was not the only totalitarian nation in the world, and that collective security against Russia was not the best means of promoting democracy and socialism which were the only true remedy for the spread of totalitarian control. The task of British socialism, then, was to heal the breach between Russia and the United States and not to act in a manner which widened that breach. Britain could in no circumstances take sides in the argument, but must continue to co-operate closely with democratic socialists on the European continent since this group was eagerly awaiting a British lead. When all was said and ended, the real Left Wing criticism of the Labour Government's policy remained its failure to provide a "socialist lead" in Europe such as it had provided at home and in India and Burma.

Midway through the pamphlet, still another version of the "revolt" in Parliament was provided the reader. It was explained that the world was already divided into blocs when Labour took office in 1945, since there had been little real wartime co-operation and the Soviet diplomatic offensive had made it impossible for Britain to maintain friendly relations. But Soviet policy had changed in the autumn of 1946 and the "revolt" was staged to draw the attention of the Government and of the British public to this change. The "revolt" had failed because Britain was already committed to a position in which her reliance upon the United States was so great that she was no longer a completely free agent. This endangered her relations with the "progressive" forces in Europe and permitted nonsocialist groups on the continent to squeeze the "progressives" out of power. A fresh start was needed which would begin with a strong Anglo-French alliance: "The goal we should work for now is a federation which binds together the nations now under Eastern domination with the peoples of Western Europe. But this goal is a long way off. For the present, it would be better to concentrate on less spectacular forms of European collaboration designed gradually to remove the iron curtain."[20]

The pamphlet went on to say that Britain was in a very strong position to take the lead in this policy because she was the world's largest consumer, and even the United States economy could not dispense with British markets. Imperial preference must, however, be maintained and Britain should try to strengthen her trading position by every means at her disposal. The Anglo-French alliance was also urged as a solution to the problem of national defense, since Britain could not survive an atomic war, and must by all means prevent such an occurrence. An Anglo-French alliance, which abjured staff conversations with either Russia or the United States, and announced that it would not manufacture atomic weapons and would submit all of its armament production centers to international inspection seemed to the writers of "Keep Left" a solution to this dilemma. Their proposal seems to follow the Soviet Union's proposal to the United Nations Atomic Energy Commission where the suggestion was discarded by all but the Eastern European representatives on the Commission.[21]

Turning to Germany, a pressing problem at the moment, *Keep Left* urged a solution which would integrate Germany into the whole European economy, and into the Soviet five-year plans. In context, the pamphlet virtually accused the United States of deliberately maintaining Germany in a divided state since: "Obsessed by fears of a Communist Germany, they [the United States] prefer to keep Germany, and Europe, divided in order to check Russian expansion."[22] The economic integration of Germany would solve that problem permanently.

The pacifist proposal for a speedy withdrawal from the Middle East was accepted completely. The Dardanelles and the Suez Canal should then be treated as international waterways. The territories of Persia and Arabia should be guaranteed by the four great powers.

In a final summary, the pamphlet listed the actions which Britain must take to regain her prestige and standing in international affairs. They concluded: a firm repudiation of the Truman proposals for "collective security against communism;" the renunciation of staff conversations with the United States; renunciation of atomic weapons; international inspection of Britain's military establishment, voluntarily established; complete withdrawal of British forces from the Middle East; and finally, integration of Germany into a *planned* European economy. The reader will by now have recognized the antecedents of most of these points, and no purpose would be served by retracing them in detail. Suffice it to note how firmly the program is grounded in the Left Wing ideology and in the traditional Left Wing attitude toward international affairs, and to call attention to the gradual increase in hostility to the center of capitalism, the United States.

The Labour party published an official reply to "Keep Left" entitled "Cards on the Table;" in it, the whole concept of a "socialist" foreign policy was repudiated. Britain's policy, it stated, must depend upon her power, and not upon the ideology of her government. Britain was also a democracy, and her actions must be supported by public opinion, within and without the country. The cardinal principle of British policy was to avoid creating a vacuum where great power conflict might take place. And, since Britain was no longer able to secure her own safety alone, she must depend upon collective security. The machinery provided by the United Nations was useless in great power disputes, therefore Britain had to protect herself as best she might through additional alliances outside the U. N. What is probably most significant for our purposes is the clear recognition that the difference between the Government and the Left Wing was dependent upon ideology, and not upon different interpretations of facts.

The influence of the Left Wing on Labour thought about international affairs is again demonstrated by the resolutions which appeared on the Agenda for the 1947 Labour party Conference. About one-fifth of the 543 resolutions listed on the Final Agenda dealt with foreign affairs, and another two-fifths were concerned with economic policy, understandably enough, of course, in the circumstances. Criticism predominated over praise, and again this is to be expected at a party Conference. But the marked hostility of many of the resolutions is striking. Nineteen of twenty-four general resolutions dealing with international affairs denounced the Government, often in very severe terms, for pursuing a foreign policy which was "unsocialist." Again, seven resolutions demanded an end to British recognition of the Franco regime. Seven others stressed the need for closer relations with Russia and implied that Britain was in some way responsible for the failure to reach agreement. No less than nineteen separate resolutions denounced the Conservative bias of Foreign Office personnel; in nearly every case making use of the term "anti-Soviet" at some point in the wording. Seventeen resolutions expressed unyielding hostility to conscription. The Left Wing had done its work well.

The temper of the Conference was shown in a trivial incident that occurred early in the meeting; an unfortunate delegate made a sarcastic remark about the use of slave labor in the Soviet Union and was immediately drowned in protests. The Conference was in no mood to hear criticism of Russia yet, and constant reference was made to the poor speaker throughout the remainder of the meeting.

A pacifist-supported resolution against conscription obtained more than half a million votes, though the union bloc defeated the proposal easily. A composite resolution was then moved by Konni Zilliacus, which began by congratulating the Government for its decision to base British policy upon the United Nations charter, and ended in a scathing denunciation of the actual policy being pursued. It urged the assumption that no war was possible in the foreseeable future; that Britain collaborate more closely with the U.S.S.R.; and that Britain associate herself more closely with the socialist nations of the world. Supporting the resolution, Zilliacus deployed a typical argument: British commitments were causing a severe drain on economic resources and this was causing the economic crisis, hence the Government must reduce the size of its armed forces drastically or else lower the living standard of the British people; but so long as Britain based her policy on the United Nations, there was no need for large military forces, hence there was no need to endanger the domestic economy. He added the further argument that Britain had received a mandate from the people to bring Russia into close collaboration in the Middle East, therefore the oil resources in this area should be developed by some form of international agreement among the great powers.

The usual resolution condemning the Government of Greece made its appearance, along with a resolution on Germany that urged Britain to resist the capitalistic efforts of the United States to prevent the socialization of Germany. It also asked that British staff in Germany be appointed only from the ranks of convinced socialists, a variation on the Foreign Office theme, which also made its appearance in the form of a strong resolution urging the appointment of Foreign Office personnel "more in touch with the aspirations of the common people of the world." A final resolution suggested that a conference of European socialists meet on British initiative to seek means of healing the breach between East and West.

The general debate on foreign affairs was, as usual, somewhat fragmented by the time limits placed on speakers. Richard Crossman and Ian Mikardo spoke on the German resolution, urging the Government to speed the socialization process in Germany to the utmost of its ability. T. E. N. Driberg spoke on the value of Soviet trade for Britain, and urged closer economic relations with that country. There were the usual requests for much closer relations with other socialist countries. In fact, the Conference saw the re-appearance of the class-conscious, economically-oriented theories of the 1930's, as in this speech by Kenneth Younger: "I believe that the present apparent deadlock is due very largely to the fear on the part of the Soviet Union that the capitalistic United States is about to lead the western world into an economic crisis, and that when that crisis occurs, the United States, like other capitalistic countries before her, will find no outlet except in aggression.'[23] This is not an isolated instance of this type of argument, but a fairly typical sample of an argument met frequently in Left Wing speeches and writings at this time.

The Foreign Secretary, Ernest Bevin, replied to the foreign affairs debate, producing for the occasion an absolute masterpiece of Labour oratory. Bevin was still smarting from the "rebellion" in Parliament staged by the Left Wing, and he proceeded to use the occasion of the party Conference to pay off his attackers, virtually ignoring the arguments of those who preceded him at the Conference. Beginning with caustic references to the "stab in the back" he had suffered while he was away in America, Bevin reviewed his policy, condemned Zilliacus in particular and his other critics in general, suggested the type of response the conference should make to the various resolutions, and resumed his seat. His suggestions, backed by the formidable power of the union bloc vote, were followed to the letter. A combination of shrewd platform strategy and trade union loyalty had again drowned the opposition but left it disgruntled and unhappy. Again, the Left Wing turned to its own press to voice its dissatisfaction, and the pages of the *New Statesman* and *Tribune* were filled with denunciations of Bevin. He was accused of lack of principle, of undemocratic prac-tices, of using the emotional appeals of the trade union movement to drown free discussion, and so on.[24] Once again the Left Wing had come to a party Conference hoping to convert international policy to an ideological basis and failed; once again the principal cause of their failure was Ernest Bevin.

VII

THE END OF THE GRAND ALLIANCE

It may be argued that the Grand Alliance never really existed, except to the extent that the western allies were willing to make it a working association through a series of concessions to the Soviet Union. Or, the Grand Alliance may be considered real and valid, a bond forged in the war against the common enemy, but lacking sufficient grounds to endure beyond the end of hostilities. Whatever the reality that may lie beneath the surface, the public end of the Grand Alliance can be dated to the second half of 1947. At the beginning of June, 1947, the western powers were still seeking a solution to world problems which could be based upon co-operation among the great powers, ostensibly at least; by the end of December, 1947, the western powers were openly charting an independent course, particularly in occupied Germany. Crudely speaking, the Marshall proposal of June 5, 1947, was the critical point in the open deterioration of East-West relations, although a final Conference of Foreign Ministers meeting was held in a futile attempt to provide a solution to the German question. This six month period is covered in the present chapter.

At some point in one of his celebrated cases, Mr. Sherlock Holmes pointed out to his assistant, Dr. Watson, that the absence of deviation from an established norm was a point of great significance. In like manner, the most significant aspect of Left Wing opinion during the critical six month period from June to December, 1947, was the absence of change. With one exception, the Left Wing attitude toward international affairs, its solution to current problems, varied not at all during a period in which the bulk of British opinion, and even of Labour opinion in Britain, swung very sharply in the direction of a new attitude. The Left Wing attitude toward foreign policy was very probably shared by a substantial portion of the Labour movement in June, 1947, and many of the arguments used by the Left Wing to support its position found favor with observers who were not necessarily committed to socialism. Few persons really prefer war to peace, armaments to civilian goods, hostility to friendliness, or anarchy to co-operation. Even careful observers realized that the past history of western-Soviet relations had created feelings of fear and suspicion which would take time to eliminate. Since the nature of the East-West relationship was in essence a question of judgment of intentions, which are particularly difficult to surmise and almost impossible to verify, the Left Wing position, when stated with moderation and due regard for the facts of day to day intercourse with the Soviets, was by no means impossible to maintain.

The Left Wing was separated from other bodies of opinion in Britain more by its processes than by its conclusions, that is, the manner in which it reached its conclusions differed in a very fundamental manner from the method used by most other opinion groups in the country. Faced by a long and continuing series of hostile and aggressive Soviet actions, western opinion gradually swung to the view that co-operation with the Soviets was not possible, and eventually to the view that the Soviet attitude was a genuine threat. It must be granted, I think, that the western governments overplayed the element of threat in the Soviet position once they had made a definite decision that co-operation was not possible; it may be that this was necessary to arouse public opinion and obtain parliamentary or congressional support for their policies. This is normal, however regrettable it might be. For it was not until the outbreak of war in Korea that the western nations began to *act* as though there was a serious danger of Soviet attack, even though they had *spoken* in this vein for some months. Nevertheless, it seems possible to affirm that none of the major western powers began the search for a postwar settlement already convinced that the effort was fruitless, and that they did not use the time to obtain suitable examples to support conclusions already reached. The timing of the western policy shift would hardly have been as it was had this been the case.

Here the line of separation between the Left Wing and the remainder is clear, for the Left Wing did begin with a predetermined position, derived from their own basic ideological principles, and, in general, consonant with the traditional Left Wing foreign policy of the 1930's. Throughout the postwar years, it clung to that position through thick and thin, rejecting any data which conflicted with the established viewpoint, or, if this was not possible, so interpreting data that they fitted the preconceptions which the Left Wing held. In the process, data were treated selectively and artificially, or even rejected outright if such data failed to conform. On some occasions, completely new data were manufactured when the data available were not satisfactory. In general, we must really deal with the methods by which the Left Wing sustained a given position through a critical period, rather

than with any changes in position, for there were no fundamental
changes.

Rightly or wrongly, most western observers considered the
Marshall proposal as the final straw which clearly indicated that
the Soviet Union had no intention whatever of co-operating on
anything except its own terms. Certainly the Soviets chose to
construe the program as a direct attack on themselves, and be-
haved in a remarkably aggressive manner thereafter. Strictly
speaking, of course, there was no Marshall "Plan" though the
term will be used here because it is so common, and in fact the
United States produced no plan at any stage in the development of
the European Recovery Program (ERP). The aid program was
evolved by the American Government in the latter part of 1946
and early 1947 to meet an obvious economic crisis in Europe.
The amount of aid provided by the program was in fact rather
less than the amount that had been provided in 1946 from governmental and private sources, but it was more efficiently used and
more easily directed because it was now channeled through a single agency. From July 1, 1945, through December, 1946, the United
States had provided some 14.3 billion dollars in public and private aid to Europe, while the Marshall Program cost only 6.6
billion dollars during its first fifteen months of operation.[1]

The chief purpose of the Marshall Program was to ensure
controlled use of funds, encourage a measure of European co-
operation and self-help, and ensure that a continuous supply of
aid would be available for the crucial years of rebuilding and
conversion. This had been pointed out by Dean Acheson, then
Undersecretary of State, as early as December 8, 1946, when he
told a group of American businessmen that: "The relief problems
of the near future are not of a character which would warrant
grants of enormous sums of money from the United States Treasury under conditions which would leave little or no effective
control by the grantor of these funds."[2] In May, 1947, Acheson
publicly noted that the United States Government would ask for
control of key areas in the economy as part of an urgently needed
program for rehabilitating the European economy.[3] The reason
for quoting these speeches is to make certain that it is clear that
the ERP antedated by far the Truman Doctrine, and that ERP had
little if any military significance at the time that it originated. In
1946 and early 1947 military threats were not a problem.

Marshall's "offer" was very simple. If the nations of Europe
would come together and work out a joint plan for effective use of
assistance, the United States Government would attempt to provide
such assistance. There were no "strings" attached to the offer,
no suggestions were made, and no nations were excluded.[4]

The British and French then invited the Soviet Union to meet with them in Paris and discuss the proposal; the meeting was duly convened on June 27, 1947.[5] Five days later, Molotov and his entourage walked out of the meeting and returned to Moscow. Molotov had proposed that each nation draw up a list of the things which it required most and send these lists to the United States to be filled; to do otherwise, he argued, would endanger the security of his country. Once Russia left the meeting, Britain and France proceeded alone to issue a general invitation to other European nations, which led to a meeting in Paris. At this meeting, working parties were established to draw up the necessary program, and this program was completed and sent to Washington by September, 1947. In the report, each nation promised to make a strong effort to increase production in basic industries, maintain financial stability, develop intra-European co-operation, and solve the "dollar shortage." In particular, each country promised to make full use of its own resources, modernize equipment wherever possible, and organize a systematic program for development of resources by mutual aid. These innocuous and self-imposed conditions were accepted almost verbatim by the American Government and incorporated in the Economic Cooperation Act of 1948.

After leaving the Paris Conference, the Soviet Union almost literally declared war upon the American aid program. Communist party agitation in France and Italy generated large scale industrial strikes that were intended to force these countries out of the aid program. The Comintern, which had been abolished during the war as a gesture of friendship, was refurbished and organized as the Cominform in October, 1947. The Soviet grip on the satellite nations in Eastern Europe, which in relative terms had been bearable through 1947, was now tightened without mercy by a series of repressive measures culminating in the final subversion of Czechoslovakia in February, 1948. These Soviet actions helped the American administration gain support for its aid program as nothing else could possibly have done, but the actions added immeasurably to the danger that the aid program would possibly turn out to be merely an "anti-communist aid program." By and large, this pitfall was avoided. President Truman, in his Message to Congress, chose to emphasize the importance of the European economy and the chief point he had urged in March, 1947, when he asked for aid for Greece and Turkey: "Our deepest concern and the chief reason for granting the assistance needed (was that). . . it is the only assurance of the continued independence and integrity of a group of nations who constitute a bulwark for the principles of freedom, justice, and the dignity of the individual."[6]

The congressional hearings that dealt with the aid program began in January, 1948, and the chairmen of the two committees made a sincere and successful effort to keep the "strings" attached to the aid bill to a minimum.[7] The basic points that emerged in the hearings in both houses were: first, the containment of the Soviet Union, though not communism as an ideology, was a clear goal of the program; second, that European prosperity was believed to have a great influence on American prosperity, hence there was an element of self-interest in the program; third, that there should be no political "strings" attached to the program. The Foreign Assistance Act, in its final form, conformed to the *CEEC Report* and the only two strings attached had no political significance whatever. The first limitation required that 50 per cent of the gross tonnage moved across the Atlantic be shipped in American vessels; the second required the Administrator to purchase surplus foodstuffs in the United States when they were available. The Act was amended in 1949 to make European integration a primary goal of the program, and this provision was strengthened in 1950. The chief concern of Congress appears to have been the impact of the program on the American economy, and no less than three reports were prepared on the subject.[8]

This brief survey of the genesis and content of the European Recovery Program contains nothing that was not made available to the world press at the time it occurred. Its mention is necessary here mainly because the interpretation placed upon the Marshall offer and subsequent events by the British Left Wing was frequently so far off the mark as to arouse suspicions about the availability of information. Very briefly, the European Recovery Program seems to have been a remarkable example of enlightened self-interest on the part of the American Administration. The program was not totally altruistic since everyone realized that the strength of the American economy depended in some measure upon a viable European economy, but there remains a worthy element of altruism in the concept and in the manner of its administration. Certainly the program was not completely dedicated to self-interest. That it was a combination, and a happy combination, of self-interest and altruism seems hardly to require affirmation, yet this particular interpretation proved quite impossible for the British Left Wing to accept.

Marshall's speech, which can hardly have been a surprise to the British Government, was a complete surprise to the general public and elicited an astonishing response from the Left Wing. It was assumed immediately that American "big business" was again faced with the danger of a severe slump and had put pressure upon the American Government to adopt this new technique for exporting its surpluses.[9] There was little enthusiasm for the proposal, partly because of the "political reservations" which Marshall had made during his speech, and partly because of the "tentative nature" of the whole conception. Only *Tribune* (June 13, 1947) was willing to concede that this had been a "bold and imaginative" gesture, though this did not prevent that journal from sharing the Left Wing assumption that primary responsibility for the proposal lay with the approaching slump in the American economy. Once again we find that the Left Wing framed an event in terms of its own preconceived views of the manner in which a capitalistic state behaves, and not in terms of the facts of that state's behavior.

Throughout the early stages of the development of Marshall aid, the Left Wing concentrated upon the more pessimistic aspects of the program. It was taken for granted that the "reactionary" American Congress would not provide sufficient funds for the program, if indeed it could be induced to provide any funds at all. Much concern was shown over the number of strings that would be attached to the program as conditions of acceptance. The more extreme elements of the Left Wing simply wrote off the entire conception as another phase of American imperialism. The parliamentary Left Wing did not advocate an outright refusal of the offer, but most Left Wing speakers in the House of Commons concentrated on the coming economic slump in the United States and implied that this was the sole reason why the offer had been made.[10] There is a curious parallel between this tendency to decry accepting assistance from capitalistic America and the absolute and complete refusal of the Left Wing to agree to the rearmament of Britain in the late 1930's so long as it was controlled by the Conservative party. Both seem to involve a clear refusal to accept any limitations whatever upon an absolute principle, even though the need for limitation seems adequately enjoined by the facts.

In the course of the debate in the House of Commons, the Foreign Secretary had made it clear that Britain intended to go ahead with the recovery program whatever the action taken by the U.S.S.R. He also stated Britain's firm intention to take its own direction without Soviet agreement if the forthcoming Conference of Foreign Ministers meeting proved unsuccessful. The breakdown of the conference at Paris and Molotov's return to the U.S.S.R. marked the second stage of the proceedings. The Left Wing explanation of Soviet behavior now began to vary somewhat. *Tribune* examined the nature of Molotov's charges against the United States and found them "patently absurd" but fell back upon the excuse it had used previously—that Molotov had "blundered"

or miscalculated in his thinking that the United States was headed
for a gigantic slump which might drag down the planned Soviet
economy if Russia participated.

The *New Statesman* (July 5, 1947) took quite a different attitude:
"Russia will not risk any American influence in Eastern Europe,
and fears any unity or reconstruction of Europe except under exclusive Communist influence. The division between the two
worlds is therefore admitted and the pretense of co-operation
abandoned." It agreed that under the circumstances the western
European nations would have to go forward without the Soviet
Union. It is interesting to note that this viewpoint was specifically challenged by *Tribune* (July 11, 1947) in a leader which denied
emphatically that great power relations had broken down, although
it agreed that the remaining countries in Europe should continue
without Russia. By mid-July, then, most of the Left Wing press
had swung slightly toward support for the aid program, always
with the firm warning that no economic penetration of British
markets should be tolerated, and that British socialism be carefully guarded.

In August, 1947, after tentatively agreeing to British participation in the ERP, the Left Wing began to have second thoughts.
It was clear that no aid could be provided much earlier than 1948,
and a recalculation of the hazards involved in accepting assistance
began early in August. By the end of the month, the Left Wing was
virtually convinced that Britain should refuse the American offer.
Professor Harold Laski urged that the British Government should
not overestimate the potential value of the assistance program.
Marshall had been vague and general, and the program could in no
case have much value unless Germany was included and this was
not possible until agreement with the Soviet Union was reached:
". . . If Russian susceptabilities are left unwounded by the omis-
sion of Germany from any proposals that may be made, is it not
clear that any plan must have gravely limited objectives in view,
since it will then take no account of what is still a vital part of
both the industrial and agrarian potential of Europe." [11] Therefore,
Laski went on, once "we get down to realities," Molotov's objections to the program were sensible and should have British support.
Others, like Fenner Brockway, suggested that the British might
by careful management build a self-reliant Europe without aid.[12]

The *New Statesman* (August 19, 1947), which argued that the
failure of the American President to call a special session of
Congress had removed the last justification for supporting the
aid program, now frankly advocated "going it alone." In the July
26 issue of *Forward* Professor Laski concentrated his attention
almost exclusively on the dangers of the aid program, and particularly the possibility that it "might divide Europe in twain."

He now accepted Molotov's argument completely, e. g., he felt that the vast overproduction of the American economy had stimulated the proposal, and that the United States was merely driving toward new overseas markets. The smaller nations who accepted aid would become mere dominated markets in a short time and the United States could then use its economic influence to stop the spread of socialism. Laski suggested that Britain organize the socialist parties in Europe and save itself and them "without losing their independence." *Tribune* held aloof for one week, then joined the new trend to the extent of publishing one leader which followed Professor Laski's arguments.

In July, 1947, then, the British Left Wing for a brief time accepted the breakdown of British-Soviet relations, contrary to their ideological beliefs, only to revert rapidly in the following month to their original position. The terms of the Marshall proposal were ignored, Soviet behavior at Paris was forgotten, and the need for economic aid was minimized. By early August, 1947, the Left Wing was urging the British Government to engage in "closer co-operation with European Socialists" in the search for a "middle way" and once again was attacking the size of the British military program as the chief source of economic weakness. When the severe financial crisis broke in August, partly at least as a consequence of British efforts to carry out the provisions of the Anglo-American Loan Agreement of 1945[13] about convertibility of currency, the Left Wing was confirmed in its belief that Britain must go forward alone, and the fiscal debacle was laid at the doorstep of the United States Government, often with the intimation that the intent had been to discredit the British socialists. The crisis led to a sharp upsweep in the demand for further reductions of the armed forces, and a swift departure from the principles of free trade and multilateralism in favor of a "planned" international economic effort. The Left Wing now suggested quite frequently that Britain had in any case only to await further pressure from American surplus production and that factor alone would "force" the United States to offer aid on better terms.

As the crisis matured and worsened, the Left Wing broke into full cry against the United States, and swung its policies around completely to sharp opposition to Marshall aid. In the process, the battle cries of the 1930's were brought out once again as were the old ideological symbols as the Left Wing found in the course of events a validation of their own previous convictions. *Tribune* (August 22, 1947) urged Britain toward a closer association with the Commonwealth and with Europe that might enable all of them to survive as independent political entities. The chief threat to

British independence now came from the West and not from the East and it took the form of economic penetration. "Hard hearted men in the American Treasury"—a paraphrase on Lord Keynes famous statement about the 1918 British Parliament and equally inaccurate—had conceived a plan for "world domination" which the American Government was trying to carry out. The *New Statesman* suggested that the price of American aid would be inspectors in British factories, and clearly envisaged something closely akin to military occupation. It was universally agreed that British socialism would be stifled as a matter of deliberate American policy, and everyone on the Left Wing felt that it was imperative that Britain find some alternative to accepting American assistance.

Professor Laski carried the current attitude as far in the direction of fellow traveling as was possible without complete endorsement of the U.S.S.R. when he suggested an immediate trade agreement with Russia that would obviate the need for aid and prevent the reactionaries in Congress from stifling British socialism. Further all that was needed from Britain was strength of purpose so that, ". . . we can find the means of full unity of purpose with Poland and Czechoslovakia, with Hungary and Yugoslovia, and with Russia that we can free from fear that a new coalition is being prepared against it."[14] He now openly declared that capitalistic America would never assist socialist Britain, and this seemed to him a striking confirmation of the validity of Marx's analysis of capitalism in its imperialistic stage.[15]

At this time, we find the first of a series of rumors regarding the state of opinion within the Labour Cabinet which imply that the split between the Left Wing and the bulk of the Labour movement had its parallel within the Cabinet. The issue on which the split was alleged to have occurred was the nationalization of steel. On August 16, 1947, *Forward* claimed that American interests were trying to prevent nationalization and had brought strong pressure to bear upon the British Government as a condition of economic assistance. This charge had already appeared in the *Daily Worker* (May 8, 1946), but not in the Left Wing press. The *New Statesman* also broached the question on August 29, asking for a shift of Cabinet offices that would insure nationalization of steel even though it meant the loss of American aid. On September 13, Kingsley Martin noted that any changes which did occur would leave Aneurin Bevan "inside the Cabinet. . . biding his time." The issue was then dropped. It is included here only in view of later developments in internal Labour politics which it appears to presage.

Once the flurry of interest created by the financial crisis died away, Left Wing thought on international affairs settled into two broad channels. One, which was simply a continuation of what had gone before, is best represented by Professor Harold Laski and to some degree by the *New Statesman*. It held that Britain should refuse American assistance and press for closer relations with the Soviet Union. Fundamentally, this view was based on the belief that this course of action was most conducive to the success of socialism in Britain and on the Continent. The other channel of opinion, for which *Tribune* became the chief spokesman, could find no reasonable alternative to accepting American aid, but cautioned the Government against allowing American economic penetration of British markets. The British Government, and apparently the main stream of British opinion supported its policies at this time, never faltered in its own course, and continued to develop a policy which assumed that agreement with the U.S.S.R. was not possible at the moment. This policy did not include any drastic revision of British military power, though both elements of the Left Wing considered this a vital necessity. On the central question of whether Russia was merely fearful and unco-operative, or genuinely aggressive and threatening, neither the Left Wing nor the Government had a great deal to say. Professor Laski clearly assumed the former condition, and the main body of Left Wing opinion sided with his view by inference, rather than by direct and open affirmation.

As in the past, Soviet policy once again placed the Left Wing in a dilemma between recognition of Soviet aggressiveness and total disregard of facts. The creation of the Cominform in October, and the savage strikes in France and Italy, followed by the final breakdown of the Foreign Ministers conferences, alarmed the western powers and roused public opinion in the west to anti-Soviet sentiment which was much strengthened by the growing repression in eastern Europe, climaxed by the flight of Mikolajczyk from Poland, and the Czech coup and the suicide or defenestration of Jan Masaryk. In this period, *Tribune* moved further and further away from the main stream of Left Wing opinion in Britain and closer toward the position of the Government and the bulk of moderate opinion in the country. It firmly denounced Soviet policy in Eastern Europe. It clearly condemned the Soviets for fomenting the strikes in Italy and France. Finally, it supported the British Government's decision to support the formation of a West German Government. By the end of 1947, *Tribune* had become a supporter of Government policy, albeit a somewhat critical supporter. The contrast between the views expressed in *Tribune* and those found in the remainder of the Left Wing press is truly striking. In general, the Left Wing group that followed this new approach to international policy is identical with the group that produced the "revolt" in Parliament and the "Keep Left" pamphlet, minus R. H. S. Crossman and, later, Ian Mikardo who disagreed with *Tribune's* editorial board and resigned.

The main body of the Left Wing, on the other hand, took a very different view of international affairs. The creation of the Cominform was taken as a sign that Soviet patience was exhausted. Mikolajczyk's flight from Poland was sharply criticized, and it was noted, caustically, that he would be welcomed with open arms by the anticommunists and by the Vatican, since he could be used to conduct anti-Soviet propaganda. The French and Italian strikes were taken to be a normal consequence of the conditions of labour in these two countries. In the *New Statesman*, for example (November 29, 1947), the strikes were subject to this commentary: "By creating the impression that the strikes, which were begun quite justifiably as a protest against inadequate wages and soaring prices, are being converted into a political demonstration that France cannot be governed without the Communist Party, M. Duclos, and M. Marty have done much to ensure the swift passage by Congress of the stop-gap aid bill." In contrast, President Truman's proposals to Congress, and the final breakdown of the Conference of Foreign Ministers were hardly noted by the Left Wing press. Kingsley Martin brought the year to a fitting conclusion with a bitter lament to the effect that the Labour party had grown so engrossed with the problem of communism that it had forgotten the existence of the Franco Government in Spain.

Since this book is concerned with the influence of ideology, it is worth noting that the group being studied, the Left Wing, very definitely believed that the ideological aspects of international affairs were far and away the most important questions to be solved in the field, and further, that the Left Wing very consistently attempted to place international events in an ideological context, particularly during and after 1947 when the gap between the western powers and the Soviet Union was clearly revealed. In the early stages of development, this commonly took the form of attacking the "antisocialist" bias of the United States. Thus the Truman Doctrine was usually interpreted as an American effort to stem the advance of communism, as was the Marshall Plan at a later date.

The chief differences between Russia and the United States were thus framed in terms of ideological principles, and the conflict which later became the cold war was characterized as an ideological conflict. This thesis was made more tenable by the public statements of the American Administration, and by extremely careless use of the term ideology in the western press.

The Soviet Union likewise encouraged this trend by its habitual treatment of all external problems in ideological terms. It appears to the writer that no serious examination of the course of international affairs after 1945 could produce this interpretation. The thesis that an ideological struggle exists, or has existed, between Russia and the West may be tenable. But if so it seems most likely that the conflict is part of existing ideologies rather than a conflict which stems from pre-war ideologies. A much better description of events can be obtained if the struggle is viewed as a simple power struggle between two camps in which aggressive actions were taken preponderantly by one party, and in which the only ideologies involved were the inevitable national-ism on both sides, and not communism and its opponent, whatever that may be.

The British Left Wing, almost without exception, took the view that an ideological conflict had arisen, and it was usually held that the United States had begun this war of ideas with the Truman Doctrine, or in its attempts to convince Congress that aid money was required for Europe. Many Left Wing writers used this thesis to justify the need for a neutral third force position.

This concept of an ideological war has come to command much support, in Britain as well as in the United States, and among Conservatives as well as radicals or socialists. It deserves some careful thought. For, if the premise is accepted, two very important conclusions can be drawn quite legitimately: first, that the American "ideology," which is little more than its own peculiar form of nationalism, is not exportable since it depends upon economic circumstances that are not duplicated anywhere in the world except in Russia where it is hardly likely to gain many adherents; second, that history is crammed with illustrations to "prove" that military force is of no use whatever against the expansion of ideas. Leaving aside the question whether history has ever "proved" anything at all in this sense, most people would agree that military force is not very likely to deter the expansion of an idea, and the possibility of creating another social unit like the United States at any other place on the globe is certainly remote. Hence these conclusions seem to be quite reasonable given the initial premise. Both of these propositions were very widely used by Left Wing spokesmen to support opposi-tion to the expansion of British military forces and at times to urge that Britain was much more closely aligned to the Soviet ideology than to that of the United States. Eventually, the ideo-logical argument was used as justification for the third force or neutral position which the Left Wing advocated for Britain.

When due consideration is given to the vagaries of day to-day journalism, the British Left followed a remarkably stable policy line in international affairs down through the autumn of 1947. One of the theses of this study is that such stability is a normal corollary to ideological conviction, and that the absence of a stable policy would be evidence of a lack of ideological conviction. This thesis is substantiated in a very significant manner by the larger and presumably more carefully considered works of Left Wing writers and propagandists. Three volumes on this larger scale appeared in Britain in 1947, and the extent to which they reflect the same premises as those found in the Left Wing press and in speeches by the parliamentary Left Wing is indicative of the stability of ideologically conceived patterns of thought. The largest and most important of these works came from Professor G. D. H. Cole;[16] another was written by Leonard Woolf;[17] a third by Professor Harold Laski.[18] All three substantiate the position found in the remainder of Left Wing writings in every respect except minor details.

Professor Cole's volume offered, literally, all things for all men. Well over the thousand page mark, the book offered advice and information on international trade, economics, domestic politics, philosophy, socialism, international affairs, and a host of related subjects. That portion of the work which impinges directly on international affairs offers an illuminating and sometimes terrifying conception of the principle of neutralism carried to its logical conclusions. Thus the Persian crisis was held to originate in the resistance offered to Soviet efforts to penetrate the Middle East by the dominant Anglo-American oil interests. Soviet policy on the Danube River Commission, where the Eastern European bloc had literally driven the western powers out of the meetings, was due to Russian economic interests in the area and her determination not to permit penetration by the capitalistic powers. There is, in fact, a strong element of economic determinism in the entire book.

In more general terms, Cole made use of the usual Left Wing view that Europe was undergoing a "social revolution" which the Soviet Union could not allow to fail. The "revolutionary forces" were busily engaged in breaking the power of the old governing classes and rendering them impotent to launch a successful counter-revolution. There had been intimidation and repression, of course, but the anti-Soviet groups in eastern Europe—he cited Mikolajczyk as an example—were "very reactionary" and seeking to destroy the new social order at the first opportunity. This, it appears in context, was ample justification for any repressive measures which the communist-dominated governments in these countries might have taken. Cole tended to follow the "Zilliacus line" rather more closely than most Left Wing spokesmen in that he accepted explicitly the need for an alliance of communist and socialist forces before a socialist victory was possible. Specifically, this alliance was still needed in France and throughout western Europe, and above all in Great Britain "as a vital factor in the international situation." For, if the British Labour party took any action that: ". . . will tend to make it harder for the French Socialists and the French Communists to act together, it will be striking a blow at the prospects of Socialism, not only in France, but also throughout Western Europe. Nay, more; if British Labour wishes for a socialist solution of the problem of western Europe it must shape its international policy along lines which French Socialists, as well as French Communists, can reasonably be expected to accept."[19]

Opposing the western powers condemnation of the farcical elections in eastern Europe, Professor Cole stated that this could provide no real solution of the problem of social revolution and the notion of settling a country's fate in the middle of such a social revolution by a general election was "absurd." Yet he insisted that the Soviet Union and its satellites were fully democratic: "I do, then, accept Soviet democracy as a legitimate form of democracy and reject altogether the notion that it is merely autocracy in disguise. But, of course, it is not, at any rate in the shape which it exists in the Soviet Union, a form of democracy at all appropriate to western conditions of fitting it in with the democratic traditions of the west."[20] Here is a very clear example indeed of the manner in which ideological conviction leads to the dual standard in social morality.

For all his sympathy with the U.S.S.R., Professor Cole did not feel that Britain should follow a conciliatory policy; not, in truth, because the Soviets did not deserve such treatment, but because they would interpret conciliation as a sign of weakness and act accordingly. Since Britain was not strong, she must act as though she were so. This was best achieved by the "Third Force" solution to the problem, e.g., placing herself at the head of a neutral bloc between Russia and the United States. The section of the book that deals with this concept is quoted below at some length because it is one of the best summaries available of the opinion trends that were developing into this "third force" conception at that time:

> (The first requisite for better British-Soviet relations) . . . is a sharp dissociation of British from American foreign policy. The first essential step towards this is an entire cessation of British support for American interferences in the politics and economics of the countries

of Eastern Europe, and a fresh recognition that these countries must be left to shape their political and economic institutions in close relation to those of the Soviet Union. We must stop backing up the claims of the Peasant Party in Poland; or of the right wing parties in Rumania and Bulgaria. We must stop supporting the American demand for an open door for capitalistic exploitation of the Danube area. And we must reverse our policy in Greece, at least to the extent of shifting our support from the Royalist to the Republican side, even if this means in effect the acceptance of a largely Communist Government.

Secondly, we must make it plain that in economic affairs we stand for an international policy based on Socialism and not on the American notion of capitalistic enterprise. This is not easy to do in the face of the most regrettable economic commitments into which Britain has been forced to enter; but we can at any rate say plainly that the British signature was given to the American trade proposals under duress and that we shall be highly gratified if the refusal of other countries to walk into the American trap relieves our obligations under them—obligations which we should never have incurred but for our imperative need for immediate financial assistance. We can . . . set to work to develop. . . state trading organizations for the management of our import and export trade; and we can try, through these institutions, to build up closer trading relations with the Soviet Union and with the countries associated with it."[21]

One cannot, of course, do justice to the arguments of a thousand page book in a few short paragraphs, but the reader will recognize many of the assumptions implicit in Cole's argument; the tenor of the work is the same throughout. It seems reasonably clear that in this case at least there is little or no difference between immediate reaction and considered opinion so far as suggested policy is concerned.

Leonard Woolf's little booklet is important primarily because it attempts to deal with the vexing question of what it meant by a "socialist" foreign policy. Woolf contended that a socialist foreign policy was possible, and had indeed been followed at times by the Labour Government, but he argued that its relation to government policy was nearly always obscure. He thought that all British socialists were agreed on the policy that should be followed in Spain, but that such examples were infrequent. Great Britain's basic policy, Woolf contended, should aim at peace and collective security, but this was not a socialist monopoly. Socialism could only affect secondary policies and not such fundamentals. By Left Wing standards, this was sheer heresy. But Woolf did believe that the Labour Government could behave in a "socialist" manner by implementing the cause of socialism at home, and by encouraging socialism abroad, by pressing for the formation of an international government, and by accepting the view that the interests of the common people were the same in all parts of the world.

Woolf expressed the opinion that world tensions were at that time due chiefly to postwar competition for strategic advantage, particularly between the United States and the Soviet Union, and that this had proved detrimental to the world's hopes for peace and security. In the circumstances, Britain could join one or the other of the two camps, or attempt to remain free of both sides. A policy of neutrality was by far the most desirable, but this did not mean neutrality in the strict legal sense. Britain should side with the U.S.S.R. "whenever possible" because she had to date sided far more frequently with the United States. For example, "with regard to Spain, Greece, and Persian oil, we should pursue a policy which ought to be supported by the U.S.S.R. and would probably be opposed by the U.S.A. . . . ."[22] Aside from this, the British Government should base its policy upon the United Nations and protest strongly when that machinery was misused. Like G.D.H. Cole and other Left Wing spokesmen, Woolf felt that Britain must dissociate herself from the close alliance with the United States which she had fallen into, even though this might involve "temporary sacrifices," an obvious reference to refusing Marshall aid. This would ease her relations with the Soviets and enable her to begin acting as mediator between the two super powers.

Woolf also agreed with the Left Wing leaders who were demanding a substantial and immediate reduction in British military estimates, and he substantiated his argument for doing so by using the United Nations as justification much as Clement Attlee had used the League of Nations as justification for opposing British armament in the 1930's. Britain should maintain such forces as her United Nations commitments required but must state clearly that she would not participate in any future war though she would be willing to take part in collective security action. This would obviate any need for atomic weapons and Britain could then renounce them completely and enter into bilateral negotiations with other countries desiring to share information about atomic processes. Having done this much, Britain was, he realized, still liable to be bombed by some "lunatic nations" but her leaders would know that they had "taken the only step capable of preventing this and leaving us masters of our destiny."

Woolf's pamphlet had an interesting postscript by W. N. Ewer, international editor of the *Daily Herald,* and a brief preface by Harold Laski. Ewer, who supported the Government's policy, pointed out that if Russia were truly aggressive there was no alternative to an alliance with the United States and that he believed this to be the case. Laski repudiated both Ewer's opinion that Russia was menacing and Wolf's view that a socialist foreign policy was an impossibility in other than general terms, though he did not attempt to make a case to the contrary.

Harold Laski's comments on East-West tensions, published in the autumn of 1947, took yet another approach to the problem. He claimed that Britain had been clumsy and unimaginative in her dealings with the U.S.S.R. after 1945, and had been particularly clumsy in the choice of criteria used to judge the "painful emergence" of democratic processes in Eastern Europe since her criteria in fact ignored the revolutionary nature of the economic and social changes which had taken place. Undoubtedly, Russia had been a suspicious neighbor, and this had to be taken into consideration. But on balance, he felt that common action between Britain and the United States would be a profound error in policy since American economic aid would "probably prove incompatble" with democracy and freedom in Britain. America's "containment policy" would ally Britain with every reactionary regime in Europe and separate her from the European socialist movement almost completely. Britain must, therefore, begin to rebuild her traditional ties with Eastern Europe as speedily as possible, beginning with large-scale trade. This should be followed by an agreement with the Soviet Union that would settle the German problem; if, for example, Russia would agree to free elections, Britain could offer to "socialize" the German economy and integrate it into the *whole* European economy. Britain must also cease haggling about the regimes in Eastern Europe, particularly so because her own policy in Greece had been far from exemplary. Russia, after all, had a right to friendly nations on her borders, and the communist-socialist coalitions now in power were an additional guarantee to Russia that the old ruling classes would not return.

Britain could also guarantee to the Soviet Union that she would not enter into any coalition against Russia whatever the circumstances. This was of vital importance for the Labour party since: "nothing would be more likely to contribute to a Labour defeat at the next General Election than the realization by the voters of this country that a Socialist Government could find no basis of common interest with the Government of Russia." Laski realized that these proposals assumed, as a matter of course, that Russia was peaceful and even potentially friendly: "I am rejecting out of hand any view of Russian policy which attributes to it an expansionist character, whether on strategic or economic grounds. I am assuming that Russia neither wants war nor is in a position to wage it on a global scale."[23] Laski was not, then, a supporter of the neutral third force concept at all; he favored a closer association with the Soviet Union along the lines suggested by G. D. H. Cole and other extreme members of the Left Wing.

To sum up briefly, the Marshall aid proposal very nearly converted the Left Wing to opposition to Russia, but the effect of this was speedily lost when the economic crisis began. From that point, there were three schools of thought within the Left Wing about American assistance, each based on a somewhat different view of the intentions of the U.S.S.R. One group, led by part of the *Tribune* staff, saw no real alternative to American aid, but urged that caution be exercised, and closer relations with the Commonwealth and western Europe be cultivated at the same time. This group tended to accept the British Government's view that Russia was hostile, un-co-operative, and unlikely to enter into close relations with Britain.

The second view, typified by *Reynolds News* and the *New Statesman* was characterized by a willingness to accept American aid, but without assuming Soviet aggressiveness, and without choosing sides in a definite manner in the East-West conflict. This group vacillated somewhat between a position near that taken by the Government to a position very close to that of the fellow-travelers. The third attitude, which favored "tightening the belt" and refusing aid, and at the same time extending relations with Russia and Eastern Europe, is more extreme and was held chiefly by independents like G. D. H. Cole and Harold Laski. They felt that if there were world tensions it was the fault of the United States and not the Soviet Union, and they believed that if Britain was in danger, the danger came from the West rather than from the East. These three groups may also be considered as the three levels of ideological influence within the Left Wing.

VIII

CRISIS IN GERMANY

By the beginning of 1948, the western powers were no longer awaiting Soviet agreement on the unsettled problems before them; they were actively engaged in the search for solutions which could be found within the limits of their own authority. Chief among these problems was the question of Germany's future. At the very least, Germany was a serious economic liability to the occupation. It was neither likely nor desirable that Germany would remain a political vacuum for an indefinite period of time. Germany needed her own government and a viable economy, and Soviet Russia could hardly be expected to give her blessing to either goal. The failure of the December, 1947, Conference of Foreign Ministers was only the overt expression of western determination to proceed unilaterally in Germany. The actions that followed led to increased tension between Russia and the western nations, and produced, among other effects, the Berlin Blockade which can be considered a turning point in the development of western hostility toward Russia.

In Britain, the new attitude toward Russia was shared fully by the Labour Government. Plans for utilization of Marshall aid were being worked out rapidly. The Labour party tightened party discipline, particularly toward the fellow travelers and other pro-Soviet elements in the movement. Already, the British Government was thinking in terms of large scale regional alliances, for Ernest Bevin made his famous "Western Union" proposal in the House of Commons in late January of 1948,[1] and the wider conception of an Atlantic Union seems already to have occurred to Britain. By May, 1948, this proposal had been broached informally to the American Government.[2]

Left Wing opposition to the British Government remained though the fellow travelers were perhaps most openly hostile to the Government's foreign policy during the early part of 1948. Most of the Left Wing had come to accept the need for Marshall aid by the beginning of 1948, although they were usually careful to add that the funds be used to aid the growth of European socialism.

In a similar fashion, the suggested "Western Union" was eagerly seized upon by the Left Wing and swiftly converted into a "Socialist Western Union" which in fact seems little different from the concept of a socialist "third force" which the Left Wing developed during the spring and summer of 1947. The Soviet coup in Prague excited some criticism by the group of Left Wing spokesmen associated with *Tribune,* though other elements of the Left Wing managed to take the event in stride. In fact, a state of uneasy truce prevailed between the Left Wing and the Government during the first months of 1948. It was clear, I think, that the Left Wing had not really changed its fundamental position and was extremely apprehensive of the formation of a German Government, but it remained silent until open Soviet hostility appeared in the Berlin Blockade.

Thus the two-day foreign affairs debate that took place late in January, 1948, following Bevin's "Western Union" speech, was rather desultory. Bevin had made a massive survey of the problems facing the government, in which he clearly denounced the policy of the Soviet Union, particularly in the countries of Eastern Europe, and pointed out that the Marshall proposal had ". . . brought out what must have been there before." Britain had agreed to friendly nations on the Soviet borders, but this did not mean a Soviet-dominated bloc in the region. He flatly accused the Soviets of attempting to sabotage the Marshall plan, and, in reply to an interjection, stated that the Government had known well in advance where and when the difficulties in France and Italy were to arise. The London Conference of Foreign Ministers had been necessary, he said, as one final attempt at co-operation and this had failed. In reference to Germany, Bevin pointed out that the drain on the British treasury was unbearable; he left the distinct impression that Britain was now prepared to discuss a German Government for the western areas, though he said nothing explicitly about this.

The debate that followed produced less criticism than had been heard from the Left Wing on any given occasion since the end of the war. There was widespread support for the "Western Union" concept, and an almost complete absence of an agreed definition of the term; indeed, Bevin himself had been less than clear about its meaning. The fellow travelers, led by Konni Zilliacus, still maintained their original view that Britain must renounce the use of force and not hope for too much from the American aid program, but most of the Left Wing ignored this issue. The Third Force concept was kept alive by Richard Crossman, but not pressed very strongly.

Though Bevin's speech had, on the whole, been well received

in the House of Commons, and elicited considerable praise in the moderate press, the Left Wing press remained critical, or even hostile; on this occasion the impetus came primarily from the fellow travelers. Thus the editor of *Reynolds News* refused to concur in Bevin's estimate of past Soviet behavior, for where Bevin saw a "lust for domination," the editor saw only an "excessive suspicion and overwhelming fear of war." Bevin was placing far too much confidence in the benefits to be derived from association with American capitalism, and did not sufficiently emphasize the danger that British socialism would be inhibited thereby.[3] The *New Statesman* concentrated on the implied proposal to form a German government and opposed it bitterly.[4] Pacifist Emrys Hughes attacked Bevin's speech vigorously, on the grounds that western policy was as much responsible for world tensions as Soviet aggressiveness, and he cited American possession of atomic weapons, and American fleet exercises in the Pacific as justification for Soviet suspicions.[5] Professor Laski likewise continued to pursue his own critical line, refusing to admit that Russia was expansive, and pointing out that the Truman Doctrine was "very nearly, if not actually, a deliberate threat to Russia." He was "not ready to believe in Russian imperialism thus far. American imperialism could be proven just as easily."[6] Thus, despite the apparent concord, or at least outward acquiescence of the parliamentary Left Wing, the Left Wing attitude toward great power relations seems to have changed very little. Ammunition with which to rebut Bevin's charges was lacking, but the will quite evidently persisted.

The proposal for a "Western Union" was, on the other hand, very well received by the Left Wing, and freely debated in the weeks that followed Bevin's speech. It was of course taken for granted that any such union would be socialist, and the possibilities inherent in the proposal were intriguing for Left Wing spokesmen, since the proposal opened the door for a return to the demand for a "socialist" policy which they had been voicing since World War II ended. When Winston Churchill proposed a Congress at the Hague to discuss the possibilities of Western Union, a note of partisan politics was also injected into the discussion, and the Left Wing made it plain that there was a definite distinction between *their* version of Western Union and that of Winston Churchill. As a result, the British Government was urged to proceed with haste toward Western Union on socialist lines. But in the final analysis, neither the Labour party nor Winston Churchill were terribly enamoured with the notion of uniting Britain too closely with the Continent, and British reluctance became the most important barrier in the way of Western Union under both the socialists and the Conservatives.

The reaction of the Left Wing to the coup d'état at Prague offers striking evidence of the degree to which their attitude toward the "social revolution" in Europe had remained constant through the vicissitudes of great power relations. The harsh clang of the iron curtain on the western borders of Czechoslovakia was heard with almost casual indifference, as though this were an event long expected and in no way an occasion for surprise. Events were variously described as a "second revolution," a "finalization of the partition of Europe agreed at the Yalta Conference," a "bloodless revolution" supported by the "overwhelming mass" of the Czech people, and a "repudiation of western democracy" by the Czechs, who had deliberately adopted the Communist road.[7] Repeated warnings were published in the Left Wing press against "giving way to hysteria" or against comparing the change in government to the rape of Czechoslovakia by Hitler and his minions. Russian interference in the process was specifically and emphatically denied.[8] While everyone agreed that certain "traditional middle class freedoms" had been lost, much more was to be gained under the new regime.[9] Even the death of Jan Masaryk, which might have been expected to change the tenor of Left Wing comment, had little effect. Thus, Professor Laski offered this explanation:

> He would never have died if Mr. Neville Chamberlain had not thrown Czechoslovakia to Hitler. . . He would not have died either if it had been possible to make Mr. Churchill understand how urgent it was to make genuine friendship with Soviet Russia an essential element in giving reality to victory over Nazism, instead of thinking of our alliance with Russia as a temporary partnership. . . He would not have died if America had grasped the vital fact that to convince Soviet Russia that its fears were groundless was the indispensable condition of enduring peace. . .[10]

He also might not have died, even after all of these events, if the Soviet Union had not made an iron-bound satellite of his country, but Professor Laski does not say this. In brief, the coup was simply accepted as another facet of the social revolution in Europe, and the cost was balanced against ideologically computed gains, to the detriment of those human values which western civilization has come to prize.

For all the interest created by Western Union, and the momentary interest in the Czechoslovakian coup, the central issue of the period remained the problem of Germany. Since 1945, little progress had been made toward economic revival or political self-government, partly for lack of preparation, but more important still, for lack of great power agreement. The Yalta decisions, though fundamental, had provided little more than general guide lines which certainly did not anticipate the situation that actually developed. The total collapse of the German Government after surrender, and the pressing demand for food, fuel, housing, and raw materials left neither time nor money nor manpower to work out the detailed policy for the future that was needed. The Potsdam Conference, ostensibly called to make such decisions, had in fact been unable to do more than make the one fundamental, and perhaps fatal decision—that each zone commander would be supreme in his own area. Perhaps it was impossible to have things otherwise. But this decision made four-power control impossible without unanimity, and practice demonstrated that there were few questions on which unanimity could be reached.

The purposes of the occupation were admirable. Germany would be completely disarmed, de-Nazified, re-educated; war criminals would be tried, the judiciary would be reformed, the government would be decentralized, and the nation would be democratized. In principle, it was agreed at Potsdam that Germany would be treated as a single economic unit; in practice, the zones were virtually airtight, though osmosis from West to East was possible until it was stopped in 1946. Total reparations payments were not fixed, but it was agreed that Russia would get a portion of the dismantled capital in the western zones, and would satisfy Poland's demands from her own share.

Until September, 1945, the Allied Control Council was optimistic in its approach to the German settlement. Two key problems, the need for central administrative agencies, and a decision on the "level of industry" to be permitted Germany, were tackled immediately. The first problem was left unsolved, mainly because of the opposition, or in effect the veto, of the French representative on the Control Council. The level of industry was finally settled at a base of seven and one-half million tons of steel production per year, after proposals ranging from nine million tons (British) through three and one-half million tons (United States State Department) had been discussed. On a third problem, the need to treat Germany as a single economic unit, no progress was made at all. This caused endless difficulty. The western powers occupied that part of Germany which had traditionally depended upon the eastern half for a portion of its food supply. Moreover, West Germany needed to import raw materials before its industrial capacity could be used. The influx of refugees, expelled from Poland and other areas of eastern Europe, or fled from

Soviet controlled East Germany, aggravated the problem. The British, French, and Americans found themselves paying an enormous food bill, while war damage and lack of raw materials prevented the manufacture of sufficient goods to offset the cost of food imports.

By the spring of 1946, the western nations were weary of this endless drain on their resources, and Secretary of State Byrnes proposed, during the Paris Conference, that the zones be fused. Only Britain accepted, and an economic merger of the British and American occupation zones took place at that time. In the Control Council, the friendly atmosphere of 1945 was now dissipated, and recriminations followed the merger, together with minor annoyances like seizure of locomotives, shooting raids across the zone borders, and political arrests. High-level efforts to arrange a solution to the problem of economic unification failed, and, in January of 1948, the British, French, and Americans began discussion of a possible West German state, which the French feared and disliked, but accepted, one suspects, because they had been told that Britain and the United States would in any event proceed. Talks began in London late in February, 1948, and the Benelux nations joined the discussions soon afterward. On March 7, 1948, a communiqué was issued which favored the establishment of a Federal Government for Western Germany.

The Soviet response was immediate and sharp. On March 20, the Soviet Commander protested these unilateral decisions, and walked out of the Council when his protests were turned down by a majority vote. The following day, he informed his colleagues that new and more stringent regulations would now be applied to all traffic bound for Berlin. All rail traffic ceased temporarily, and air transport was pressed into emergency service. On April 5, a serious accident occurred, involving a British passenger aircraft and a Soviet fighter plane which collided near Gatow Airfield in Berlin. Tension ran high for several days, and the British Government firmly stated its intention to remain in Berlin.[11] The crisis passed, however, bringing temporary relaxation.

A Six-Power Conference met in London from April 20 to June 1 to discuss the proposed West German Government. It agreed to call a Constituent Assembly in the western zones, and allow the German people to form a national political organization. On June 18, 1948, the western powers introduced a new currency into their zones of Germany. The Soviet Commander refused to allow this currency to circulate in his zone, and once again tightened his control over Berlin. All road traffic to the city was halted and rail traffic ceased, ostensibly because of "technical difficulties." Despite Soviet warnings, the western currency was then introduced into the western-controlled areas of Berlin and the full blockade followed swiftly thereafter. On June 24, 1948, the last transport line between Berlin and West Germany was cut and the Blockade began. The western airlift began the following day, though on a small scale.

The impact of the Berlin Blockade on Left Wing opinion in Britain was enormous, as it was throughout the world. It had the same effect, much magnified, as the economic crisis of August, 1947. Prior to the Blockade, criticism of the British Government was at a minimum. All of this agreement was swept into the discard and the Left Wing once again turned full circle. Since the contrast is so great, a quick survey of the trend of opinion during the 1948 Labour party Conference may serve as a focal point for discussing the changes which later ensued.

The Conference met under the most favorable of auspices. The American Congress had just passed the Foreign Assistance Act money bill, and aid was now assured. Further, even the most assiduous of Left Wing critics could find little in the Act to support the view that this was another phase of American imperialism, heavily laden with political "strings." True, the recent preliminary crisis in Berlin still caused concern, and the well-remembered economic crisis remained in the background. But the general attitude of the conference was sanguine; Britain was going ahead and the future looked more hopeful, if not particularly secure.

This changed attitude is reflected in the marked decrease in concern with foreign relations, and the more conciliatory tone of the resolutions submitted to the conference. The opening address, for the first time since 1945, contained not one reference to the conduct of foreign affairs. An early attack on Bevin by fellow traveler Konni Zilliacus was beaten down very easily. The National Executive Committee's sharp criticism of the Czechoslovakian coup was approved with little dissension. The disciplinary action taken against fellow traveler John Platts-Mills for his part in the "Nenni Telegram," a cable of endorsement signed by a number of Labour M.P.'s and sent to the pro-communist portion of the Italian Socialist party, in which there was evidence of misuse of some of the names, was likewise endorsed, though more than one million votes were polled against the action.

In a more positive sense, a lengthy and interesting discussion took place on Western Union, in which the Labour party, as might be expected, took sharp issue with Winston Churchill's concept of a United Europe, and discussed alternate means of promoting a socialist Western Union. A few members of the Left Wing, including Fenner Brockway, spoke in favor of the Third Force ver-

sion of Western Union, but there was no real issue involved, since
the official Labour party view differed little from that of the Left
Wing. As Hugh Dalton put it:

> In my opinion, speaking also for my colleagues on the
> Executive, we are quite confident that any scheme for a
> United States of Europe, however defined, is going to de-
> pend upon the success of those Democratic Socialist
> parties in each of these countries taken separately and in
> all of these countries taken together. If we could assure
> an equal strength for our Socialist comrades in all these
> countries as we command here, then indeed it would not
> be difficult to make a triumphant success of a United
> States of Western Europe. [12]

But if "reactionaries" were in power throughout Europe, then
Britain would certainly look twice before she committed herself
to any close association with Western Union. There was some
measure of discord when R. W. G. Mackay asked the delegates to
stop talking idly of a socialist Europe when socialist strength in
European parliaments was declining rapidly, and he asked for due
toleration for non-socialists. A Labour party Conference, however, is a poor place to ask for tolerance of non-socialists, and
Mackay was hooted down and referred to in rather angry tones
through the remainder of the Conference.

The tone of the foreign affairs debate was equally amicable.
The National Union of Mineworkers moved a resolution asserting
the "loyal support" of the conference for the Government's foreign
policy, welcoming Marshall Aid, and expressing the hope that
speedy rehabilitation of the European economy would follow soon.
The mover, Will Lawther, made it clear that the unions did not
take kindly to "blacklegging" by the Left Wing and urged resolute
support for his old comrade Ernest Bevin. Only the fellow travelers and a handful of diehard Left Wing spokesmen continued to
oppose the Government. Konni Zilliacus moved a long resolution
containing the usual demand for an end to staff talks with the
United States, lower service estimates, withdrawal of British
forces from Greece, full partnership with the Soviet Union in exploitation of oil resources in the Middle East, nationalization of
the basic German industries, full trade relations with Eastern
Europe, and closer co-operation with European "workers" whatever their party association. His amendment was defeated by
more than four million votes, and subsequent speakers were in
most cases careful to point out that they were in no way sympathetic with Zilliacus's position. Even the more prominent pacifists,

Rhys Davies and Victor Yates, refused to follow Zilliacus on this occasion.

Thus the Conference ended, for the first time in the postwar period, with only the fellow travelers in forthright vocal opposition to the Government's foreign policy. From the remainder of the Left Wing there was either conditional support, or at least tacit acquiescence to the Government's policy. The key questions of military alliances, defense spending, and German re-armament remained, but for the moment there was peace in the Labour movement.

This happy condition was not destined to last. The Labour party Conference adjourned on May 21, 1948; within six weeks, the outward unity was shattered, and the Left Wing was again in full cry against its own Government. The palpable cause of this reversal was the Berlin Blockade. But it seems more reasonable that the Blockade, coming at the end of a long sequence of hostile Soviet moves, would stimulate national feeling sufficiently to consolidate the Labour party rather than press it apart. Going beyond the surface appearance of the issue, one can speculate on the effect that the potential military consequences the Blockade presented might have had on the Left Wing. Historically, the Left Wing record shows a consistent tendency to revert toward pacifistic socialism at the first sign of international crisis, as in 1914, in 1935, and again in 1939. The Berlin Blockade was the first occasion after 1945 in which the possibility of military action was plainly to be seen, and serious consideration was given, at one stage in the blockade, to a plan for pushing a land force across the territory that separated Berlin from West Germany. Though argument by analogy is not fundamentally sound, this aspect of the Left Wing reaction to the crisis should not be ignored.

When the initial crisis arose over Berlin early in April, 1948, only the *New Statesman* had commented in any great detail on its implications, and these comments are singularly instructive in view of subsequent developments. The tone of the commentary was defeatist: it would be impossible for the western powers to remain in Berlin if the Russians took away the transport facilities, and evacuation was taken for granted.[13] Perhaps even more important, the Soviet argument, that the western powers were in Berlin on suffrance, and not as a matter of right, was accepted explicitly, for the *New Statesman* spoke of the limited facilities "so far conceded" by the Soviets. Once the crisis passed, the question dropped out of the *New Statesman's* pages until June.

In the reaction to the Blockade proper, beginning on the 25th of June, a careful distinction must be made between the small group of Left Wing spokesmen associated with *Tribune* and the remainder of the Left Wing. *Tribune* supported the Government consistently throughout the crisis, and refused to accept the Soviet claim to legal control of entry and egress from Berlin. In the early stages of the Blockade, *Tribune* was rather pessimistic about the ability of the western powers to maintain their hold in Berlin, though this is not surprising, for many British—and American—people felt precisely the same way. Through the middle of July, *Tribune* tended to mock the "bravado" of the airlift, but, once it was clear that the lift was succeeding, it came down firmly behind the allies and remained a staunch supporter. By September, *Tribune* was urging the Government to remain in Berlin "at any cost," and even contemplated the possibility of an armed effort to make contact with the beleaguered city without flinching. For practical purposes, if we include both Labour and Conservative opinion, *Tribune* can be taken as a typical example of the general trend of opinion in Britain as the blockade developed.

On the remainder of the Left Wing, however, the general response was a wave of near hysteria, followed by a sharp revulsion against militarism and armaments. The Blockade had the effect of placing the pacifists in the vanguard of the Left Wing once again, together with the fellow travelers. Thus a situation emerged in 1948 which bore remarkable resemblance to the condition of the Labour movement at the beginning of the 1930's. The alignments which had emerged since 1945 were dissolved and the new alignments were more along the lines of the pre-1939 Left Wing. The "Keep Left" group, for example, dissolved completely and a new group did not emerge until 1949, this time with quite a different composition.

The chief point in the Left Wing argument against the Government's foreign policy became opposition to armaments. This line was supported by the pacifists and the fellow travelers for obvious reasons. In other cases, fear of the potential effect of armaments on the social services undoubtedly played a vital part in the opinion-forming process. Beyond this point, precision is more difficult to achieve though there undoubtedly were traditions and other complex causes which entered into the making of opinion. The point which is of prime importance here is that the Left Wing divided, at this point in time, into those who supported the Government, or more accurately those who continued to support the Government, and those who opposed the Government, or who once again began to vocalize their opposition. It might also be said that the leadership of the British Left Wing changed hands, though one can never be certain of this, and the Left Wing once again came under the direction of its traditional elements, pacifists and fellow travelers and other extremists.

The Left Wing justified its opposition to the Government and to armaments either by avoiding the Berlin issue completely, or by a reinterpretation of agreed data which produced a new evaluation of the crisis. The responsibility for the Blockade was either placed at the door of the western powers, or in some few cases shared between the West and the Soviet Union with the former bearing the lion's share of the burden.[14] The chief justification for this division of responsibility was the alleged failure of the western powers to carry out the social and economic reforms which Germany so badly needed.[15] In one extreme case, it appeared that the western powers were attempting to drive the Soviet Union out of Berlin and not vice versa, for a writer in *Forward* asserted that this attempt might lead to full scale warfare in Europe.[16] Other spokesmen pointed to the presence of American bombers in England as proof that the Soviet Union was being forced to negotiate under duress. In almost every case, it was taken for granted that the western powers had no *right* to remain in Berlin and a speedy withdrawal was assumed. In fact most Left Wing spokesmen suggested that Britain and the western powers withdraw to Frankfort where they could begin socialization of the German economy. Once this was accomplished, negotiations with Russia would prove fruitful.

The airlift, when it began, was dismissed as a "short-term summer expedient" which was bound to fail as soon as bad weather appeared, if not much sooner. The following is typical of the Left Wing view of the airlift: "But every expert knows that aircraft, despite their immense psychological effect, cannot be relied upon to provide the Berliners in the Winter months, let alone provide them with fuel. If the blockade continued, therefore, or if the blockade were now lifted but reimposed next Winter, we should be compelled to retreat from Berlin, or re-open communications with it by force."[17] This latter possibility rendered the writer nearly speechless with apprehension, and he urged that "any offer" which the Soviets were willing to make should be accepted immediately. Yet, when it was clear that the airlift was in fact successful, the whole subject dropped out of the Left Wing press completely.

Two of the best examples of the reaction engendered by the Berlin Blockade are a manifesto entitled "Stop the Coming War," issued by a small group of Labour M.P.'s at the height of the crisis and an "Open Letter" to Foreign Secretary Ernest Bevin, signed by forty-five Labour M.P.'s, which was produced late in July, 1948. Both contain a combination of pacifist ideals and fellow traveler inspried principles which are typical of the influences dominant at this time in Left Wing circles.

The "Stop the Coming War" manifesto was inspired by Sydney

Silverman and William Warbey, both of whom were prominent fellow travelers. It was signed by thirteen other M.P.'s, all recognized members of the Left Wing, but none of whom was a prominent pacifist, or fellow traveler. Yet the manifesto was a frank appeal to pacifist sentiment, and relied heavily upon principles associated with the fellow travelers after 1945. The manifesto in fact reads very much like the resolution moved by Konni Zilliacus at the 1948 Labour party Conference.

The manifesto attracted attention by its heavy, black, scarehead warning of the dangers of atomic warfare, particularly to Great Britain. The opening paragraphs were a frank appeal to pacifist sentiment, or fear of atomic attack. The writers went on to urge the need for an independent socialist United States of Europe, and suggested that Britain use Marshall aid to make herself independent of the United States as speedily as possible, and then go on to create this socialist bloc. This bloc would then be complementary to the Soviet bloc in Eastern Europe, and negotiations should immediately be opened with them in search of a peaceful settlement. The specific demands made on British foreign policy will be familiar to the reader: Britain must end staff talks with the United States immediately; American troops should not be allowed to use bases in Britain—a reference to the American bombers sent to Britain during the Berlin crisis; Britain must stay clear of any alliance with the United States aimed at the Soviet Union; there must be no more interference with the social revolutions in Eastern Europe—Britain should adopt a more "tolerant" attitude toward these regimes and not try to dictate their affairs. The influence of the fellow travelers is fairly obvious.

The concluding portion of the manifesto was devoted to a series of criticisms of the United States. This capitalist nation, it claimed, was faced with a situation in which she must either export her surplus or face economic collapse. This accounted for the Marshall offer. Britain was therefore in a strong position to resist American pressure to join in the "witch hunt" against communism. An ideological struggle was taking place in which communism would only be beaten by an ideology offering a better way of life, i.e., British democratic socialism. Once again, the manifesto had little to offer that was new; these proposals were a commonplace in Left Wing criticisms of the Government prior to the Berlin Blockade.

The open letter to Ernest Bevin poses a similar problem, in that the fundamental thesis of the letter is pacifistic, but the list of signatories appended to the letter contains only a few pacifists.[18] Again, the initial approach is a rather morbid reference to the horrors of war, and the belief that the world was at that moment trembling on the brink of an appalling catastrophe. The letter urged the British Government to make a "bold effort" to avert this disaster and restore good feeling among the Great Powers. This "bold effort" should include: immediate action to ensure a fresh discussion of world problems by the Great Powers, e.g., a meeting of the "Big Four"; British initiation of disarmament proposals immediately, without waiting for the outcome of the meeting; unilateral repudiation by Britain of all atomic weapons, followed by the destruction of all existing stocks and the plants necessary to produce them; *after* stocks and plants were destroyed, a proposal for systematic international inspection of atomic plants and international control of all atomic materials. The last is, of course, identical with the proposal made by the Soviet Union at the meetings of the United Nations Atomic Energy Commission. The letter offered support for the "Western Union" concept, but only if the union was socialist, and then only in economic and social matters. The writers realized the risks which Britain would undertake by following such a policy, but, "Whatever the risks involved in the pursuit of this policy, they are less than those inherent in power politics, with their menace of European annihilation." Again, the letter puts forward what are essentially the same proposals, and the same arguments, that were commonplace on the Left Wing in the 1930's. Both the letter and the manifesto are in fact a curious re-statement of the traditional policies of the British Left Wing.

The Left Wing, then, responded to the Berlin Blockade by a sharp reversion to the pacifistic traditions of the 1930's with the exception, of course, of the small group associated with *Tribune* at that time. The British Government, for its part, made a quick re-assessment of its military capabilities, and began to move toward an Atlantic alliance system, formalized the following year in the North Atlantic Treaty.[19] "Negotiation from strength" became a stock phrase on both Government and Opposition front benches, though the concept was not accepted by the Left Wing. In September, 1948, the British Government halted its demobilization of wartime forces, and shortly thereafter moved to increase the period of service for conscripts from twelve months back to its original proposal of eighteen months. If we date the beginning of the "cold war" to the Berlin Blockade, as seems reasonable, the British Government's chief problem is easily seen as providing for its own defense, as it must do, and in the meanwhile avoiding if possible an excessive armaments burden on the badly shaken economy. The solution, as Ernest Bevin stated to Parliament, was a large defensive alliance: "Once we can, in the West, get this basis of collective security, with the United States and

Canada and the Western Powers, and others if they will come in, it should be possible to work out a rationalized system of defense so that we can ensure our collective security while we shall not be drawing off too much manpower. . ."[20] This basic policy had a number of repercussions on the Left Wing.

In the first place, Bevin's policy statements were assumed, and probably correctly, to mean that Western Union had changed meaning for the British Government. So long as Western Union was synonymous with a "socialist" union of western Europe, it was supported by the Left Wing; given a concept of Western Union as a military alliance, the Left Wing immediately shifted ground and began to question its feasibility. In this, the Left Wing was consistent, for it had opposed military alliances well before the Berlin Blockade arose, arguing that, ". . . the job of democracy in Western Europe is not to organize armed forces sufficient to defeat Russia but to construct a Western Union whose social system makes Communism unnecessary and refutes the prophecies of the Kremlin sages."[21] The Berlin Blockade had the effect of seriously inhibiting Left Wing support for Western Union. [22]

A second effect of the Blockade on Left Wing thought was to arouse strong antagonism against the proposed German Government. Speculation began about the revival of German militarism and this was used later as a convenient device for attacking German economic recovery after Germany again began to compete with Britain for overseas markets. These problems, however, arose in 1949 and 1950. In 1948, the Left Wing was still thinking in terms of a socialized Germany in which the trade union movement would play an important part, and the more immediate effect of the Blockade was to impart greater urgency to the demand for socialization.

Far and away the most important effect of the Berlin Blockade, however, was the impetus given to antimilitaristic sentiment on the Left Wing. The sentiment was not new, of course, nor had it died out in postwar years, for Left Wing opposition to the size of British arms estimates put forward in March of 1948 was quite strong. But that particular effort to reduce the military estimates had been led and supported primarily by the pacifists, together with a few fellow travelers. After the Berlin Blockade, the main body of the Left Wing, excepting only the relatively small *Tribune* group, fell back upon antimilitaristic sentiment as their main line of attack on the Government. *Tribune* had supported the demand for a reduction of military estimates in March, 1948, along with the remainder of the Left Wing press, and those associated with *Tribune* had been instrumental in the reduction of the length of service for conscripts from eighteen to twelve months. But the

Berlin Blockade brought about a reappraisal of Britain's military requirements, and a different policy line.

When the British Government announced the end of demobilization, *Tribune* was not hostile, though it did note that Britain did not have the manpower supply that would enable it to maintain a very large military force. When it was clear that the Government planned to divert a portion of its resources to military supplies, *Tribune* again agreed that this was necessary, though once again it cautioned against excess. In brief, the need to rearm was faced without flinching, the hostility of the Soviets was taken for granted, and the notion of a neutral Third Force was abandoned.[23]

But the remainder of the Left Wing did nothing of the sort. They emphasized, with increasing frequency, the growing danger of war and pointed out that armaments "always" led to war—an historical cant that was very popular in the Labour movement. The need for additional armaments was firmly denied, usually by denying that Russia had been in any way aggressive after 1945. If the need for arms was ignored, as frequently happened, the argument simply stated that Britain could not afford them, and great stress was placed upon the danger that an arms program might pose for the British economy, and even more frequently, for the British social service program. Against this trend, the argument most commonly met is that British socialism, suitably supported by socialists elsewhere, was a much better guarantee of peace than military forces, or American aggressiveness. It was commonly believed, particularly by those who relied heavily upon the theory of economic determinism, that the United States was drifting toward an imperialist stage in her development. The dangers of the "coming slump" in the United States were very consistently underlined, and it was taken for granted in some quarters that the instability of the American economy was in fact responsible for the aid program. The pacifists, of course, went one step further, and opposed all arms and all military spending upon principle; armaments, they argued, depleted the economy, lowered the standard of living, and did not make anyone more secure. Wars, they said, had never settled anything—a dictum that deserves a bit more examination, since wars have settled a great many things.

The bifurcation in the Left Wing press had its parallel in the House of Commons, where some spokesmen from the Left changed their position and began supporting the government, while others maintained their original views. The group of M.P.'s who produced *Keep Left* was broken up in 1948, and the new group that began to meet in 1949 was differently composed. Michael Foot, Geoffrey Bing, Fred Lee, Benn Levy, Ronald Mackay, J. P. W. Mallalieu, Ernest Millington, and Woodrow Wyatt, the hard core of the *Keep Left* group, were excluded when the new group was formed that later produced *Keeping Left*.[24]

In two major debates in the House of Commons that took place in the last six months of 1948, the division of the Left Wing ran between those who continued to maintain the position they had adopted in 1945, and those who found that changing circumstances demanded a change in policy.[25] The latter group was much the smaller of the two. The former included the pacifists, the fellow travelers, and a substantial number of Labour—and Liberal— M.P.'s.

IX

THE PROBLEM OF SECURITY

The course of public opinion, whether of the Left Wing or of some other body of persons, does not appear to move in a smooth curve. Rather, it seems to move in a series of sharp, rapid fluctuations much like an oscillograph of a very brief electrical pulse, rising very rapidly in values to peak strength, then "damping" more slowly back to its normal level. The stimulus that gives rise to this response seems always to come from without the opinion body; self-stimulation of the Left Wing, for example, occurs very rarely. In most instances, the stimulus is easily identified. Spurts of Left Wing opposition to armaments, for example, date to the spring of 1946, when they stemmed primarily from the Persian crisis; to the economic crisis of 1947; to the Berlin crisis, and, as we shall see in the later parts of this chapter, to the Korean War. Briefly, each international crisis of any proportions led to a demand for less military spending.

The Berlin crisis of 1948 in a sense set the international stage for some years to come; the Korean War of 1950 provided the necessary impetus to fill the stage with characters and action. The Berlin crisis produced the North Atlantic Treaty; the Korean crisis transposed the mechanism from paper plans into some semblance of real military force. The Berlin crisis assured the emergence of a German state; the Korean War led to German rearmament. Both events are part of the general pattern of action followed by the western powers as they sought suitable interpretations of the meaning of Soviet actions, and policies that would meet the challenge posed by these interpretations. When all was said and done, much remained that was pure speculation, and the Left Wing capitalized upon this element of the western position in much of its propaganda.

The Left Wing had received the Brussels Treaty of 1948 with complete equanimity, mainly, it seems, because the treaty was not primarily a military alliance but an economic and cultural arrangement, and quite innocuous. But the North Atlantic Treaty which Britain signed in the spring of 1949 was first and foremost a military alliance, clearly aimed against Soviet expansion, and only secondarily if at all concerned with non-military matters. The Left Wing responded to the Treaty as it had responded to the Berlin crisis. *Tribune* alone of the Left Wing press conceded that the pact was necessary, ruled out neutrality and a possible alliance with the Soviet Union, and supported the British Government's position on the pact, though it remained acutely conscious of the economic dangers involved. *Tribune* at this time believed that it was possible to maintain a defense system, with the necessary men and materials, without ruining the European economy, but it cautioned against complacency. This attitude caused a split in the editorial board of the newspaper when the treaty was signed, for Ian Mikardo felt that it was not compatible with the Anglo-Soviet Treaty of 1942, and resigned when the board refused to adopt his position. On May 20, *Tribune* published full explanations by both sides which show clearly the difference of approach.

Mikardo argued that the first task of the British Government must be the prevention of a Third World War which would lead to the total destruction of Britain. Since only the United States or the Soviet Union could begin a conflict on this scale, the Third Force position was ideal for Britain, since this would leave her free to work for peace, and not bound to the views of one side or the other. Mikardo believed that the *Tribune* editorial board had abandoned the Third Force position too quickly, and joined the Government in its demand that Russia evacuate areas which were part of her vital interests. The Russians realized that evacuation by them would leave these areas open to American economic penetration, and refused to do so. Michael Foot, speaking for the remainder of the editorial board, countered by stressing the fact that no British or American political leader had accepted the inevitability of war, and that American policy had assisted and not hindered the economic recovery of Europe. Foot believed that Mikardo was disregarding the events of the postwar period, and his opinions were thereby rendered unsound.

It must be said immediately that Mikardo's viewpoint commanded far more Left Wing support than did that of the *Tribune* editorial board. The distinction between offensive and defensive alliances was swept aside as mere window dressing. The pacifists assumed that Russia would construe the pact as a direct threat to its security, and might even take the pact as justification for an attack.[1] There were more mutterings about the "high price of security," and fear of the economic consequences of rearmament which the pact clearly presaged, was widespread. The justification of the Treaty was attacked along familiar lines: "The military case for the Atlantic Pact is that the West is exposed to the threat of armed Soviet invasion. There is absolutely no evidence that Moscow intends such a step."[2] Moreover, even if this assumption were true, defense of western Europe would not be possible unless very large contingents of American troops were stationed on the Continent and this was politically impossible. The United States, for its part, was depending upon its long-range bombers, and this amounted to suicide for Europeans. The pact could be used to suppress "popular revolutions" just as easily as it could be used to oppose Soviet expansion, and this would have disastrous consequences for Europe. The pact went far beyond the "regional arrangements" clause of the United Nations Charter, and was technically not legal. The pact was an expression of American pressure for a formally united "anti-communist nations" bloc, and this would make war inevitable. The American Government had been driven to the pact because she must rearm or go through a major slump. Finally, the German crisis was brought into the picture, and it was argued that the pact made it necessary to reconstitute German military power, a spectre that had long haunted the Left Wing. Most of these opinions appeared in the Left Wing press, chiefly in the leading articles in the *New Statesman*, which was violently opposed to the North Atlantic Treaty.[3]

When the treaty came before the House of Commons, however, the chief opposition came from the pacifists, who argued that the pact would certainly lead to a war in which Britain would be destroyed, and from the fellow travelers, who were unwilling to accept the basic premise of the pact, Soviet aggressiveness. The treaty was actually approved by 333 votes to 6, with a substantial portion of the Left Wing abstaining.[4] The argument of the fellow travelers, as set forth in Parliament by William Warbey, is interesting. The Soviet Union, he claimed, had tried very hard to prevent the division of Europe, but failed. If the western powers would only try once again to find a four-power basis for agreement in Germany, there would be no need for the Atlantic Pact, and the possibility of war would be reduced. This would be particularly beneficial to Britain, since she would be only a very junior partner in an alliance with the United States, and the expenditure required to maintain the military commitments required by the pact would ruin the British economy. This in turn would lead to the ruin of the social system in Britain and the rebirth of capitalism. The similarity of the arguments employed by Warbey and of the views put forward by the pacifists is quite clear. This becomes one of the characteristic features of Left Wing propaganda after 1949 as pacifist sentiment becomes increasingly important on the Left Wing.

Labour interest in the Atlantic Pact, and in the whole course of international affairs, declined substantially in the later portion of 1949 as the forthcoming General Election began to assume increasing importance. When the Labour party met in Blackpool in June, interest in foreign affairs reached its postwar nadir. About 10 per cent of the resolutions on the Conference Agenda dealt with international affairs, though in fact most of the conference time was devoted to the discussion of the manifesto prepared by the party for use at the coming election.[5] Pacifist Rhys Davies, supported by Richard Crossman, attempted an attack on the Government's rearmament policy, but the question was brushed aside by an uninterested conference. This was not the place to begin criticizing the policy of a Government about to go to the polls. Further, the status of international affairs at that time was conducive to this attitude; most of the issues at hand were technical, little understood by the general public, and not sufficiently noteworthy to become an election issue. The communist success in China aroused some comment, but most of the conference time spent on foreign affairs dealt with the two key questions of the German future and British rearmament. Neither was exhaustively discussed.

On the eve of the General Election of 1950, a new group of Left Wing M.P.'s published their own manifesto of party aims under the title *Keeping Left*.[6] The relation between this new group, and the M.P.'s who had produced *Keep Left* was limited. The older group had dissolved in 1948; the new group began to meet in the summer of 1949, and the *New Statesman*, rather than *Tribune*, put forward the opinions with which the group agreed. Their deliberations led to *Keeping Left*, which devoted about one-fifth of its space to the subject of international relations. The pamphlet drew heavily upon two lines of thought that had been developing in the Labour movement in recent months: the growing concern with the economic effects of British rearmament, which has been dealt with sufficiently for the moment; and, less important though portentous, rising opposition to any western effort to rearm the people of Germany.

Once the western powers abandoned hope of a four-power agreement on Germany and began constructing a West German state, Left Wing interest in the future of Germany increased rapidly. This was quite natural, since the assumption of German independence at some future date had to be made once a central political system was permitted; none of the occupying powers contemplated a permanent occupation. Given a measure of political independence, Germany was certain to regain her sovereignty eventually and with it the right to rearm and pursue her own interests. Left Wing memories of the 1930's, and the consequences of an armed Germany, were still very strong, and considerable thought was given to the search for some means of allowing Germany to re-enter the family of nations without becoming a potential threat to world peace. In the nature of international relations, the search was futile, for sovereignty is not conditional, and the only means by which this might have been accomplished was in fact not to permit Germany sovereign authority. Without saying this in so many words, the Left Wing nevertheless conceived a number of plans for securing against future German aggression which had this effect.

The two more important suggestions for dealing with Germany which appeared on the Left Wing were: first, to integrate Germany into a planned European economy; second, to integrate Germany into a planned Western Union. As a matter of course, it was assumed that socialism should be installed in Germany, e.g., that the German economy should be "socialized." The hope for a Germany integrated into the whole European economy had foundered on East-West antagonism; the hope for a socialist western Europe was drowned at the polls. While there was still hope that the German Socialist party might succeed in gaining control of the German Government, the Left Wing remained relatively quiet. When the elections were held in 1949, a solid victory for the "capitalist" Adenauer ensued, and the socialists ran a poor third. The Left Wing view of the future of Germany grew increasingly pessimistic.

Keeping Left relied heavily upon these two attitudes for its commentary on international policy, for both rearmament and an independent, rearmed Germany were now probabilities for the future. The arguments are ingenious. Labour had fought the General Election of 1945 on the foreign policy issue, and won the election because the British people felt that Labour, unlike Winston Churchill and the Conservative party, would maintain friendly relations with both Russia and the United States, and act as a mediator between them. This Third Force concept had become unworkable when the Soviets refused to join the Marshall Aid Program. Britain had rightly joined the Atlantic Pact group, and had rightly supported the formation of a German Government, since there was no acceptable alternative.

Now, Britain must decide whether or not she would accept the enormous arms bills that her policies entailed, and further, whether she was willing to accept the polarization of the world into two hostile blocs. The writers rejected these two concepts, and suggested that Britain should instead return to an independent socialist foreign policy. Britain was not secure, despite the size of her armaments bills, and would not become secure, however much she might spend. For western Europe could not be defended unless Germany was rearmed, and this was impossible. Had not Neville Chamberlain tried this policy in the 1930's with disastrous results? Worse yet, it would destroy all hope of a true German democracy and thus play into the hands of the communist parties of western Europe.

Having ruled out German rearmament, and thus made it impossible for Britain to be secure against attack, the problem of British security remained unsolved. But the pamphlet decided this question in a simple and attractive manner: it denied the need for arms entirely by denying that there was any likelihood of attack, and, what is more, used the existence of the North Atlantic Treaty Organization to justify the position. For the value of the treaty was that "It is surely clear that the danger of a war begun by direct Russian act of aggression is very small." Armaments, then, were definitely a second priority: "The most vital need for today is that Britain and America should accept the view that the first line of defense is social and economic, and that armaments are the second line."[7] The most pressing need was for economic assistance to the backward nations of the world, and help for "social revolutions" taking place in these areas. There was included the usual proposal that Britain make new proposals for the control of atomic energy, meanwhile renouncing herself in advance the use of such weapons. Western Union was specifically abandoned, because British socialism was "in opposition" across the channel, but the pamphlet conceded that in some areas co-operation between socialists and nonsocialists was possible or even desirable.

Keeping Left was much less discussed than *Keep Left* had been, and had almost no effect on the General Election of 1950, although it appeared just before the election: ". . . for some reason by no means clear, however, not much was heard of it (*Keeping Left*) in the six weeks that followed."[8] Perhaps the chief reason for this was the lack of interest in international affairs during the election, for the General Election of 1950 was extremely unsatisfactory to Labour, and to the Left Wing in particular. Though Labour retained a small majority, it was clear that a new election would have to be held in the near future, and this was a great disappointment to those who had felt that the General Election of 1945 heralded "fifty years in power." The issues on which the election was fought are difficult to discern. As one leading British commentator put it: "Nevertheless the fact remained that at a moment when our national survival was at stake, the fundamental issues were most of the time buried beneath other considerations which, important enough in themselves, were by comparison almost grotesquely trivial and irrelevant."[9] Looking back at the General Election, the Left Wing drew its own conclusions as to the cause of the failure, and this had important consequences for the future. Left Wing socialists are by definition a dedicated group, and they had felt strongly that the electorate, given an opportunity to see socialism in practice, would continue to return Labour to power by substantial majorities. When the electorate failed to do so, they concluded that the failure of the Government to follow a sufficiently socialist policy was responsible; it would be impossible, of course, for them to assume that the Government had been *too socialist* for the electorate.

Thus the near defeat in February, 1950, was taken by the Left Wing as a vindication of their own demands for "more socialism," both in domestic and in foreign policy. Through the life of the 1945 Parliament, this demand had been voiced consistently by Left Wing spokesmen, and the Government had failed to give heed, pursuing instead a more moderate policy less clearly distinguished from traditional British policies than the Left Wing desired. During the election, grievances were put aside and the Left Wing supported the Government, though pamphlets like *Keeping Left* were really criticisms of the past actions of the Government. The outcome was difficult to evaluate, since the actual voting change was small, and there were few clearly defined issues. These doubts were easily resolved by the Left Wing, which concluded that the next election would certainly be lost if a more socialist program was not adopted.[10] For practical purposes, "more socialism" meant more in line with the pattern of opinion on the Left Wing.

A further effect of the election, which raised before the Left Wing the spectre of the political crisis of 1931, was the slim Labour majority, which effectively precluded highly controversial issues, since the slightest defection might lead to a no-confidence vote. The Left Wing pressed hard for a quick General Election, and electoral considerations were very much in the Left Wing mind during the interregnum from February 1950 to the General Election of 1951. This makes it particularly difficult to decide whether Left Wing spokesmen supported a particular line for ideological or for practical reasons. Until the Schuman Plan appeared in May, 1950, there was no substantial issue among the political parties in the international area. The recognition of Communist China was approved by both parties, though the Conservatives tended to deplore the timing employed by the Government. The Left Wing, as might be expected, took the view that Mao Tse-tung was in some manner different from Soviet Communists; perhaps more an agrarian reformer of some sort. Neither Conservative nor Labour spokesmen were really interested in furthering closer relations between Britain and the European continent, though this was now one of the major objectives of the American aid administration.

The Council of Europe was doomed to a life of fruitless discussion by British unwillingness to accept any real unity of purpose with the Continent, and, reasonably enough, because Britain was unwilling to relinquish her status as a great power. The Schuman Plan was accepted by the Left Wing, but under conditions which rendered it nonsensical, since they insisted that a precondition must be socialization of the countries taking part. When the British Government finally refused to enter the agreement, the Conservative party put down a motion of censure, which was enough to ensure Left Wing support for the Government's policy, whatever their private opinions.

The outbreak of war in Korea in the early morning hours of June 25, 1950, found the British Left Wing floundering in the wake of the recent General Election, and as yet undecided on a course of action for meeting the challenge of the coming election. The leadership of the Left Wing was sundered, since *Tribune* had deviated from the traditional Left Wing attitude toward international affairs and had begun supporting the Labour Government's foreign policies. The two chief issues at hand, the future of Germany and the level of armaments, were being pursued rather haphazardly since it was as yet uncertain which direction events would take. The effect of the war on the British Government's policy was first to force a substantial increase in military expenditure, and second, under strong pressure from the United States, to force agreement to the rearmament of Germany. As in the United States, the war marked a turning point, in that statements of intention were soon replaced by deliberate actions. Military budgets rose quickly, military research was emphasized strongly, and military strategy began to weigh with increasing heaviness in the determination of policy.

The effect of the war on the Left Wing was remarkable. Within six months, the Left Wing was converted from a leaderless body of opinion with a very low level of political effectiveness into a relatively cohesive group with an agreed-to program of action and a clearly established group of leaders. In effect, there was a sudden and sharp reversion to the foreign policy principles of the 1930's, led by *Tribune* and its associated spokesmen for socialism, following one of the strangest reversals of opinion in the postwar history of the Left Wing.

The course of the war itself, and the political decisions that it produced, have been well documented by the Royal Institute for International Affairs.[11] Roughly, the initial attack by North Korea (much disputed in the Left Wing press) was followed by a meeting of the Security Council from which Russia was then absent. A resolution was passed by the Council demanding an end to hostilities and the withdrawal of attacking forces. Member nations were asked to help the South Koreans stave off the invasion. The United States Government authorized munitions supplies for South Korea, provided air support, and for reasons of its own sealed off the Island of Formosa from the China mainland with the Seventh Fleet. The Security Council resolution was ignored, and North Korean forces continued to advance southward with little effective opposition. On June 27, the Security Council requested member nations to furnish assistance to South Korea, and American troops were sent into the peninsula on June 30. The western powers were now committed to military action in Korea involving their own forces.

The war that followed can be divided into four fairly distinct stages: in the first stage, the initial thrust of the North Korean armies nearly drove western forces from the peninsula; next, a counterthrust by the United Nations troops broke the fighting ability of North Korean troops, and forced them back toward the border of China; the third stage brought Chinese "volunteers" into the conflict, forcing United Nations troops back toward the 38th parallel; finally, the fighting line stabilized, roughly along the 38th parallel, and negotiations for truce or armistice began.

The two main patterns followed by the Left Wing in its response to the war in Korea are exemplified by the behavior of the *New Statesman*, which was entirely consistent with its previous line of opinion, and *Tribune* which underwent a remarkable transformation during the course of the conflict. The remainder of the Left Wing press—*Forward* and *Reynolds News*—remained consistent, but in fact published little direct comment on the war in Korea. A comparison of the views of the two leading Left Wing journals is particularly useful because these views were paralleled by the division of opinion within the House of Commons, and further, it offers some explanation of the remarkable course of events within the Labour party following the Korean War.

The *New Statesman* was remarkably consistent. When the fighting began, it immediately joined with the "legalists," i.e., those who believed that the actions taken by the United States were illegal, and therefore, by implication, should not be supported. The essence of the charge was as follows:

> Jumping the legal gun by more than five hours, America announced its intention to protect Southern as against Northern Korea, and also formally declared its determination to prevent an attack on Formosa. . . American Imperialists welcome this new move. . .[12]

This became the first point in the case against the United States: it had acted too rapidly, and with hidden intentions. The second aspect of the "legalist" case emerged a week later, when the right of the Security Council to act in the absence of the Soviet representative was raised, and denied. Concurrently, American defense of Formosa was severely criticized, and General Douglas MacArthur was singled out for particularly violent denunciation. Throughout the first phase of the war, the editor of the *New Statesman* pressed for admission of Communist China to the United Nations and cession of Formosa to the mainland government. The lack of comment about the actual issues involved in Korea, i.e., the fact of aggression, is representative; the *New Statesman* never faced this issue at all but spent its time and effort impugning the motives of the United States and worrying about the possibility of conflict with China.

The Government's proposal for a 3.4 billion (United States) pound arms program, released soon after the war began, was received in silence by the *New Statesman,* though by mid-August a limited program was suggested as a substitute. A capital levy was also proposed to replace regular taxation as a means of financing the arms program, since this would remove any danger of strain on the social services program. This question became increasingly important later on, because the Left Wing believed that Labour's electoral chances were in some measure dependent upon the success of the medical and other socialization programs.[13]

In the second phase of the war, as Korean forces disintegrated and began to retreat, more and more apprehension arose about the possibility of war with China. The *New Statesman* was strongly opposed to crossing the 38th parallel, and expressed the belief that this might well lead to a third world war. It was now urging peace in every issue, whatever the "cost" might be. Chinese assistance for North Korea was clearly anticipated by the editor, and repeated warnings were issued against further antagonizing of Chinese sensibilities. When United Nations forces approached the Chinese-Korean boundary, the *New Statesman* expressed violent opposition to this act of "pure provocation" and blamed MacArthur for deliberately fostering a large scale war. Opposition to U.N. troops crossing the 38th parallel was consistently reiterated.

When Chinese forces were first noticed in Korea, the *New Statesman* issued a solemn warning of the possible consequences of full-scale intervention. It advised Britain to withdraw its forces from Korea if MacArthur were not curbed immediately. When it was clear that China had in fact intervened in force, the pessimistic attitude of the journal became even more marked; "Once Manchurian cities become targets for American bombers, the Third World War has begun. Let it also be clear that United Nations forces can be driven out of Korea by the Chinese and Russians as easily as the cities of China and Russia can be bombed."[14] There was no question but that evacuation of western forces would be necessary; merely whether it would be done immediately or later. It noted that Mao Tse-tung would demand full recognition and admission to the United Nations as a price of peace, and expected, in context, that this would have to be granted: "Having successfully driven him (North Korea) out, they proceeded gratuitously to provoke a third country into war, and were thrown back in headlong retreat. If they now admit that they were in the wrong, and make peace on the best terms they can, what possible reason is there for calling them 'Municheers.' "[15] However, once the fighting line stabilized, the *New Statesman* subsided once again, though it vigorously denounced the United Nations resolution which "branded" the Chinese Communist Government as an "aggressor."

The pattern of response to the Korean War found in the *New Statesman,* which was representative of the major portion of the Left Wing, is fundamentally consistent. There is little or no concern with the "principles" which may have been involved in the United Nations action in Korea; even less concern with the merits of North Korean actions. The points which most Liberal and Conservative newspapers considered essential to an evaluation of the conflict and western policy were simply ignored by the *New Statesman.* Its goal was peace, whatever the conditions that might be necessary to achieve it. It feared the effects of the war on the British social service program, and denounced the rearmament program sharply when it was first announced. It turned against Germany shortly thereafter, and opposed rearmament of that country as well. It was sympathetic to the Chinese communists, and unwilling to associate them too closely with the Soviet Union. The distinct impression gained by a thorough reading of the *New Statesman's* pages is that the paper was essentially not concerned at this time with international affairs at all except as they affected internal British politics, and particularly the progress of British socialism.

By way of contrast, the editorial pages in *Tribune* show loyal support for collective action in Korea, and for the British Government's decision to rearm, though in the last analysis political ambition or ideological conviction—the decision is impossible to make with certainty—forced a sharp change of policy and aligned the *Tribune* group with, or rather at the head of, the Left Wing.

In the initial phase of the war, *Tribune* offers a complete contrast to the *New Statesman*. The United Nations action in Korea was warmly welcomed as "correct and inevitable," and the "legality" of the action was specifically endorsed. It decried the quibbling of those who were arguing the "legal" aspects of the police action, and pointed out the principle involved in the defense against aggression. It agreed that the government of South Korea was scarcely a worthy object of such support, and that Communist China should have a seat on the Security Council, but insisted that these questions were not really relevant to the point at issue. Even the isolation of Formosa, which was criticized, was kept separate and distinct from the policy in Korea. This does not mean that *Tribune* was a supporter of General MacArthur; it was not, and denounced him roundly for his behavior as United Nations commander when he visited Formosa. But the principle of repelling aggression by military force was firmly supported.

Significantly, the first break in the *Tribune* line came in mid-August, shortly after the Government announced its changed rearmament program. Through late August and early September, a series of special leaders appeared which examined the proposed rearmament program with care and stressed the caution needed to prevent any impairment of the socialist program at home. On September 15, confidence in the ability of the British economy to stand firm under the additional burden proposed by more armaments was suddenly and drastically shaken. Concern was replaced by genuine anxiety, and a suggestion that perhaps, a capital levy was necessary if the extra taxation burden was not to cause economic damage. While it is true that *Tribune* had consistently expressed concern over the economic effects of armaments, it had previously been confident that the economy, if carefully managed, could withstand the shock. Why this sudden change?

No clue to the change can be found in the Labour party Conference which opened at Margate on October 2, for the Conference was concerned primarily with wages, prices, and costs. Various Left Wing spokesmen proposed a capital levy to meet the additional expense of the rearmament program, and there were the usual speeches against conscription, against colonialism, against atomic weapons, and against submission to American pressure. Significantly, the Conference did produce a decided revival of the Third Force concept, which now gained the support of the pacifists, possibly out of fear engendered by the recent outbreak of fighting in Korea.[16] But the Conference was a model of unity, on foreign affairs as well as on domestic affairs; the election was too close for dissension in the ranks.

Shortly after the Conference closed, *Tribune* published the first of a series of pamphlets or small booklets which continued the singular departure from its previous line in international relations, and marks the beginning of a very important force in Left Wing thought.[17] Entitled *Full Speed Ahead,* the pamphlet took as its point of departure the unity displayed at the recent Labour party Conference; this unity, and the dangerous impasse that existed in the House of Commons, might conceivably lead to a dangerous situation;

> . . . if doubts should grow about the main direction, if the belief should prevail that the leaders accepted an awkward Parliamentary situation as a fortunate release from the necessity of declaring a bold initiative, then all the lesser irritations and doubts would be kindled into a more destructive flame.[18]

Clearly, this is a thinly veiled threat to the leaders of the parliamentary Labour party, reminiscent of Aneurin Bevin's warnings to the Prime Minister during the Second World War.

In Chapter IV, entitled "Arms and the State of the Nation," the pamphlet turned to the problem of collective security. It agreed that the Government's policy enjoyed more support in the Labour movement than it had managed in the past five years, and suggested that Molotov's behavior had done more to obtain this support than any positive action by the Foreign Secretary. But it feared that the Government was growing complacent, since many of the rank and file party members retained serious misgivings about the course of Labour's international policy. Even the choice of the Anglo-American alliance, which was the only feasible policy for Britain, was fraught with some danger for Britain, though Britain had thus far proved an excellent balancing force in the alliance.

Having agreed this much, the writer(s) launched a subtle attack on the entire rearmament program, first, by ascribing the need for armaments to the "Fulton Policy," and secondly, by attacking the view that only American atomic weapons restrained the Soviet Union from hostilities: "There is no evidence from Soviet history that the challenge of general world war is part of the strategy of making the world communist."[19] The pamphlet goes on to say that American productive capacity alone, being so much greater than that of Russia, was an adequate deterrent against war. The present emphasis on armaments was based upon a grossly exaggerated view of Soviet strength and aggressiveness. The argument on which this assumption was based is worth quoting in some detail:

It is necessary to have arms, but policy can be more important than arms. All the arms in the world could not have saved us before 1939 so long as the Government of that day was pursuing a policy directed against collective security in alliance with or friendly submission to the dictators.

It was right to resist in Korea, and it is right to build forces needed to prevent the success of any further Soviet-promoted adventures in the future. But it is no less necessary to resist military demands which would strain our economy to the breaking point. That resistance will not come from the Tories or the military chiefs. It must come from a Labour Party helping a Labour Government to keep a cool head. The task of the Labour party is to prevent such a distortion of our economy through exaggerated notions of Soviet strength that military expenditure destroys our hard-won social gains and gives the Russians a bloodless victory. [20]

This is the fundamental argument on which Left Wing opposition to armaments came to rest thereafter. It is essentially based upon the needs of domestic policy, and not upon the status of international affairs at all.

The pamphlet next resuscitated the old Left Wing concept of a "socialist foreign policy," which was now held to be compatible with agreements or even alliances with nonsocialist states. The first principle, however, was no longer support for friendly groups in Europe, but, ". . . to help strengthen the progressive forces behind the American Government. The British alliance is worth much more to the United States and to the United States Government than Republican acquiescence in Congress."[21] Nevertheless, the "real" criticism of Ernest Bevin's foreign policy remained his failure to assist the socialists of Europe to achieve power in their respective countries.

Full Speed Ahead is not a direct commentary on the Korean War. Instead, it is an attack on the premises on which the Government's defense policy was based. Within a matter of weeks, this line of attack had been taken up by the remainder of the Left Wing, and *Tribune* became once again the leader of Left Wing criticism of the Government's policy. This abrupt change took place as the Korean War entered its third phase, featuring Chinese intervention in the conflict. In sharp contrast to its previous attitude, *Tribune* was horror-struck, and complained that the attack should never have taken place. It now urged that a neutral zone be created in Korea, and that negotiations with the communist Government be undertaken immediately. Significantly, the publication of this attack on the policy of the United Nations in Korea coincided with the publication of a second leader suggesting that Aneurin Bevan, John Strachey, and G. R. Strauss were at odds with the rest of the Cabinet about the price of armaments, and a third leader which suggested that the level of armaments be fixed with reference to the social services' requirements, and maintained sufficiently low to avoid any change in their framework. These three leaders are very closely connected with further changes to follow.

By the beginning of 1951, *Tribune's* editorial policy had reverted to a position which was reminiscent of its attitude toward international relations in the 1930's. A strong tinge of pacifism appeared in its editorials; it was most uncharacteristically defeatist, and pressed very strongly for negotiations with China "at any cost." When proposals to name Communist China as an aggressor nation were brought into the United Nations, *Tribune* insisted that this would lead to American landings on the Chinese mainland, and eventually to full-scale warfare which would be a catastrophe for Britain. Even the long-dead issue of "four-power agreement" in Europe was reopened, mainly as a basis for opposing any action toward the armament of Germany. The January 26, 1951, edition of the weekly carried large headlines proclaiming an "Anglo-American Crisis," based upon allegations of American refusal to accept any peace proposals in the Far East. The "fight to save the peace" now proclaimed was used as a very convenient instrument to drub the United States: "The danger of war no longer arises solely from Soviet policy. It arises also from the temper which has been aroused in the United States and the foolhardy policies on which the erstwhile progressive Government in Washington has been launched at the bidding of an ever more raucous and hysterical reaction."[22] Among the specific American policies denounced in the article were American armament of Japan, support for Chiang Kai-shek, and pressure for German rearmament.

By the early weeks of 1951, then, the Left Wing press had grown together until the policy that appeared in *Tribune* could not be distinguished from that found in the *New Statesman*. The three issues involved were: the Korean War and the danger of large-scale involvement on the mainland of China; the level of British armaments and the danger that arms costs might in some manner damage the British social services program; and the German armaments issue, which was in a sense opposition to American proposals for German armaments, since the British Government

was firmly committed to a disarmed Germany at this time. The
driving force behind the Left Wing attitude toward these three issues came from the traditional policies of the 1930's. Pacifism,
opposition to armaments, the theme that armaments inevitably
lead to war, and a strong revival of anti-American sentiment, (the
United States being the pre-eminent capitalist nation of the time)
all made their appearance in the arguments of the Left Wing.

The same issues, and the same general approach to them,
characterize the Left Wing approach to international affairs in the
House of Commons during this same period in late 1950 and early
1951. In the first phase of the war in Korea, the action of the
United Nations was opposed by an alliance of pacifists and fellow
travelers, the latter relying heavily upon the "legalist" version
of events and ignoring the fact of the North Korean attack. The
pacifists ignored the legal quibble, but refused to support the intervention. A small portion of the Left Wing actively supported
the United Nations. Though the position of many of those opposing
the United Nations was the same, the justification differed very
widely from individual to individual. Thus Zilliacus refused to
accept the competence of the Security Council, holding that what
had occurred was "a civil war, in which our sympathies should lie
with native Communism as against American capitalism (although
I believe the truth to lie somewhere between the two positions)."[23]
In any event, the Security Council had no authority to intervene in
this case. D. N. Pritt, on the other hand, simply insisted that
South Korea had first attacked North Korea, and presumably
thought the United Nations should be supporting the North Koreans.[24] H. N. Brailsford, no fellow traveler, also supported the
view that the Security Council had acted illegally, but again on different grounds, since he believed that Russia's absence had deprived the Security Council of its authority.[25] But in any case,
Brailsford believed that the United States had acted without waiting
for authorization. Sydney Silverman, another of the prominent fellow travelers, felt that the absence of China from the Security
Council rendered that body's authority nugatory.[26]

These various attitudes were bound together into an Amendment to a Government Motion for Approval which was moved in
the House of Commons on July 5.[27] The Amendment called for the
immediate withdrawal of American troops from Korea, and referred to the war as an act of aggression *by the United States*
against Korea. The mover, S. O. Davies, and the seconder, Emrys
Hughes, exemplified the alliance of pacifists and fellow travelers
standing behind the motion. Another motion against the use of
atomic weapons was tabled by Emrys Hughes and James Carmichael which received some support in the Left Wing press, but

it was not debated and did not really become an issue, now or later.[28]

The Left Wing M.P.'s who provided support for the United Nations action in Korea were few in number. Michael Foot was perhaps the strongest supporter of resistance to aggression,[29] with some assistance from Henry Usborne,[30] Seymour Cocks,[31] and Woodrow Wyatt.[32]

Apparently a substantial portion of the Left Wing remained on the fence at this time. There was little active opposition to the Government, and little real support for its policies. There was great concern over the attitude that Communist China would take toward the war, and almost universal support for the admission of Communist China to the United Nations Organization. There was some difference of opinion as to the importance of American action in Korea, it was denounced by some and supported by others. The hesitations and misgivings were cleverly bundled together by Sydney Silverman, now a leading figure among the fellow travelers, and placed upon the order paper as a motion, which was not debated:

> That this House, having without a division supported His Majesty's Government in its acceptance of the United Nations Security Council's decision on Korea, nevertheless remains profoundly anxious that the peace of the world shall be preserved, and to that end urges His Majesty's Government to prepare the way for world settlement: (a) by using its best endeavors to limit the area of conflict; to bring about a cessation of hostilities and mediation in Korea under the auspices of the United Nations; to urge the withdrawal of United States forces from Formosa; to secure the admission of the recognized Chinese People's Government into the Security Council; to take the initiative in bringing about an early meeting of the representatives of all the Great Powers, including India, to consider what action can be taken, either on Trygve Lie's proposals or otherwise, to strengthen the United Nations and to end the cold war which is fraught with such dire perils to the survival of civilization and mankind.[33]

This is a reasonably good summary of the questions which were at this time causing considerable concern to the Left Wing.

The German rearmament issue remained dormant in the House of Commons until late in the Autumn of 1950, largely because of the statements made by Government spokesmen on the issue. Emmanuel Shinwell, speaking in the Defense Debate in July, put the

Government's policy as: "His Majesty's Government have repeatedly. . .declared their opposition to the rearmament of Germany. Any change in this policy must necessarily be the result of a joint allied statement."[34] And in September, the Prime Minister, while announcing that the British armament budget would increase considerably, clearly stated the Government's intention to remain firm on the question of arms for Germany: "We hold the view that the eventual participation of Germany in the defence of Europe can be considered only within the framework of the common defence of the West."[35] Perhaps soothed by these rather imprecise statements, the Left Wing had little to say about German rearmament until Ernest Bevin returned from a meeting of the NATO countries in Washington committed in principle to some measure of German armaments in the near future. When Attlee informed the House of Commons that Germany would be permitted to make some contribution to the common defense of the West, the statement was sharply attacked by Michael Foot, Richard Crossman and James Carmichael.[36]

When Parliament returned to the discussion of foreign affairs late in November of 1950, a two-day debate revealed serious disagreement between the Labour Government and its back benches.[37] The two chief issues were American policy in Korea, now roundly denounced from all sides, and the commitment to rearm the Germans. In the course of the debate, pacifist Victor Yates condemned the decision to arm Germany and demanded a reconsideration of that policy. Ellis Smith pleaded for a mutual aid plan for the backward nations, and some action by the British Government to resolve great power differences. Frederick Jones noted the grave suspicions which oriental people entertained of American intentions in the Far East, and urged that Communist China be admitted to the Security Council. Ian Mikardo claimed that the United States was convinced that war was inevitable and was no longer seeking a peaceful solution to world problems. Sydney Silverman, in a lengthy speech, reasserted the old Labour view that armaments always led to war, and attacked the rearmament of both Britain and Germany. Woodrow Wyatt, Tom Driberg, and other Left Wing speakers all expressed great anxiety about the course of events in the Far East, and condemned the American, and to a lesser extent the British government for its current international policy.

Whether by coincidence or intent, Prime Minister Attlee then journeyed to the United States for consultations, and returned to Britain to inform the House of Commons of his success.[38] In the brief debate following Attlee's statement, only a few Left Wing speakers were heard, and these, without exception, devoted most of their attention to European affairs.

Following the Christmas adjournment, foreign affairs came up for debate again in mid-February 1951. The Government had already announced that it would support the American resolution before the United Nations to denounce Communist China for aggression in Korea,[39] and had announced a still further increase in its armament program from 3.4 billion pounds to 4.7 billion pounds over the next three years.[40] The Prime Minister himself opened the debate with a review of the premises on which Britain's Korean policy was based.[41] It differed much less from the premises of the Left Wing than might have been expected from the uproar in the Left Wing press. Britain, Attlee stated, was widely experienced in the Far East, and the United States was not. They did not feel that the resolution before the United Nations was good for British interests, and did not think that China had "spoken the last word." There would be no final solution until the Formosan question and the status of Communist China in the United Nations had been settled. Speaking in relation to German rearmament, Attlee produced a new set of "Attlee Conditions" when he stated that although Britain had agreed in principle to German rearmament, this must not be done until all of the armed forces needed in Europe had been created and suitable arrangements made to ensure against German aggression. These conditions were not stressed very much in this particular debate, but became very important later on. The debate showed clearly that the Left Wing had abandoned the Korean War in favor of German rearmament and British arms expenditures as suitable objects of attack in the field of international affairs.

The Left Wing still desired an immediate and peaceful settlement of the Korean War, however, and the work of a "Peace With China" group might be mentioned in this connection. Its avowed purpose was negotiated peace with China, admission of Communist China to the United Nations, and the return of Formosa to the control of the mainland government.[42] Its adherents included Kingsley Martin,[43] Norman Bower,[44] William Warbey, Sydney Silverman, and Wilfred Vernon.[45] This program enjoyed the nearly unqualified support of the Left Wing, and very likely of a substantial portion of the Labour party, though this is only conjecture. The program was supported by a widely diversified group. Victor Gollancz, the publisher, Will Elliot, Eric Messer, Leslie Hale, and Fenner Brockway even combined to form another organization called "Victory for Socialism" for the same purpose.[46] As an individual, G. D. H. Cole favored the same opinions and published two important articles in the *New Statesman* on the subject on February 3 and 24. The Korean War had been a civil war, he claimed, in which he personally had hoped for a North Korean victory; it was certainly not an object for Security Council action. He could hardly blame the Chinese for intervening when American forces appeared on their borders. He did not believe the United States was motivated by imperialistic desires, but that she was only muddled and uncertain. American pressure for German armaments was the result of a profound failure to understand that Europe could not afford this policy, and did not desire it. He closed his second article with the hopeful suggestion that he could not really discount the possibility of a massive American attack on China, even at this late date. This attitude was common at the time, and led to such actions as a parliamentary motion denouncing the American proposal to name China as an aggressor nation, which was signed by a number of M.P.'s, not all of whom had pacifistic or fellow traveler inclinations.

The Korean War was undoubtedly an important turning point in post-1945 international affairs. It hardened the policy of the United States toward the Soviet Union, and, perhaps even more important, instilled in many people the fear that Russia was not merely aggressive and grasping, but actually very likely to begin all-out war if it suited her purposes. The western nations, under American guidance and pressure, plunged into feverish activity as they hastened to turn themselves into an armed camp. Military expenditures soared. They nearly quadrupled in the United States; doubled, then increased 50 per cent more in Britain. The military potential of Germany, and its essential position in any meaningful defense scheme for Europe, hastened the day when all was forgiven and Germany was hurriedly placed on the road to rearmament. Special arrangements for Japan were put into effect which reached fruition in 1952 when the Peace Treaty with Japan was signed.

This militarization process was watched by the British Left Wing, and by many others as well, with growing apprehension and concern. It impinged directly on two particularly sensitive areas of Left Wing ideology. First, the Left Wing was antimilitaristic. It associated militarism with capitalism, the deadly enemy. It likewise assumed that military activity invariably flowed from economic conflict, which was also a product of the capitalist system. It feared that militarism in the western nations would undermine the foundations of the social revolution taking place in Europe and particularly in the backward countries of Asia and Africa, and thus stay the progress of the world toward the ultimate socialist goal. In a very real and meaningful sense the Left Wing conceived militarism as essentially anti-socialism, and opposed it accordingly. Second, and perhaps even more important, militarism threatened the progress of the British people themselves toward socialism when the military estimates assumed such proportions that the British economy was unable to maintain both military expenditure and social service costs. The Left Wing feeling of dismay was augmented substantially by the results of the General Election of 1950, and the strong feeling that Labour might well go down to defeat in the approaching election if its socialization program was curtailed. In the last analysis, fear of the effects of militarization on the domestic economy probably outweighed the fear of its effects internationally, though this is only speculation.

By the early summer of 1951, the general agreement on international policy which the Labour movement displayed early in 1949 was gone, and in its place had come an uneasy tension, and genuine concern for the future. It required only a spark to ignite these tensions and to bring about an impassioned protest against the current trend toward militarism and the dangers of war that were being incurred. The spark was provided by wartime firebrand Aneurin Bevan and a handful of Labour M.P.'s following Bevan's resignation, together with his followers, from the Labour Cabinet. The arrival of leaders capable of reaching a nationwide audience concentrated and unified the British Left Wing to a degree it had not hitherto reached. For there can be little doubt that Bevan and his supporters participated in a deliberate attempt to unify the opposition to the leadership of the Labour party beneath a single banner. Most of this development lies beyond the scope of this study, but the arguments used to accomplish this unity of purpose are instructive. Significantly, the leaders chose arguments which dealt with a foreign policy issue; more significantly, the leaders made use of the oldest principles of the Labour movement to accomplish their purpose.

The political credo of the Labour Ministers who resigned in 1951—*One Way Only*—was not published until July, 1951.[47] Yet the arguments in this pamphlet were derived from the earlier pamphlet *Full Speed Ahead,* published by *Tribune* in September, 1950.[48] *Full Speed Ahead* had marked a clear and sharp break in the policy line *Tribune* had been pursuing since it made peace with the Government in 1948. Bevan and his associates made no claim to authorship of the entire pamphlet, though they accepted responsibility for the whole: "With the main argument which runs through this document we are in full accord. Inevitably, in a pamphlet composed by a number of persons there are nuances of meaning and expressions here and there which are different from those we should have used ourselves had we been the sole authors. But that does not weaken our essential agreement."[49] The pamphlet, they claimed, offered the only possible alternative to the present course of British policy, which would lead to war or self-destruction.

As a matter of fact, the exact nature of this "only" approach to international politics is hardly made clear in the pamphlet itself. There is opposition to the level of British armaments, and more opposition to militarism, but the pamphlet abounds in reasoning like the following:

> Every one of us repudiates the idea that war is inevitable. Every one of us knows that rearmament must end in war unless it is halted by a negotiated settlement. Every one of us admits that you cannot kill Communism with atom bombs, and that even if the present regime (in Russia) were miraculously wiped off the face of the map, millions of colonial people would still demand that the fantastic inequality between their standard of living and that of the industrialized western nations should be ended. The Social Revolution in Asia is the dominant fact of the twentieth century. It is a challenge which Tories will always try to avoid but which Socialists must face. The danger is twofold: that hysterical fear of Russian aggression will blind us to that challenge, and secondly that breakneck rearmament will render us impotent to meet it.[50]

The most valuable contribution that British Labour could make was, of course, to hasten their own road toward socialism.

The chief complaint voiced in the pamphlet was aimed at the "retreat from socialism" alleged to have occurred in the past year. The writers proposed to halt this drift from socialism by the application of five basic principles to Britain's foreign policy: first, that war was not inevitable but that it might become inevitable if the armament program continued; second, that the underprivileged peoples of the world had a right to their own social revolution; third, that military armaments should be subordinated to a world plan for mutual aid; fourth, that any further armaments should be financed by "socialist methods," by which was meant the use of the capital levy; finally, that additional measures for the socialization of the British economy were necessary and should be put into force immediately.

The first principle is simply a restatement of the old Left Wing assumption that "armaments always lead to war." The second principle is a variation on the support for social revolutions pledged by the Left Wing during World War II, and more distantly, the consistent support given the "socialist experiment" is Russia. The third is again a restatement of the necessity for world cooperation on socialist lines before true peace can be established. The fourth principle is an attempt to make the capitalists, who profit from wars, pay for them. Finally, there is the unqualified Left Wing assumption that quicker and more thorough socialization of Britain must be the primary goal of the Labour party. By skillful use of the traditional appeals of the Labour movement, the leaders of the new Left Wing movement soon acquired a very substantial influence in the Labour movement; an influence that was considerably increased by the loss of the General Election of 1951, since the Left Wing claimed that the loss was due very largely to the failure of the Labour Government to press for greater measures of socialization. What is perhaps most important for our purposes is the clear ideological basis of the appeal launched by the new Left Wing leaders, and its unquestioned effectiveness.

Leaving the British Left Wing, which has served its purpose as a case study, we can now return to the general question of the relationship between ideology and international affairs and summarize the principles which appear to hold good for that relationship. This occupies the concluding chapter.

X

CONCLUSIONS AND APPLICATIONS

To recapitulate briefly, this study set out to determine whether or not there were any general principles that hold true for the relationship between ideology and international affairs; to determine the effect of ideology on individual and group behavior, using behavior in the broad sense which includes both thought and action. To that end, a theory or hypothesis governing the relationship was proposed in Chapter I, and examined in the light of the actual behavior of an ideology-dominated group during a recent time period. It was argued that ideology would necessitate the use of a priori absolutes which would be applied to the course of events in a very rigid manner, ensuing in a consistently dogmatic approach to affairs. The theory also held that the ideological group would make extensive use of symbolism and gross over simplification of issues, and that a distortion of data, a manipulation and even outright evasion of facts would result from the effort to force events into a predetermined framework derived from the basic principles of the ideology. The ideological group could be expected to maintain a dual moral standard, depending more upon the group standing of the individuals involved in an issue rather than the evaluation of the actual course of events. In addition to these primary aspects of the hypothesis, numerous corollaries were proposed as possible consequences of the application of ideology to international affairs.

This theory, which is stated here only in broad outline, was subjected to comparison with the behavior of the British Left Wing in Chapters II through IX. Again, let me say that the purpose of the case study was not to demonstrate only that the theory could be substantiated by data taken from Left Wing behavior, but also to determine whether or not the theory would give an adequate explanation of the characteristic behavior of the Left Wing, or even supply a basis on which future actions could be predicted with some consistency. For this reason, the case study was organized to demonstrate the chief behavior patterns of the group, and not to follow either the general outline of the theory or the general outline of events. This creates a more difficult situation for the reader, perhaps, but it has the advantage of providing all of the information needed for a critical evaluation of the theory. The case study does not, then, pretend to be a complete survey of international affairs from 1945 to 1951, although a complete survey was made prior to the selection of material for the study. Various issues were omitted which were better illustrated on other occasions, or because the line of reasoning that occurred was an isolated phenomenon. No significant aspect of the behavior of the Left Wing was omitted.

It remains, then, to examine the validity and significance of the theory. It must, of course, be understood that even a perfect correlation in this one specific instance does not do more than indicate that the theory is valid for the case of the British Left Wing. The theory was framed from materials derived from a number of ideologies—socialism, communism, Confucianism, Christianity, nationalism, etc.—and it appears to fit these cases as well. Nevertheless, this reservation must be made until much additional material has been made available. As a first effort in the direction of better understanding of the influence of ideologies, the study is offered without apology despite its limitations; the subject is an important one and it has not been given the attention it deserves.

How well does the case study of the British Left Wing substantiate the assumptions in the theory? The reader will by now have formed his own opinion, but it is suggested that the theory explains Left Wing behavior remarkably well, and that the number of aberrations from expected behavior is not large in comparison to the number of areas in which the generalizations of the theory can be shown to hold good. In a surprising number of cases, a trained observer making use of the theory and in possession of sufficient information about the Left Wing to derive its principles from its past history should have been able to predict with some accuracy the reaction of a number of elements of the Left Wing to specific events. This is both gratifying, as a substantiation of the theory, and alarming, because of the implications it contains.

The writer is aware of the use of statistical generalizations to predict human behavior in the mass—predictions of the type on which insurance premiums are based—but he has always felt that such generalizations are quite worthless in relation to any specific individual. The type of predictability which the theory of the influence of ideology appears to give is different from this, in that the future behavior of even single members of the Left Wing, as for instance the pacifists and fellow travelers, seemed to be amenable to prediction. If this is generally true, it follows that the more strongly a society is committed to an ideology, the more likely is individual behavior to be predictable. For anyone concerned with the essential worth of individual choice, this is hardly a satisfactory state of affairs.

In two areas, the British Left Wing did not conform precisely to the theory outlined in Chapter I: it made no use of "sacred gospels" or absolute written authority; further, it did not develop into an authoritarian organization, and in fact, there are a number of reasons to assume that the Left Wing would bitterly resist any attempt to impose an authoritarian regime upon itself. Neither of these objections is fatal, but they are worth closer examination.

The classic ideologies, like communism and Christianity, all depend in some degree upon a body of "sacred writings" which contain the fundamental dogmas of the ideology. In Britain, this simply is not the case. None of the indigenous fathers of British socialism produced a magnum opus of sufficient stature to become such an authority, and the writings of Marx and the continental socialists are not held in sufficiently high regard to achieve such a position of eminence. The early British socialists were, for the most part, reformers and propagandists whose talents lent themselves more to the production of pamphlets than magisterial tomes of biblical proportions. Perhaps even more important, the heterogeneous nature of British socialism, compounded as it is of a number of threads of thought in which there is no one dominant element, mitigates against the creation of an absolute authority for the entire socialist movement.

Nevertheless, the British Left Wing did find it necessary to make use of a substitute for its missing "bible"; the gap was filled by the dogmatic use of the fundamental principles of its own thought, such as "armaments always lead to war," "capitalism always leads to imperialism," "socialism brings peace and harmony." These propositions, many of which are highly dubious to say the least, are commonly used to "prove" Left Wing arguments, or simply taken as correct without even the possibility of argument, in much the same way that a convinced communist quotes Marx. This characteristic of the Left Wing is both interesting and useful. For modern nationalism, which has its heroes but usually not its prophets, in fact makes use of this same technique. The elevation of popular cant into infallible dogma is, therefore, a method of providing a substitute for an ideological authority, and in this case the theory will still hold.

The failure of the Left Wing to develop into an organized body, and then to tend toward authoritarian control within that body, is a more serious departure from theory. The explanation of the failure seems to lie in a number of factors. First of all, the Left Wing was not, strictly speaking, an ideological group, but only a part of a broader group which definitely inhibited Left Wing attempts to constitute itself into an organized body of opinion. Nevertheless, the Left Wing is singularly attached to the "bourgeois" freedoms which it sometimes disposes for others, and there is no reason whatever to suppose that members of the Left Wing would acquiesce in authoritarian control, and several excellent reasons to suppose the contrary. This aspect of the theory must therefore be abandoned as untenable, even though it does appear to have some validity for some ideologies.

By way of compensation, the study of the British Left Wing produced two additional principles which appear to hold good for the relation between ideology and international affairs that were not anticipated by the theory. First, the evidence supports the view that strict adherence to the principles of an ideology is not really compatible with the responsibility of high political office, or the need to deal in a practical manner with the problems of international relations. Second, it seems fairly clear that periods of international tension or crisis invariably produce a sharp increase in the influence of ideology and a reversion to first principles of ideology.

In relation to the first of these points, the study demonstrates quite clearly that members of the Left Wing who were elevated to high office almost immediately deviated from their Left Wing views. Even when due regard has been paid to the principle of Cabinet solidarity, the reversal seems far too significant to be accidental or conditional. The classic example is Prime Minister Attlee, who was very close to the Left Wing during the 1930's and constantly at odds with the more conservative of the trade union leaders, but who became after 1940 a very moderate influence in the Labour movement. An even better example, perhaps, was the late Sir Stafford Cripps, who changed from a roaring lion of the Left Wing into an icy pillar of responsibility when he was taken into the Government. Even Aneurin Bevan, who resigned his Cabinet position in 1951 to return to the Left Wing, later lost his affinity for Left Wing principles—after he had gained a leading position in the parliamentary Labour party.

This generalization, to which there appear to be no vital exceptions, raises a number of important and intriguing questions. Does it mean, for example, that ideologies are in practice nothing more than means to domestic political power, and of no use whatever in the conduct of international affairs, or perhaps any of the affairs of government? This would not be too much to assume if the same pattern emerges elsewhere, and there are numerous instances in which the pattern would appear to be valid. Does the lack of evidence on this point mean that hypocrisy is in fact a

necessary adjunct to ideological leadership and that the dual approach to the basic principles of any creed which is postulated by
the theory is in practice valid? Unfortunately, the data presented
here are far from conclusive, though the point is well worth further
inquiry. Would a comparison of the views of Franklin D. Roosevelt and the leaders of the British Labour party show any paral-
lels that would support this assumption? What of Lenin's behavior
before and after the communist revolution in Russia? The answers
to these questions would have great significance for the evaluation
of the current view that the leaders of the U.S.S.R. are in fact
slaves to the demands of a rigorous ideology.

The effects of crisis on ideology—the sharp reversion to fundamental principles and dogmatic insistence on their correctness
which the Left Wing displayed—also has considerable importance
for students of international affairs. For times of crisis are, by
definition, periods in which the need for clear, balanced thought
and objectivity are at a maximum. If, as seems probable, the
effect of ideology is to produce the precise opposite of what is
most needed, then its influence is pernicious indeed, and ideology
bodes ill for the rational conduct of international affairs so long as
it affects those conducting the relations of state. This it cannot
fail to do, since even though the leaders of the state, as postulated
above, may in fact be able to ignore the effects of ideology on
themselves, they must nonetheless make their explanations in the
societies to which they belong, and such explanations will in the
nature of things be framed, at the very minimum, to suit the national ideology. In fact, on this basis, the democracies, as nations
in which the leaders are theoretically more responsible to their
followers than in any other form of government, would in theory
be more amenable to the influence of the ideology than the dicta-
torships. Apparently the uncertainty and fear that accompany
crisis lead to a strong psychological need for stability which is
sought by a swift reversion to principles most strongly held. This
assumption lies behind the wartime slogan "There are no atheists
in foxholes," which assumed, wrongly perhaps, that the fundamental principles of Americanism were religious. The parallel is
most likely to be found in the response of the followers of religious
creeds to the great persecutions in history, and in the reaction of
nationalism to external threats.

With these exceptions, then, the case study of the Left Wing
seems to produce data which validate the fundamental postulates
made at the beginning of the study. Further, it appears to supply a
valid framework for the explanation of particular examples of Left
Wing behavior in international affairs. There were differences in
emphasis among the various elements of the Left Wing, but this is

to be expected in so large and diverse a group. Within reasonable limits, the Left Wing response to international events followed the pattern which the basic tenets of the ideology dictated. Further, the reaction was remarkably consistent throughout the five year period detailed in the study, and indeed it seems to have been equally consistent in the interwar years as well.

Perhaps the most striking characteristic of Left Wing opinion as it appeared in the study was the consistency, or even the dogmatic persistence, with which it adhered to its principles during a period of time in which enormous changes were occurring in international relations. From World War I through World War II, and well into the postwar period, the principles of socialism, symbolized broadly, were the guiding ends of Left Wing policy in international affairs. The socialist world, variously interpreted, was the prescribed nostrum for every conceivable sort of political ailment. Left Wing opposition to rearmament, for example, was merely intensified by the advent of Hitler in the 1930's and by the growing international tensions of the post-1945 period. The fear and suspicion of capitalism which led the Left Wing to oppose arming its own Conservative government in the 1930's was carried over with little loss of intensity and applied to the United States after 1945. Left Wing support for fellow socialists, personified since 1917 in the Soviet Union, never faltered even when faced with the German Pact of 1939, the invasion of Finland, the partition of Poland, or the cynical domination of Eastern Europe after 1945. Other key principles of Left Wing belief could be traced in a similar manner.

This truly remarkable consistency, partly the result of agreement on absolute political ends and partly the consequence of extensive use of symbolism and emotional imagery which made agreement more apparent than real, was purchased at a terrible price in terms of the traditional western political morality. Consistency, bought at the price of rigidity and unwillingness to compromise, is an expensive trait. Time and change in social matters produced enormous logical difficulties as the Left Wing struggled to maintain its traditional symbols and to find in events its own preconceptions. The solution of the logical problems involved was never achieved. Instead, the Left Wing was forced further and further into an unreal picture of international affairs, in which the actors became mere caricatures, and the frame of reference totally distorted. The United States that appeared in Left Wing thought bears little relation to the United States of 1945-1951; one may in fact seriously doubt that the stereotyped capitalistic state envisaged by the Left Wing ever existed at all other than in the imaginings of the human mind. Similarly, the

Soviet Union of Left Wing ideology, the harbinger of social revolution and the emancipation of the masses from the oppressions of the capitalistic system, was certainly a myth by 1945, and again one may reasonably doubt that it ever really existed. Even Britain, which was closer at hand, was often pictured as the haughty Britain of the Victorian age rather than the Britain of the twentieth century. Left Wing consistency was made possible only by the willingness of the Left Wing to accept the distortion of reality which accompanied such consistency.

Left Wing behavior consistently followed the pattern to be expected from the closed group; friend and foe were differentiated according to group status and not according to behavior. In many instances, even the behavior of the participants in a particular international event was determined by group status rather than by data reported by observers. There was a marked feeling of group superiority. The Left Wing assumed quite casually that *its* traditions were the true traditions of British socialism, and that its *principles* were the true application of socialism to everyday affairs. This appeared most plainly, perhaps, in the discussion of British policy in Greece and Spain, but it also played a significant part in political controversy over other problems. There is a frightening intolerance in the attitude of the Left Wing toward friend and foe, particularly the latter. There is no room for disagreement, for conditional acceptance, or for neutrality. The Left Wing decision to support or reject, believe or not believe, depended upon the standing of the issue, or the individual, within the ideology. In the last analysis, moral judgment was predicated upon group status.

The extent to which the British Left Wing made use of symbolism within its ideology seems adequately demonstrated by the study. Some of the consequences of the use of symbolism, both within and without the Left Wing, are worth a closer examination. Symbols were widely used to describe the aims of the group—socialism, peace, justice, etc.—and to some extent to provide the group with a standard of values. One important effect of symbolism was to render it very difficult indeed for anyone outside the Left Wing to comprehend the true meaning of Left Wing propaganda. Most of the propaganda coming from the Left Wing seemed to be intended for internal consumption; for the maintenance of friends rather than the conversion of enemies. This characteristic is commonplace, of course, in national propaganda as well.

Negative symbols were used far more often than positive symbols, although the significance of this usage will depend upon its psychological explanation. Often it appeared that the sole purpose of Left Wing propaganda was to convince its adherents that it was possible to place current events within the context of the ideology; to prove that a socialist viewpoint on the question existed. The symbols derived, in the main, from past Labour history and were usually associated with the Left Wing interpretation of such history. Even when a contemporary issue was adopted for use as a symbol, as proved the case with Winston Churchill's Fulton Speech, the new symbol took on a meaning that derived from the existing Left Wing attitude toward Conservatives, and would in fact have been meaningless, or at least wholly inexplicable, to anyone who lacked information about the whole of the Left Wing ideology.

Left Wing symbols were invariably laden with overtones of this nature. The Truman Doctrine, for example, appears on the surface as a simple continuation of British policy in Greece and Turkey, justified, perhaps, on slightly different grounds. In Left Wing opinion, the Truman Doctrine was taken as a manifestation of American opposition to socialism, as a step in the direction of the imposition of an imperialistic design on Europe, as a flagrant threat to Soviet security, and as the beginning of ideological warfare. All of these interpretations are value judgments, and each of the value judgments is predetermined by the status of the Truman Doctrine within the ideology.

Another peculiarity of the use of symbols was the apparent failure of the Left Wing to recognize the existence of any conflict in the application of symbols to specific events. Indeed, it sometimes appeared that the prime concern was the use and respect of the symbol, and not the actual behavior which the symbol was supposed to represent. Despite the bitter controversy over British recognition of the Franco Government in Spain, for example, the Left Wing demand for a socialist policy toward Spain proved in practice to be strongly hedged with reservations. This appeared when the Polish resolution was debated in the United Nations perhaps more clearly than at any other time. The Left Wing apparently desired the British Government to denounce Franco and manifest other signs of disapproval, but the Left Wing was quite unwilling to countenance any overt action which might lead to a serious conflict. The two aims might well be held mutually exclusive, and to some degree they were so, yet the Left Wing was quite unwilling to accept only one and reject the other.

The end result of the interaction of the pattern of beliefs called ideology and the series of events in international affairs surveyed in the study was an almost sublime disregard for empirical data, and a rigid and dogmatic approach to complex and shifting political questions, and the development of a dual standard of morality which relied upon the ideological affinities of the characters in international drama far more than the evaluation of the behavior of the characters. The case study provides numerous examples of distortion, denial, and even replacement of empirical data when the pattern of thought demanded by the ideology was violated by the course of events. Without making a fetish of empirical data, it is none the less true that any system of thought which ignores it completely in the absence of a better basis for thought seriously endangers the validity of its own conclusions. One searches in vain for any sign of criticism of friends of the ideology, or praise for its enemies. In the interests of ideological affinity, the Left Wing proved willing to countenance ruthless political repression, political imprisonment, fabricated elections, rigorous control of the information media, denial of the right to speak, write, and even think freely, and a host of similar violations of what appear to most observers the basic political values created by western civilization. The theory of ideology postulated in the beginning of the study proposes that the characteristics of Left Wing thought which gave rise to these results will in fact ensue in time from any ideology.

The vagaries in the behavior of the British Left Wing, though interesting, are scarcely of sufficient importance of and by themselves to merit the attention of those who are not specialists in that area. But the general principles which these behavior patterns reveal are a matter of great importance to all students of the relations between states. For every state has an ideology, or rather every political society produces, in time, an ideology which is called nationalism. Most states in fact contain within their bounds a number of ideologies, most of which have little or no effect on the conduct of international affairs. Leaving aside the particular problems that may be raised by the detailed content of nationalism, the significance of nationalism as an ideology is still overwhelming.

For ideology presupposes that each individual state will proceed from a fundamental conception of what the course of action in international affairs *should* be, and it will, within the limits of its ability, endeavor to describe the course of events in such terms. The nature of these objectives will be extremely vague, and perhaps even meaningless, and the use of symbolism will render the meaning even less precise than it might otherwise be. Ends like "making the world safe for democracy," "fulfilling manifest destiny," and similar woolly conceptions are a natural product of the ideological approach to international affairs. Lack of precision in the statement of objectives makes it possible to present almost any action which has the approval of the leaders of the ideology as a necessary step in the direction of ends already accepted. If the practice of the British Left Wing is a sufficient index to the methods of ideological groups, the fact of accepted ends will suffice to ensure approval of the means, whatever their merits may be. When the ideological goal becomes something as meaningless and undefinable as "national security," the current watchword in virtually every national ideology, almost any action can be rationalized to fit the necessary framework. The fact that such means may be decried in others has no relevance to the decision, since moral judgment is in this case a function of ideological conviction and not of neutral examination of consequences.

In more general terms, the existence of ideologies would seem to preclude any possibility of a rational consideration of the course of international affairs, and even the possibility that the data necessary for such consideration will be made available. The data of events, passing through the refractory apparatus of ideological conviction, emerge garbed in suitable symbolism to evoke the condemnation or approbation which the agency transmitting the information feels that the situation requires. One need hardly mention, for example, the fact that the people of the Soviet Union presently learn of the international behavior of the United States in these terms: that American aid programs become "economic imperialism," and American assistance to beleaguered nations like South Korea become "internal aggression" in Korea. It takes rather more care, however, to recognize with equal clarity that the version of Soviet behavior which appears in the bulk of the American press inverts the process almost precisely, subjecting Soviet behavior to the "interpretation" of the American ideology, so that Soviet aid to the backward nations becomes "communization" of these areas, and Soviet assistance to China becomes a part of a malignant plot to install communism throughout the world. One may well prefer to accept the latter interpretation rather than the former, or even to argue that the degree of distortion is substantially larger in one case than another, but the principle at issue is not affected by this sort of rationalization. Both approaches to international affairs produce inaccuracies, biased judgment, and a dual standard of moral behavior. Neither can be used as a basis for fruitful discussion.

Ideology will tend, in theory at least, to divide the whole world into friend and foe, and allow no room for neutrality. In the case of nationalism, it seems reasonable to assume that ideology—usually that portion referred to as the "national interest"—will make enemies of all other states, though perhaps in different degree. In the face of serious danger, the need for self preservation may allow temporary compromise, but the recession of danger should be followed by a return of natural antagonism. In these terms, the historical truth that the victors in an engagement seldom remain united much longer than the time required for the division of spoils seems a reasonable consequence of the invidious influence of nationalism. It is not in the nature of ideology to be tolerant of criticism, not to speak of competitors. Critics and competitors alike are, by definition, men who have not learned the error of their ways and who must be placed in possession of the truth. The proselytizing tendency of those who believe themselves to know or possess knowledge of the ends most suitable to man, whether in religious matters or in relatively minor social questions, materially strengthens the tendency of all ideologies to issue in a narrow and dogmatic approach to the management of human affairs.

Perhaps most important of all, ideology will act to make international agreement very difficult, or even impossible, by making compromise a treason upon the ideology. This seems particularly relevant in those states in which the opinion of the general public is an important factor in politics; but it is not wholly irrelevant to the "totalitarian" states in which opinion is more tightly controlled from above. For neither side in an ideological dispute, or rather a dispute in which both parties maintain an ideology which has relevance to the question at issue, will in reality be disputing the same data nor will they attach the same meaning and import to the same terminology. The term "Fulton Speech" does not have the same meaning to a member of the British Left Wing and a member of the New York Stock Exchange. Further, it is a function of ideology to determine ends, and yet a peculiarity of ideology that discussion of ends is inhibited or enjoined completely. If the end position is already determined by the ideology, retreat is impossible, and compromise out of the question. Interestingly enough, this problem seems to be aggravated rather than eased by the existence of quantities of information within the society, that is, the states in which access to information is limited are far less susceptible to this kind of influence than are those in which information can circulate freely. In either case, suggested solutions to international problems will be judged in part by the source of the suggestion, and in part by comparison with the ends which the ideology approves.

Finally, and at the risk of censure from those who object to the intrusion of moral questions into the discussion of affairs of state, it seems highly probable that an increase in the influence of ideology substantially reduces the quality of moral judgment in relation to international affairs. For the tendency of the supporters of an ideology to approve the conduct of the members of their own group, or of the leaders of the ideology, seems nearly irresistible. This, I submit, is a catastrophe of the first order. It is impossible to agree with those who are able, by some process of transmutation, to separate the behavior of individuals acting as their own moral agents from the behavior of these same individuals acting as responsible representatives of a political society. When the members of a society consider it wrong in principle for an individual person to behave in a certain manner toward his fellow men, yet approve precisely the same action in another individual, or even the same individual, acting in his capacity as an officer of the society, a contradiction must appear at some point in the process. One need not agree with every moral concept supported by every society to feel that reason urges consistency in the application of such principles. The arguments used to rationalize such inconsistency are familiar, but to make of the state an organic entity, devoid of moral scruples, when it in fact remains a dead and lifeless thing without human direction, seems a travesty.

This attitude may, perhaps, be open to criticism on the grounds that reasons of state are, in fact, sufficient grounds for allowing individual behavior to differ according to the level of political authority exercised by the individual, though I cannot concur in this judgment. It remains true nonetheless, that the application of moral principles to the behavior of states must still be equitable, and that to condone in state "A" behavior which is condemned in state "B" is both logically impossible and morally indefensible. This, it must be said, seems an almost certain consequence of ideology and the extent to which the practice has gained headway in current international politics can be demonstrated easily. The Soviet Union condemns the United States for supporting a "reactionary" political regime; its own support for equally unrepresentative governments in Eastern Europe is judged by a quite different standard. The Government of the United States denounces the Soviet Union for supplying aid and comfort to the Communist Government of China; its own support for the Nationalist Government on the Island of Taiwan is also judged by another standard. If we laud in our friends what we condemn in our enemies, we reduce morality to self-interest, and moral judgment to the distinction between friend and enemy. A moral act becomes an act which furthers our own real or imagined self-interest.

It is customary, on occasions of this sort, to proceed from the distressing to the sanguine, and conclude on a note of optimism. In this instance, custom must yield to conviction, and optimism to what may appear to be black pessimism. The influence of ideology is increasing and not waning in our century, and it gives every indication of augmenting its influence with increasing rapidity. The growth of the world's population, the steady increase in fear and international tension as the potential of military action is expanded with each new advance in technology, the ignorance and intolerance that characterize so much of human relations in our time, all relentlessly intensified by the inability of the modern state to withdraw from the international arena however much it may desire to do so, has made a shambles of the hopes of those who believe that the exercise of the rational faculty contains the best hope for a sane solution to man's political difficulties. For there is nothing whatever in the history of mass action, whether religious, political, or economic, that offers much hope for a sudden burst of tolerance and understanding. Nothing in the history of ideology helps us believe that the tolerant, self-critical, human approach to political affairs will be in any way furthered by its expanding influence. One hesitates to predict internal conflict and perhaps self-annihilation, for ignorance and intolerance are not total madness though they at times appear to be. But no one, surely, can study the manner in which the British Left Wing approached the immensely complex questions of international affairs, turn to see the constant expansion of ideological influence on the lives of every human now living, and look forward to the future with hope and confidence.

NOTES

Chapter II

1. Cited hereafter as *New Statesman.*

2. *New Statesman,* July 27, 1946.

3. *Royal Commission on the Press: Report* Cmd. 7700, His (Her) Majesty's Stationery Office (London, June, 1949), p. 13.

4. Vicount Camrose, *British Newspapers and Their Controllers* (Viscount, July, 1947), p. 151.

5. The 100,000 figure for "One Way Only" is quoted in "Quo Vadis," p. 2, also published by Tribune Publications, Ltd. The quarter of a million figure for "Guilty Men" is quoted on the frontispiece of "Still At Large." Both were published by Tribune Publications, Ltd. No date.

6. *Cmd. 7700,* p. 12. Only the *Sunday Times* and the *Observer* had smaller circulation figures among the Sunday papers.

7. For example, about one-third of the Labour M. P.'s elected in 1945 were Fabians. Cf. Carol Bunker, *Who's Who in Parliament* (London, 1946).

8. *Labour Party Annual Conference Report: 1940,* p. 20. Hereafter will be abbreviated *LPACR.*

9. *LPACR: 1948,* p. 17.

10. *LPACR: 1949,* p. 17. Zilliacus has since been readmitted.

11. Vigilantes, *Inquest on Peace* (London, 1935). See also *The Road to War* (London, 1937).

12. The following table, compiled from party reports, indicates the decline of union strength in Parliament.

Year	Total Candidates	Trade Union- sponsored	Total Returned	Trade Union Returned	Per cent Trade Union
1931	491	129	46	32	70
1935	539	132	154	79	51
1945	601	125	393	120	31
1950	617	140	315	110	35
1951	617	139	295	105	35

Chapter III

1. For an interesting and brief summary of these problems, see G. D. H. Cole, *A Guide to the Elements of Socialism* (London, June, 1957). Not an official policy statement.

2. See Francis Williams, *Fifty Years March* (London, 1948), pp. 134-137.

3. See R. B. McCallum, *Public Opinion and the Last Peace* (London, 1944). Also R. Bassett, *Democracy and Foreign Policy: A Case Study of the Manchurian Crisis* (London, 1952).

4. In 1930, for example, Miss Susan Lawrence, M. P., claimed that a great step toward peace had been taken because German soil was at last free of "invading armies." *LPACR: 1930,* p. 157.

5. Cf. R. Bassett, *Democracy and Foreign Policy,* and R. Bassett, *Political Crisis: 1931* (London, 1958). The latter is a very detailed study of the events of 1931 and some of their consequences and is sympathetic to MacDonald and his followers.

6. *LPACR: 1932,* p. 230.

7. *LPACR: 1933,* p. 186.

8. For text, see *TUC Report: 1933,* p. 425, or *LPACR: 1933,* pp. 266-268.

9. The best survey of Labour opinion in the 1930's is contained in a doctoral dissertation by S. Davis entitled "British Labour's Foreign Policy: 1931-1939," available at the University of London. I have relied upon it considerably for general information about the period, although the specific problems considered in this study were supplemented by additional research.

10. Text in *LPACR: 1934,* pp. 242-246.

11. Statement of July 30, 1934. Quoted in R. Bassett, *Democracy and Foreign Policy*, p. 584.

12. *LPACR: 1937*, p. 206.

13. *Ibid.*, p. 209.

14. Clement Attlee, *The Labour Party in Perspective* (London, Victor Gollancz, Ltd., 1937), p. 214.

15. Clement Attlee, *Labour's Peace Aims* (Labour Party Publication). No date.

16. *Labour, the War, and the Peace* (Labour Party, February, 1940).

17. *The Old World and the New Society* (Labour Party, 1940).

18. Harold J. Laski, *Is This An Imperialist War?* (Labour Party Publication, 1940).

19. *LPACR: 1940*, p. 134. The voting was: 2,413,000 for; 170,000 against.

20. *LPACR: 1942*, pp. 99-100.

21. *LPACR: 1943*, pp. 127-128. The voting was: 2,243,000 for; 347,000 against. The opposition was extremely vocal, but never large.

22. For example, Victor Gollancz, *Betrayal of the Left* (London, 1940).

23. *Tribune*, August 25, 1939.

24. *Ibid.*, September 22, 1939.

25. See *Labour, the War, and the Peace* (Labour Party Publication, 1940), p. 3.

26. *365 House of Commons Debates*, November 5, 1940, c 1314.

27. *372 House of Commons Debates*, June 24, 1941, c 992-993.

28. *383 House of Commons Debates*, September 8, 1942, c 246.

29. Harold J. Laski, *Britain and Russia: The Future* (National Peace Council, April, 1942).

30. G. D. H. Cole, *Europe, Russia, and the Future* (London, 1941).

31. For example, see *Plan For Britain* (Labour Book Service, London, 1943). Essays prepared for the Fabian Society by G. D. H. Cole, Harold Laski, Aneurin Bevan, James Griffiths, *etc.*

32. *Labour's War Manifesto* (Labour Party Publication, 1940).

33. In *Labour's Aims in War and Peace* (London, 1940), p. 133.

34. *Labour, the War, and the Peace* (Labour Party Publication, 1939).

35. *LPACR: 1940,* p. 125.

36. *The Old World and the New Society* (Labour Party Publication, 1942). Emphasis added by the author.

Chapter IV

1. For typical Left Wing reactions to the Italian "revolution," see *391 House of Commons Debates,* August 3, 1943. Also, *Tribune,* March 24, 1943. Most other accounts follow this general pattern.

2. C. M. Woodhouse, *Apple of Discord* (London, no date).

3. Reginald Leeper, *When Greek Meets Greek* (London, 1950).

4. Denys Hamson, *We Fell Among Greeks* (London, 1946).

5. W. Byford-Jones, *The Greek Trilogy* (London, 1945).

6. Richard Capell, *Simiomata* (London, 1945).

7. *Documents Regarding the Situation in Greece,* Cmd. 6952, His (Her) Majesty's Stationery Office (London, January, 1945). *Report of the British Legal Mission to Greece,* Cmd. 6838, HMSO (London, January, 1946).

8. *What We Saw In Greece,* published by the Trades Union Congress (London, 1945).

9. Korizis apparently committed suicide early in 1941.

10. W. Byford-Jones, *The Greek Trilogy,* cites conversations with an EAM schoolmaster (p. 73), and Nitsos Partsalides, Secretary General of EAM, (p. 97) on this point. Woodhouse, *Apple of Discord,* concurs, pp. 60-61.

11. *Cmd. 6592,* His (Her) Majesty's Stationery Office (London, 1945), p. 9.

12. Woodhouse, *Apple of Discord,* p. 188.

13. Hamson, *We Fell Among Greeks,* is a description of the mission.

14. Appendix "C" in Woodhouse, *Apple of Discord,* contains the agreement.

15. Leeper, *When Greek Meets Greek,* pp. 31-33, and Woodhouse, *Apple,* pp. 151-158.

16. For text, see Woodhouse, *Apple of Discord,* appendix "F."

17. *393 House of Commons Debates,* November 9, 1943, c 1080.

18. *395 House of Commons Debates,* December 14, 1943, c 1435-1436.

19. *397 House of Commons Debates,* February 22, 1944, c 695-696.

20. *402 House of Commons Debates,* August 14, 1944, c 898-899.

21. *Tribune,* June 2, 1944, June 9, 1944. *New Statesman,* June 3, 1944.

22. *Tribune,* September 8, 1944. *New Statesman,* September 9, 1944. Both are good examples of the Left Wing reaction.

23. *Tribune,* April 14, 1944. *New Statesman,* April 15, 1944. Aneurin Bevan, in a special leader in *Tribune,* referred acidly to "so-called" mutinies in Cairo and demanded that British personnel stop interfering in Greek politics.

24. *Tribune,* November 12, 1943. *Tribune,* derided the story. The "real truth" was that Zervas was one of the King's guerrillas.

25. *402 House of Commons Debates,* August 14, 1944, esp. c 1550-1551.

26. *406 House of Commons Debates,* November 30, 1944, c 246.

27. *Ibid.,* December 5, 1944, c 356-360.

28. *Ibid.,* December 8, 1944, c 908.

29. *Ibid.,* December 8, 1944, c 957.

30. *LPACR: 1944,* p. 143.

31. *Ibid.,* p. 148.

32. *Ibid.,* p. 150.

33. *406 House of Commons Debates,* December 20, 1944, c 1877-1878.

34. For example, *Tribune,* January 18, 1945.

35. *Tribune,* December 29, 1944.

Chapter V

1. *LPACR: 1945,* p. 104.

2. This is a complete reversal of attitude for the leaders of the Labour party as well. Compare Attlee, *Labour Party in Perspective,* p. 226, with Attlee's election address, mimeographed copy, Transport House.

3. Lord Strabolgi at the 1945 Labour Party Conference: *LPACR: 1945,* p. 93.

4. Denis Healey in *LPACR: 1945,* p. 114.

5. *Forward,* June 21, 1945; June 28, 1945; July 4, 1945.

6. Typical examples can be found in *Tribune,* July 6, 1945; July 13, 1945, and *New Statesman,* August 4, 1945.

7. Quoted in the *London Times,* August 18, 1945.

8. Typical reactions can be found in *New Statesman,* August 11, 1945; *Reynolds News,* August 12, 1945; *Tribune,* August 17, 1945; *Forward,* August 11, 1945.

9. See in particular: *New Statesman,* August 25, 1945; *Tribune,* August 31, 1945; H. N. Brailsford in *Reynolds News,* August 26, 1945.

10. *413 House of Commons Debates,* August 16, 1945, c 78-93.

11. *Ibid.,* c 336-341.

12. For example, John Platts-Mills and Lyall Wilkes, *413 House of Commons Debates,* August 18, 1945, c 307, 326.

13. For example, James Hudson, *413 Debates,* c 326.

14. Richard Stokes, Michael Foot, Lyall Wilkes, and Lt. Fred Peart all made mention of "continuity" in their speeches.

15. For example, Woodrow Wyatt, letter to *New Statesman,* September 8, 1945; H. N. Brailsford and T. E. N. Driberg in *Reynolds News,* August 26, 1945. Every issue of the Left Wing press published during the last week of August and the first week in September, 1945, contains similar letters.

16. *413 House of Commons Debates,* August 23, 1945, c 875-887.

17. See *New Statesman,* September 22, 1945; September 29, 1945; October 6, 1945; October 13, 1945; *Tribune,* September 29, 1945; October 5, 1945; *Reynolds News,* September 30, 1945, also has several references to the question.

18. *New Statesman,* November 13, 1945; *Tribune,* November 12, 1945; *Forward,* November 13, 1945.

19. *415 House of Commons Debates,* November 7, 1945.

20. See *Daily Herald,* November 8, 1945, and *News Chronicle,* November 8, 1945.

21. *416 House of Commons Debates,* November 22, 1945. The Prime Minister's statement can be found in columns 600-610.

22. *Ibid.,* c 709.

23. *Ibid.*, c 824–832.

24. See particularly *New Statesman,* December 1, 1945, and *Tribune,* November 30, 1945.

25. *Forward,* January 26, 1946. A special leader by Harold Laski in this issue praised the Soviet action highly. Also *Tribune,* January 25, 1946, and *Reynolds News,* January 27, 1946.

26. In *Daily Herald,* January 29, 1946.

27. *Tribune,* February 8, 1946. Harold Laski in *Forward,* February 9, 1946; *New Statesman,* February 9, 1946.

28. *419 House of Commons Debates,* February 21, 1946, c 1322.

29. *418 House of Commons Debates,* February 4, 1946, c 1439.

30. For example, Bertrand Russell in *Manchester Guardian,* October 2, 1945.

31. Mimeographed copy. Conservative Political Centre, London, no date.

32. See *420 House of Commons Debates,* March 11, 1946, c 1293 for reference to number of signatures.

33. Mimeographed copy. Conservative Political Centre, London, no date. Copy includes a list of signatories.

34. From *Forward,* March 9, 1946; March 16, 1946; *New Statesman,* March 9, 1946; March 16, 1946; *Tribune,* March 8, 1946; March 15, 1946; March 22, 1946.

35. *423 House of Commons Debates,* June 4, 1946.

36. *Final Conference Agenda: 1946* (Labour Party Publication), Labour Party Library, Transport House, London.

37. *LPACR: 1946,* pp. 105–106.

38. *Ibid.,* p. 151.

39. *Ibid.,* p. 154.

40. *Ibid.,* p. 155.

41. *Ibid.,* p. 157.

Chapter VI

1. *430 House of Commons Debates*, November 18, 1946, c 525.

2. *Ibid.*, c 527-530. The points are paraphrased and not quoted exactly except those phrases in quotation marks.

3. *Ibid.*, c 530.

4. *Ibid.*, c 576.

5. Woodrow Wyatt, *Into The Dangerous World* (London, Weidenfeld & Nicolson, Ltd., 1952), p. 140.

6. *Tribune*, November 22, 1946.

7. For example, see Konni Zilliacus in *Forward,* November 23, 1946.

8. G. D. H. Cole, *Labour's Foreign Policy* (London, 1946), p. 6.

9. *420 House of Commons Debates*, March 4, 1946.

10. Geoffrey Bing, *430 House of Commons Debates,* November 18, 1946, c 610.

11. See Foreign Affairs Debate, *433 House of Commons Debates,* February 27, 1947; Debate on the Army Estimates, *434 House of Commons Debates*, March 13, 1947; Defense Debate, *435 House of Commons Debates*, March 20, 1947. This characteristic appears in each case.

12. Royal Institute for International Affairs, *Documents on International Affairs: 1947-1948* (London, 1952), pp. 2-7.

13. *Ibid.*, pp. 4-5.

14. *Ibid.*, pp. 4-5.

15. *Ibid.*, pp. 4-5.

16. In *Forward,* March 22, 1947.

17. See *New Statesman,* March 15, 1947, March 22, 1947, April 5, 1947; *Tribune*, March 21, 1947; Zilliacus in *New Statesman,* April 5, 1947.

18. *435 House of Commons Debates*, March 31, 1947. The Division List appears in columns 1965-1966.

19. *Keep Left* (London, 1947). Those who signed the pamphlet included: R. Crossman, M. Foot, I. Mikardo, Geoffrey Bing, Donald Bruce, Harold Davies, Leslie Hale, Fred Lee, Benn Levy, Ronald Mackay, J. P. W. Mallalieu, Ernest Millington, Stephen Swingler, George Wigg, and Woodrow Wyatt. The group began to meet soon

after the debate on the King's Speech. Wyatt, *Into The Dangerous World*, p. 143.

20. *Keep Left*, p. 38.

21. See Official Records, Special Supplement, *First Report to the Security Council*, December, 1946; *Third Report to the Security Council*, May, 1948.

22. *Keep Left*, p. 42.

23. *LPACR: 1947*, p. 173.

24. For particularly virulent specimens see *Tribune*, June 6, 1947; *Forward*, June 6, 1947; *New Statesman*, June 7, 1947. One Left Wing journalist even hinted that Bevin was anti-Semitic, the worst possible accusation that could be made within the Left Wing.

Chapter VII

1. Brookings Institution, *Major Problems in United States Foreign Policy* (Washington, D. C., 1948), p. 152. For a good summary of the aid problem see Bank for International Settlements, *20th Annual Report* (Geneva, 1950).

2. *Department of State Bulletin*, December 15, 1946, p. 1108.

3. Royal Institute for International Affairs, *Documents on International Affairs: 1947-1948* (London, 1952), pp. 17-20.

4. Royal Institute for International Affairs, *Documents on European Recovery* (London, 1949). James Forrestal notes that American officials were astonished when the Soviet Union walked out. See James Forrestal, *The Forrestal Diaries*, ed. by Walter Millis. (London, 1952), p. 273.

5. *Committee on European Cooperation Report*, Department of State Publication 2930, 1947.

6. Royal Institute for International Affairs, *Documents: 1947-1948*, pp. 59-72 for text.

7. *Hearings in the Senate Foreign Relations Committee on the Foreign Assistance Bill: S 3101* (U. S. Government Printing Office, 1948); *Hearings on House Bill: H. R. 2362* (U. S. Government Printing Office, 1948).

8. The Krug Report, *National Resources and Foreign Aid;* the Nourse Report, *The Impact of Foreign Aid Upon the Domestic Economy;*

the Harriman Report, *European Recovery and American Aid* (U.S. Government Printing Office, 1948).

9. See particularly *Tribune,* June 13, 1947, June 20, 1947; *Forward,* June 14, 1947; *New Statesman,* June 14, 1947, June 21, 1947; *Reynolds News,* June 22, 1947, contains an article by Harold Laski dealing with the Marshall proposal which follows this general pattern.

10. *438 House of Commons Debates,* June 19, 1947.

11. *Forward,* July 19, 1947.

12. *Ibid.,* July 19, 1947.

13. *Anglo-American Financial Agreements,* Department of State Publication 2439 (Washington, D. C., December, 1945).

14. *Forward,* August 23, 1947.

15. *Ibid.,* August 30, 1947.

16. G. D. H. Cole, *The Intelligent Man's Guide to the Post-war World* (London, 1947).

17. Leonard Woolf, *Foreign Policy: The Labour Party's Dilemma* (London, 1947).

18. Harold J. Laski, *Russia and the West* (London, 1947).

19. Cole, *Intelligent Man's Guide,* p. 1035.

20. *Ibid.,* p. 802.

21. *Ibid.,* pp. 1031-1032.

22. Woolf, *Foreign Policy,* p. 15.

23. Laski, *Russia and the West,* p. 13.

Chapter VIII

1. *446 House of Commons Debates,* January 22, 1948, c 387.

2. *450 House of Commons Debates,* May 4, 1948. Also James Forrestal, *Diaries,* pp. 371-372 for date of proposal to United States Government.

3. *Reynolds News,* January 25, 1948.

4. *New Statesman,* January 24, 1948.

5. *Forward,* January 31, 1948.

6. In *Forward,* January 31, 1948.

7. See *New Statesman,* February 28, 1948, March 6, 1948.

8. *Ibid.,* March 6 and March 13, 1948.

9. See particularly *Reynolds News,* March 14, 1948.

10. In *Forward,* March 20, 1948.

11. *499 House of Commons Debates,* April 6, 1948, c 35.

12. *LPACR: 1948,* p. 179.

13. *New Statesman,* March 27, 1948; April 3, 1948; April 10, 1948; April 17, 1948.

14. For typical examples, see *New Statesman,* June 26, 1948; July 10, 1948; *Forward,* July 3, 1948; July 24, 1948; *452 House of Commons Debates,* June 30, 1948.

15. This was particularly true of the Left Wing speakers in the June debate in the House of Commons. See *452 House of Commons Debates,* June 30, 1948.

16. *Forward,* July 24, 1948. The writer, Emrys Hughes, is a well-known British pacifist.

17. *New Statesman,* July 10, 1948.

18. A copy of the letter is in the Labour Party Library, Smith Square, London. Five M.P.'s signed both the manifesto and the letter: Harold Davies, Leah Manning, Ernest Millington, Maurice Orbach, and T. C. Skeffington-Lodge. Other M.P.'s who signed the letter were: W. Ayles, J. Battley, James Carmichael, W. G. Cove, Rhys Davies, C. Dumpleton, E. Ferneyhough, A. Greenwood, D. Grenfell, J. Harrison, P. Holman, J. Hudson, W. Jeger, C. Kenyon, A. Lewis, F. Longden, H. McGhee, F. Messer, P. Morris, M. Nichol, G. Pargiter, F. Paton, J. Ranger, J. Rankin, R. Richards, M. Ridealgh, G. Roberts, P. Shurmer, J. Silverman, F. Skinnard, R. Sorenson, J. Sparks, G. Thomas, F. Viant, G. H. Walker, T. Watkins, O. Willey, E. Willis, V. Yates. Cove, Davies, Hudson, Sorenson, and Yates were prominent pacifists. Oddly enough, there were no prominent fellow travelers in this group, although many of the principles contained in the letter were a hallmark of the postwar fellow-traveler group.

19. See the exchange between Ernest Bevin and Winston Churchill, *454 House of Commons Debates,* July 29, 1948.

20. *459 House of Commons Debates,* December 9, 1948, c 583.

21. *New Statesman,* March 6, 1948.

22. For a typical example, see Harold Laski in *Forward,* September 25, 1948.

23. See in particular, *Tribune,* July 1, 1948; September 17, 1948; October 1, 1948; February 4, 1949.

24. See below, p. 152.

25. *456 House of Commons Debates,* September 22-23, 1948. Also the debate on the bill to extend the length of service clause for conscripts, *459 House of Commons Debates,* December 6, 1948. Those voting against the Government included: T. Braddock, R. Chamberlain, C. Davies (Liberal), Rhys Davies, M. Lloyd George (Liberal), E. Granville, James Hudson, E. Hughes, W. Kendall, H. McGhee, L. Manning, I. Mikardo, M. Nichol, F. Paton, J. Platts-Mills, E. Roberts, G. Roberts, J. Silverman, E. Smith, S. Swingler, and Victor Yates.

Chapter IX

1. See *Forward,* March 26, 1949, in particular; also all issues in April.

2. *New Statesman,* March 12, 1949.

3. See *New Statesman,* March 26, 1949; April 9, 1949; April 16, 1949; *Forward,* April 9, 1949; April 16, 1949; *Reynolds News,* April 10, 1949.

4. *464 House of Commons Debates,* May 12, 1949. Opposing the motion were: T. Braddock, communist William Gallacher, communist Phil Piratin, fellow travelers J. Platts-Mills, D. N. Pritt, and Konni Zilliacus, pacifist Emrys Hughes, and Ronald Chamberlain. There were a substantial number of abstentions, but they cannot be identified because of the practice of "pairing" in the House.

5. *Labour Believes in Britain* (Labour Party Publication, London, 1949).

6. Signed by Sir Richard Acland, Donald Bruce, Barbara Castle, Richard Crossman, Harold Davies, Leslie Hale, Tom Horabin, Marcus Lipton, Ian Mikardo, Stephen Swingler, George Wigg, Tom Williams. Some significant figures of the *Keep Left* group are missing, although Bruce, Crossman, Davies, Hale, Mikardo, Swingler, and Wigg belonged to that earlier group.

7. *Keeping Left* (London, 1950), p. 23.

8. H. G. Nicholas, *The British General Election of 1950* (London, 1951), p. 78.

9. *Ibid.*, p. 305.

10. The Left Wing press devoted much space to this question after the election. In particular see *Tribune*, March 3, 1950; March 10, 1950; March 31, 1950; and *New Statesman*, March 4, 1950.

11. Royal Institute for International Affairs, *Documents on International Relations: 1949-1950* (London, 1953).

12. *New Statesman*, July 1, 1950.

13. See particularly *New Statesman*, October 21, 1950; October 28, 1950; November 18, 1950.

14. *New Statesman*, December 2, 1950.

15. *Ibid.*, December 16, 1950. Also December 23, 1960, especially the article by "Critic" (Kingsley Martin).

16. *LPACR: 1950*, especially 141 ff.

17. *Full Speed Ahead* (London, 1950).

18. *Ibid.*, p. 7.

19. *Ibid.*, p. 13.

20. *Ibid.*, p. 14.

21. *Ibid.*, p. 21.

22. *Tribune*, February 9, 1951. See also January 26 and February 2, 1951.

23. Letter to *New Statesman*, July 8, 1950; letter to *Forward*, July 8, 1950.

24. *Letter to New Statesman*, August 5, 1950.

25. *Letter to New Statesman*, July 8, 1950, and July 29, 1950.

26. In *Tribune*, July 28, 1950.

27. *477 House of Commons Debates*, July 5, 1950.

28. *476 House of Commons Debates*, June 29, 1950. See also Ian Mikardo in *Tribune*, July 14, 1950.

29. In particular, see *Tribune*, July 28, 1950.

30. *477 House of Commons Debates*, July 28, 1950.

31. *Tribune*, August 11, 1950. Letter to *New Statesman*, July 15, 1950.

32. *477 House of Commons Debates,* July 26, 1950. Letter in *Tribune,* August 25, 1950.

33. Text in *Tribune,* July 21, 1950. Also *477 House of Commons Debates,* July 19, 1950, c 2251.

34. *477 House of Commons Debates,* July 26, 1950.

35. *Ibid.,* September 12, 1950, c 963.

36. *480 House of Commons Debates,* October 31, 1950.

37. *Ibid.,* November 29-30, 1950.

38. *483 House of Commons Debates,* December 14, 1950.

39. *Ibid.,* January 23, 1951.

40. *Ibid.,* January 29, 1951 (United States billions).

41. *484 House of Commons Debates,* February 12, 1951.

42. *Forward,* February 17, 1951; March 10, 1951.

43. *Forward,* February 17, 1951.

44. *Ibid.,* March 10, 1951.

45. Letter to *New Statesman,* February 17, 1951.

46. Letters to *New Statesman,* February 24, 1951; March 17, 1951.

47. *One Way Only* (London, 1951).

48. Similar to the extent of virtually identical wording in some paragraphs; Cf. p. 21 of *Full Speed Ahead* with pp. 10-11 of *One Way Only* for example.

49. *One Way Only,* p. 3.

50. *Ibid.,* p. 4.

INDEX